IMPACT
ANALYSIS FOR
PROGRAM
EVALUATION

IMPACT
ANALYSIS FOR
PROGRAM
EVALUATION

Lawrence B. Mohr

The University of Michigan

The Dorsey Press

Chicago, Illinois 60604

© THE DORSEY PRESS, 1988

This book was set in Century Schoolbook by Compset Inc.
The editors were Leo Wiegman, Waivah Clement, and
    Jane Lightell.
The production manager was Bette Ittersagen.
The designer was Michael Warrell.
The drawings were done by Tom Mallon.
Arcata Graphics/Kingsport was the printer and binder.

ISBN 0-256-05623-4 (casebound)
ISBN 0-256-06006-1 (paperbound)

Library of Congress Catalog Card No. 87–70721

Printed in the United States of America
1 2 3 4 5 6 7 8 9 0 K 5 4 3 2 1 0 9 8

To my wife

FIGURE 4–1 Characteristics of design (placed here for the ease of the reader's reference)

	Design			Selection/ assignment type
No.	Chapter	Name	Diagram	
1	4	One-shot case study	T Y	Either/none
2	10	Ex-post facto	Assorted	Decentralized/ nonrandom
Elementary quasi-experimental designs				
3	4	Before-after	X T Y	Centralized/ nonrandom
4	4	Comparative posttest	$\dfrac{T \quad Y_E}{Y_C}$	Centralized/ nonrandom
Quasi-experimental designs				
5	7	Comparative change	$\dfrac{X_E \quad T \quad Y_E}{X_C \qquad Y_C}$	Centralized/ nonrandom
6	9	Interrupted time series	X.... T Y....	Centralized/ nonrandom
7	9	Comparative time series	$\dfrac{X_E... \quad T \quad Y_E...}{X_C... \qquad Y_C...}$	Centralized/ nonrandom
8	11	Subobjective	Assorted	Centralized/ nonrandom
Mixed designs				
9	8	Random comparison group	$\dfrac{X_E \quad T \quad Y_E}{R \quad X_C \qquad Y_C}$	Centralized/ part random
10	6	Regression discontinuity	$\dfrac{A_E \quad T \quad Y_E}{A_C \qquad Y_C}$	Centralized/ near random
Experimental designs				
11	4	R-comparative posttest	$\dfrac{R \quad\ T \quad Y_E}{R \qquad Y_C}$	Centralized/ randomized
12	4	R-comparative change	$\dfrac{R \quad X_E \quad T \quad Y_E}{R \quad X_C \qquad Y_C}$	Centralized/ randomized

		Threats to internal validity				
				Contamination		
Spurious-ness/time order	History	Selection P	Q	Assignment	Treat-ment	Controls
NA	NA	NA		NA	NA	NA
X	NA	X	X	X	X	X
NA	X	NA		NA	X	(X)
NA	—	X	X	X:div. events, div. attr.	X	X
NA	—	—	X	X:div. events, mat.,attr.,regr.	X	X
NA	X	NA		NA	X	X
NA	—	—	X	X:div. events, matr., regr.	X	X
NA	—	— (At best)	—	— (At best)	X	— (At best)
NA	—	—	—	—	X	X
NA	—	—	—	—	X	X
NA	—	—	—	—	X	X
NA	—	—	—	—	X	X

Preface

The subject matter of this book is usually called just Program Evaluation by those who practice it and write about it. I have found that some people object rather strenuously to the usurpation of that title. They have convinced me that many other approaches to the evaluation of programs and policies have as much claim to the label as the approach reflected here, but are different in many fundamental respects; for example, benefit-cost analysis. I have therefore put the words *Impact Analysis* in the title, and have used that terminology frequently throughout the book to make clear what the subject matter is. I eventually found this change helpful in conceptualizing and attacking the kinds of issues to which I wanted to give priority. For example, I have not emphasized the politics and diplomacy of program evaluation and have felt justified in the omission because these aspects are rather distant from the discipline of impact analysis. I do not by any means disparage their importance; but I wanted to concentrate on those aspects that are rooted in logic rather than art and that are susceptible to criticism based on system and rigor. Some of the similarities and differences between impact analysis and other conceptions of program evaluation are treated in the final chapter.

Campbell and Stanley made an important contribution to policy-making in their handbook chapter of 1963 that well deserves the attention it has received from both practitioners and scholars during the past twenty-four years. My central purpose here is to contribute to a basic understanding of the core and central thrust of their original subject matter. Several characteristics of the book reflect this aim.

For one, I felt that the body of material they offered has remained largely in pieces, and it is difficult to learn something important about one piece through the mastery of another. What is a design? What, then, is a quasi-experimental design? What is this thing called an ex-post-facto design? How is one design to be distinguished from another? Why is a particular threat to internal validity a threat to one design and not another? What is the connection between impact-analysis designs and classical statistical inference? What is the connection between statistical inference and the quality of a design? Which is more important for quality; internal validity or generalizability? What connections, if any, are there between design and generalizability? What are the ways—conceptual rather than empirical—in which a design can be improved? These are the kinds of questions that, if answered, would begin to impose an integration on this subject matter as a body of scholarship.

I am convinced that such integration is possible, but its implementation is difficult. Integration demands consistency. Smoothing the surface into shape in one place tends to produce a bulge in some other place. Most of the time, the resolution of such puzzles seems to improve the rationality of the overall scheme. However, I surely have not resolved all of the problems; my hope is that this general framework provides a good beginning.

I have also addressed the question of goals as well as methods. Most of the time the goal or objective or outcome of the program, and therefore the criterion or dependent variable used in the analysis of its impact, is taken for granted. I have felt that this mindset contributes substantially to the ambiguity of results. At the same time, I am convinced that the selection of the dependent variable is not purely arbitrary, that it is possible to say something at least faintly rigorous on that important issue. Therefore, Chapters One through Three and Chapter Twelve address it in two of its different but related aspects.

The process of developing those sections led me to see the great importance of Scriven's (1972) concept of formative evaluation—evaluation that aims at improving a program instead of just finding out what it did. I find that a certain kind of outcome, one that I and others call subobjectives, can be crucial here and can contribute to the quality of a research design. Subobjectives are treated in Chapters Three and Eleven. Much of the material on subobjectives has been of concern to others under headings such as process analysis—an analysis of the process by which the activities undertaken supposedly accomplish the ends desired. Greater attention to subobjectives is one of the ways in which the practice of impact analysis can perhaps best be improved.

Third, I have used regression analysis as a common language for talking about all designs—not just about statistical calculations, but about strengths and weaknesses and the meaning of what is being done in the application of a particular design to a particular problem. An elementary knowledge of multiple regression is therefore a prerequisite for closely following the development of the text. The application of multiple regression to the needs of impact analysis for program evaluation is outlined in Chapter Five; parts of Chapters Six through Eleven then specialize and elaborate this material to contribute to an appreciation of the niche of each individual design. I hope that some readers will find, as I did, that this use of regression analysis to conceptualize program evaluation improves one's perspective on the first as well as the second.

This book is addressed to scholars; but at the same time, it is primarily a text. As a result it is not a compendium of scholarship, as many texts are, but rather a summary and interpretation with several additions. Therefore, I feel that it will serve best as a text when it is used as a basis rather than a handbook or field guide. I have tried to be clear and methodical in presentation. Yet, for the student with only two courses in statistics, the going will be rough unless the instructor fills in many gaps and elaborates with perspectives on selected topics. For writers in the field, instructors, and evaluation practitioners with a good background and an intellectual savor for the subject matter, I hope that the material will stimulate both reflection and criticism. The ultimate aim, as always in this field, is strongly dual: to contribute both to the rewards of scholarly discussion and the soundness of evaluation practice.

ACKNOWLEDGMENTS

Under acknowledgments, without question, my first debt is to the literature cited in the references, plus much else read but not specifically mentioned. I have tried to put a lot of it together, and in so doing have learned far more from it than would have been possible for me in a more passive relation. If I have not always used it correctly, the fault is undoubtedly mine; to the extent that the end result is thereby imperfect, as it surely is, I welcome continued critique. I owe much to the Institute of Public Policy Studies of The University of Michigan for support, including the gracious assistance of the clerical staff. The Sloan Foundation provided partial support for the writing of Chapter Twelve through its grant for studies in public management to the Institute of Public Policy Studies. Lynn Deniston and George Downs provided valuable criticism along the way. I would also like to thank reviewers Jerry Goldman, Northwestern University; Gloria Grizzle, Florida State University; Albert R. Roberts, Indiana University; and David M. Rocke, University of California, Davis, for their constructive suggestions and guidance. The public policy and political science students who took my evaluation course over the past several years were extremely important in the development of many of the ideas. Finally, and most of all, I thank my wife, Elizabeth Hawthorne, who motivated me to do this thing in the first place and encouraged my belief in it throughout.

Lawrence B. Mohr

Contents

List of Figures   xvii

Chapter One   The Evaluation Framework   1
The Evaluation Framework   2
Some Quantifiers of Program Effectiveness   2
Coverage Level of the Quantifiers   7
Summary   8

Chapter Two   Outcomes and the Problem   10
The Problem   10
The Outcome Line   12
    Finding the Outcome of Interest   14
Relation of the Problem to the Outcome Line   18
    Distraction from the Problem   18   Failure to Recognize
    Multiple Concerns   19   Failure to Recognize the Targeted
    Problem   19   Failure to Recognize Levels of Coverage   20
    Failure to Acknowledge the Counterfactual   21
Joint Use of Complete Outcome Line and Problem Definition   21
Summary   23

Chapter Three   Subobjectives and Other Components   25
Formative and Summative Evaluations   25
The Formative Analysis of Subobjectives   27
Activities: Implementation Analysis   31
The Operation of Subobjectives   32
    The Discovery Subobjective   32   Behavior Prerequisites   33
    The Omission of Subobjectives   34   Example: The Kirtland's
    Warbler   35
Types of Diversity within Programs   39
    Multiple Outcomes and Parts   39   Comparative Methods   41
    The Multichannel Treatment   42

Chapter Four   The Quality of Design: Experiments and the Elementary Quasi Experiments   44
Introduction to the Issues   44
The Basic Experimental Designs   45
The Threats to Internal Validity   48
History and Related Threats: The Before-After Design   49   The Threat of Selection: The Comparative-Posttest Design   58   The Threat of Contamination   62   Summary of Threats to Internal Validity   66
External Validity   66
Summary   70
Appendix: The Regression Artifact   71

Chapter Five   The Regression Framework for Impact Analysis   80
The Basic Bivariate Equation   81
Regression as an Impact Statement   82
Extending the Regression to Include Control Variables   83
The Relation between β_T and Gain Scores   88
Significance Testing of the Impact Parameter   90

Chapter Six   The Regression-Discontinuity Design   97
The Logic of the Regression-Discontinuity Design   99
Threats to Validity   104
Fuzzy Cutpoints   105   Random Measurement Error   107   Nonrandom Measurement Error   108   Curvilinearity   110
Summary   114

Chapter Seven   The Comparative-Change Design   115
Selection-Q Bias and Comparative Change   117
Intercept Bias, Matched Groups   118   Intercept Bias, Unmatched Groups   122   Bias in Slopes   126
Random Measurement Error   130

Chapter Eight   The Random-Comparison-Group Design   132
The Design in Concept   133
The Population of Concern   134
Estimating the Treatment Effect   135
Threats to Validity   142
Internal Validity   142   Interaction   143   External Validity   144
Conclusion   145

Chapter Nine   Time-Series Designs   146
The Interrupted-Time-Series Design   147
Regression Analysis   151   Visual Analysis   154   ARIMA Modeling   157

The Comparative-Time-Series Design   158
Summary   162

Chapter Ten   Ex-Post-Facto Evaluation Studies   163
The Ex-Post-Facto Design in Concept   164
Spuriousness as a Source of Selection Bias   168
The Volunteer Problem   170
Coincidence as a Source of Selection Bias   178
Contamination and Time-Order Problems   182
Conclusion   184

Chapter Eleven   Subobjectives as Design   185
The Logic of the Method of Subobjectives   187
Applications of the Method   191

Chapter Twelve   Multiple Outcomes   193
Benefit-Cost Analysis   195
Multiattribute-Utility Technology   197
    Summary   199
Impact Analysis   200
    Finding   200   Limiting   204   Assessing Impacts   207
    Common-Scaling and Weighting   207
Postscript: Utilization   208

References   210

Index   i

List of Figures and Tables

Figure 2–1   Outcome line   13

Figure 2–2   Outcome line for a wiretapping program   13

Figure 2–3   Outcome line for a program of home energy
                  audits   17

Figure 3–1   Formative results   28

Figure 3–2   An example of the discovery subobjective and
                  the behavior prerequisites   34

Figure 3–3   Direct and indirect effects   35

Figure 3–4   Outcome line for the cowbird control program   38

Figure 4–1   Characteristics of design   50–51

Figure 5–1   The basic regression equation   82

Figure 5–2   Bivariate regression for program evaluation   83

Figure 5–3   The control-variable regression   86

Figure 6–1   The regression-discontinuity design shows that
                  the treatment has lowered the E-group scores   100

Figure 6–2a   No treatment effect   106

Figure 6–2b   Fuzzy cutpoint with biased allocation—
                  pseudotreatment effect   107

Figure 6–3   Misclassification. Pseudotreatment effect
                  created by the assumption of linearity   110

Figure 6–4   Interactive treatment effect confounded with
                  null-case curvilinear relation—solid line =
                  observed data; dashed line = linear
                  assumption; dotted line = curvilinear
                  assumption   111

Figure 6–5   Curvilinear null-case assumption needed to
                  contradict a treatment effect when the highs
                  are made higher   113

Figure 7–1   Weight change in two groups, where the
                  average initial weights and the slopes are the
                  same, but the two intercepts are different   120

Figure 7–2   Intercept bias due to selection-Q effects or

	random measurement error in unmatched groups	123
Figure 7–3	Selection-Q bias tends to yield a higher R^2 within groups than in the population as a whole	125
Figure 7–4	Evaluation results in which the slope of posttest on pretest is different for the two groups	126
Figure 7–5	Experimental design—the difference in slopes may appropriately be incorporated into the treatment effect using an interaction model	127
Figure 7–6	Treatment effect erroneously inferred when both slopes are identically false	129
Figure 8–1	Interval estimates of program effect	138
Figure 9–1	The counterfactual series; the result series	148
Figure 9–2	Time-series analysis compared with analysis of two time points	149
Figure 9–3	Visual analysis of well-behaved series	155
Figure 9–4	Series in which changes in level or slope or both are difficult to estimate by visual analysis	156
Figure 9–5	Effect of introducing a law in the experimental state requiring repayment of welfare costs from the deceased recipient's estate on the old age assistance case loads—monthly data have all values expressed as a percentage of the case load eighteen months prior to the change of the law	161
Figure 10–1	Z is a source of spuriousness	167
Figure 10–2	X_1 is an intervening variable	183
Table 3–1	Summative evaluation of the cowbird control program	37
Table 3–2	Formative evaluation of the cowbird control program	39

IMPACT
ANALYSIS FOR
PROGRAM
EVALUATION

Chapter One

The Evaluation Framework

Let us take the term *impact analysis* to mean determining the extent to which one set of directed human activities (X) affected the state of some objects or phenomena ($Y_1, \ldots, Y_k$) and—at least sometimes—determining why the effects were as small or large as they turned out to be. We will usually think of X as being some established program and each Y as being one of the many possible outcomes of that program. Until the final chapter, we will generally simplify by considering only one Y per program, an unrealistic simplification, but one that is not ultimately misleading. Notice that in concentrating on impact analysis we will not be concerned in this book with the worthwhileness of a program, as in benefit-cost analysis, for example, but rather, we will limit our concern to certain of its accomplishments. In the final chapter, however, I will present some reflections on this approach as compared with others, such as benefit-cost analysis, so that some of the strengths and limitations may be brought into perspective.

As an organizing device, we will assume that there is in each instance a "program theory." The program theory always states that the program's activities will have certain specified results in terms of Y, perhaps through the medium of some intermediate events or accomplishments that were also specified. Testing this theory once it is given substantive content is what impact analysis is all about. It is important to accept fully at the outset that the program theory is purely a formal device; what matters is only that someone is interested in the truth or falsity of the theory that X results in Y and is willing to devote some resources to testing it. The theory that a program has a certain outcome may in fact often be tested primarily to show that it is *not* true. This was the case, for example, with the Kansas City Preventive Patrol Experiment (Kelling et al. 1976), whose supporters suspected that preventive police patrol might not stop enough crime to make this nearly universal practice worthwhile.

THE EVALUATION FRAMEWORK

The framework for the study of program evaluation that we will use is generated largely by the program theory concept and the intent to test it. This framework has three major divisions. (1) The theory has component elements; impact analysis consists largely of making observations about these elements and relating them to one another. The primary elements are the problem, the activities, the outcome of interest (sometimes called the objective), and the subobjectives. For good evaluation to develop, a sound working knowledge of these concepts, the differences among them, and their respective functions both in the conduct and evaluation of the program are critical. Considerable attention will be devoted to elaborating and clarifying these elements and their offshoots to foster a useful intuitive grasp of the edifice of impact analysis. (2) There must be some means of determining whether the theory is correct. Whatever means one uses can be called a design. Most of the book deals with probing the advantages and disadvantages of different impact-analysis designs (which will sometimes be referred to as evaluation designs). (3) There must be a way of quantifying the program's effectiveness. This is best accomplished through statistics such as a regression coefficient, a difference between two means (for example, the experimental-group mean and the control-group mean), or a difference between two proportions, and, when appropriate, through tests of the statistical significance of such measures. There are two additional quantifiers that are not often used but that could profitably be considered much more frequently. These are the *effectiveness ratio* and the *adequacy ratio* (see Deniston et al. 1968). Finally, in quantifying program effectiveness, one must be concerned with the *coverage* level of the measure. Specifically, one must determine whether the measure refers to the population actually treated or the population at risk.

SOME QUANTIFIERS OF PROGRAM EFFECTIVENESS

In the ensuing chapters, the explicit and organizing subject matter will be either the elements of the program theory or impact-analysis design, while attention to the quantitative measures of effectiveness will be woven into the discussion only as needed. Often, such attention need be only indirect or coincidental to the primary focus of a chapter. Let us begin, however, with an orientation to the idea of the scaling of effectiveness, including an explanation of the two underemployed measurement devices noted above.

The crux of impact analysis is *a comparison of what did happen after implementing the program with what would have happened had the program not been implemented.* We may call this comparison the *impact* of the program. Events in the what-would-have-happened category must obviously be troublesome. As Hardy put it (1905, p. 357): "what they would have been remains forever in the darkness of the unfulfilled." This element can never be observed and can never be known for certain. Its paramount importance in assessing the impact of a program and, at the same time, its fundamental inaccessibility, makes this the pivotal point of all impact-analysis designs and a major point of reservations about the validity of evaluative conclusions. We will refer to this element with the term *the counterfactual* (see Larkey 1979), and symbolize it as "C." In using the term, the reference will not be to general states of things on a host of variables at once, but only to one variable at a time, usually the outcome of interest (objective) being considered, at least for the moment, in connection with the evaluation of a particular program. Hence, the counterfactual will usually refer to the quantitative score or level at which the outcome of interest would have been found had the program not been implemented.

The other major component of impact assessment is the actual state of the world (i.e., of the treated subjects) on the same outcome of interest after the program is implemented, or the "resulting" state of the world. It will be symbolized here as "R."

The simplest and probably the most common quantifier of program effectiveness is the explicitly presented difference between R and C. The statistic used for R − C is the difference of means or of proportions. For example, if one were evaluating the efficacy of an employment counseling program for prisoners soon to be released, one outcome of interest would no doubt be some operationalization of the concept of unemployment. One might assess program impact by stating the difference between the mean number of days unemployed in a six-month postrelease period for the group that received the treatment (R), and a similar group that did not (C). The statistic here is the difference of means. Alternatively, one might subtract the proportion of the treatment group not holding a full-time job six months after release (R) from the proportion of the comparison group in that same category (C). In this second operationalization of the term *unemployment,* the difference of proportions is the statistic that quantifies program impact.

While a simple R − C as expressed by a difference of means, a difference of proportions, or, as we will see later, a regression coefficient, may be straightforward and common, it often has a noteworthy shortcoming as a measure of effectiveness. A simple number such as − 23, − 15 percent, or − .66 does not really answer the question "How effective?" Does a difference of means of − 23 say that the program has been quite effective or only minimally so? In certain instances one may legitimately run a statistical test and learn that the difference of − 23 is "significant," but that finding merely allows one to conclude that the program had *some* causal impact. One does not learn from the test itself whether the impact was substantial or weak. If the measurement scale used for the outcome of interest has become intrinsically meaningful through extensive use, as with measurement in dollars, for example, a simple R − C may be communicative enough; otherwise, some standard is needed by which a number such as − 23 or − 16 percent may be interpreted.

One possible standard (perhaps the most obvious one) is the *planned* impact of the program. If, for example, the program directors had desired and sought an impact of − 46, then their attainment of − 23 tells them that their efforts were only 50 percent effective. Thus, Deniston et al. (1968) have proposed (using other notation) the following "effectiveness ratio" as a quantifier of effectiveness:

$$\text{Effectiveness} = \frac{R - C}{P - C}$$

where P indicates the planned state of the world on the outcome of interest. The function may be readily interpreted as expressing the ratio of the actual to the planned impact of the program. The planned impact, as a standard, would seem to be an eminently reasonable basis for expressing degree of effectiveness, and the effectiveness ratio has the additional characteristic, which many would consider desirable, of leading program personnel actually to think about how much they hope to attain. Here it should be noted that while the evaluation and planning literatures pay considerable lip service to the necessity of having "objectives" or goals, no planned attainment is actually required by the ordinary impact quantifier R − C.

Looking at the effectiveness ratio, one readily sees that a high rating may be attained by modesty in planning. But while the effectiveness ratio could surely be used to deceive and impress (as with so much in program evaluation), its proposed use is for the self-guidance of thoughtful and serious program managers and personnel. The possibility of deceit is present, therefore, but will not occupy us further in this context. There are, however, other possible limitations to consider. One is that, as an outside evaluator, it is extremely difficult to get program personnel to do the planning required to specify P. Even a program manager him- or herself has difficulty finding the motivation to do the required planning! A second limitation lies in the frequent difficulty of estimating the counterfactual accurately ahead of time, which must be done if the planned impact is to be established before the evaluation is carried out.

Let us take an example that illustrates some of the pros and cons. The road commissioners plan to reduce average travel time along a stretch of road from 15 minutes to 10 minutes by widening it to three lanes. Let us suppose that when the project is completed average travel time is 10.5 minutes. Then,

$$\text{Effectiveness} = \frac{R - C}{P - C} = \frac{10.5 - 15}{10 - 15} = \frac{-4.5}{-5.0} = .9 \text{ or } 90\%.$$

First, one presumes that there is something to be learned by program personnel from the difference between planned and actual impact—perhaps, for example, about the unanticipated extent to which additional motorists were attracted to the road by widening it. The counterfactual (15 minutes) is readily estimated beforehand. Indeed, it must be estimated beforehand in this case, because the design, as we will see, is the "before-after" type in which the baseline measure must generally be obtained before implementation of the project if it is to be obtained at all. Finally, some would say that the quantity 4.5 fewer minutes is so clearly understandable and interpretable that no further indicator of effectiveness is necessary. (This would by no means always be the case. Consider attitude scaling, for example. The quantity of conservatism, tolerance, job satisfaction, and so on that is represented by the distance of one point on the scale is not likely to be very clear, almost regardless of how the attitude is measured.) To others, however, the figure 90 percent may be highly informative additional information that will improve future planning and program management.

An alternative to the planned state of the world as a standard that yields another quantifier of effectiveness is the extent of the problem, usually indicated by the counterfactual itself. The measure that results may be called the adequacy ratio, formulated as

$$\text{Adequacy} = 1 - \frac{R}{C}.$$

This measure quantifies effectiveness by conceptualizing it as the proportion of the problem eliminated by the program. It is applicable without modification only when complete elimination is relevant, which is commonly the case. Sometimes, however, it is not the case, as in the example of the street-widening project just explored. The formula suggests that

$$\text{Adequacy} = 1 - \frac{R}{C} = 1 - \frac{10.5}{15.0} = 1 - .7 = .3 \text{ or } 30\%.$$

To say that the project was only 30 percent adequate, however, is to mislead substantially since 100 percent adequate, or 100 percent elimination of the problem, would mean a travel time of zero. The trouble is that we do not want to consider the entire quantity fifteen to be a problem. The remedy for this sort of case will be presented momentarily. To take a more appropriate illustration first, consider the results of a voter registration drive:

$$\text{Adequacy} = 1 - \frac{R}{C} = 1 - \frac{25\%}{30\%} = 1 - \frac{5}{6} = \frac{1}{6} = 16.67\%.$$

Here, 30 percent would have been unregistered if there had been no program and 25 percent were left unregistered at the close of the drive. We might feel comfortable considering the entire 30 percent unregistered as a problem. The ratio R/C indicates the proportion of the problem remaining—here 83⅓ percent—so that the program was 16⅔ percent adequate.

The adequacy ratio forces the evaluator to take an interesting measurement stance. To reflect the degrees of a problem, the counterfactual (and therefore the actual outcome) must be seen as an undesirable condition rather than a desirable one so that the higher the number the greater the problem. If the adequacy ratio is put the other way around, it will communicate nothing whatever of interest, as the reader can tell by experimenting. In the above illustration, for example, we spoke of the percent unregistered rather than the percent registered. Frequently, the undesirable is the natural way of looking at a condition in program planning and evaluation, as in the case of travel time, incidence of disease, death rates, pollution, birthrates (as a concern of birth control), crime, unemployment, and so forth. Sometimes, the desirable and undesirable sides of the coin are nearly equivalent for purposes of evaluation so that the adequacy ratio using the undesirable side is still quite straightforwardly applicable, as in registered versus unregistered, or literate versus illiterate. Sometimes, however, the need to focus on the undesirable demands extra effort, as in a special education program to increase the achievement of gifted children, an agricultural program to increase crop yields, a management program to improve morale, or a physical therapy program to improve body function. Such ideas as achievement, crop yields, morale, and body function cannot readily be expressed as undesirable conditions; they have no reverse side that is "bad" in the same way that they themselves are "good."

The remedy to the adequacy ratio is to decide on the level of crop yield, morale, and so on that is considered desirable and to *render the measures of R and C in terms of a gap.* For example, if the desired yield were forty bushels per hectare and if the yield without the program would be only fifteen bushels, then C becomes the undesirable *gap* of twenty-five bushels. Similarly, if actual yield after implementation were thirty, then R becomes a gap of ten. Thus

$$\text{Adequacy} = 1 - \frac{R}{C} = 1 - \frac{10}{25} = 1 - \frac{2}{5} = .6.$$

One sees that 40 percent of the undesirable *shortfall* remains and the program has been 60 percent adequate in problem elimination. One may always measure R and C using a gap in this fashion.

We may now return to street widening, where the adequacy ratio was not directly applicable because problem elimination expressed as zero travel time was not a realistic possibility. It is only necessary to establish the travel time that *would* signify elimination of the problem, say 9 minutes, and express R and C as gaps or distances from this standard. Here, R = 10.5 − 9 = 1.5 (i.e., a 1.5 minute gap between actual and optimal), C = 15 − 9 = 6, and

$$\text{Adequacy} = 1 - \frac{1.5}{6.0} = 1 - .25 = .75.$$

The necessity of expressing R and C as an undesirable condition and of thinking in distances from elimination of the problem is constructive. In the case of a special education program for gifted children, for example, what is supposedly wrong with their current levels of achievement? What is wrong with current rice yields in a region of Indonesia? There should not be a program unless there is a problem, but current achievement and yields do not in themselves express the problem. The adequacy ratio draws program personnel away from an orientation to simple unconsidered "improvement" as a goal and toward an explicit appreciation for the difference between what can and should be, on one hand, and what will be without intervention, on the other.

It was suggested above that the effectiveness and adequacy ratios are underemployed. It would be both futile and undesirable to recommend that they be used more often as substitutes for the standard statistics that reflect impact, or R − C, alone. There is much to be gained, however, in using them in evaluation reports *in addition to* the standard measures, and in using them in discussions with program personnel at both the planning and evaluation stages to help them gain further insight into the logic of their activities.

COVERAGE LEVEL OF THE QUANTIFIERS

Impact statistics may refer to either of two levels of *coverage* or inclusiveness: the population treated or the population at risk. This distinction is important because the first group is often smaller than the second and a program that is effective concerning the subjects actually treated may still leave a good deal of the problem unmet. Sometimes the program is not administered to all subjects that might need it because it is a pilot project or experiment to test the efficacy of a new method. Examples are the negative income tax experiments (e.g., Kershaw 1980) or a comprehensive care program for the treatment of severe arthritis (Deniston and Rosenstock 1973). In such cases, the larger population that might benefit from the program is not relevant to the evaluation of effectiveness. Sometimes the decision to target a smaller group than the population at risk is well known to all and is mainly a matter of the limited availability of funds, as with a program of loans to minority businesses or a program to rehabilitate the housing stock of the poor. Sometimes, however, it would be possible and desirable to reach the whole at-risk population, but the program does not do so. This might be the case, for example, with a program to ensure that all women in a certain age group have a periodic Pap smear for cervical cancer detection, or a program to counsel high school students on employment opportunities and job-seeking skills, or a program to make the housing stock of a community more energy efficient. It is particularly in such cases that the program may be effective with those treated but ineffective in that it fails to reach enough subjects. Even when small scope is necessitated by lack of funds, it may be important to know how much of the larger problem remains unsolved.

When both the smaller and larger levels of coverage are germane, any of the quantifiers of impact may be applied to either level, but each may demand its own data and research activities. Consider, for example, a program that offers energy audits to the owners of business and residential buildings, with the further objective that the owners will then retrofit the buildings for energy conservation. Once audited, a substantial proportion may proceed to retrofit, but only a small proportion of owners may request or receive audits. The adequacy ratio tends to be particularly well suited to the larger population since it tells directly the proportion of that population that is not in the desired state (e.g., the proportion of buildings in the community that need conservation measures but still lack them). An ordinary impact statistic or the effectiveness ratio may often be a better choice with the group actually treated (in this example, audited). The impact statistic would communicate the extent to which the audits and other activities led to conservation measures that would otherwise not have been taken, and the effectiveness ratio would indicate the percent of planned or estimated successes actually achieved among those who were audited. In any case, recognizing that the choice of quantifier will depend on just what information is needed in each instance, it is well to ask in all impact analyses whether the issue of coverage has been adequately treated.

SUMMARY

In this chapter, the rudiments of the evaluation framework were set out in terms of the elements of the program theory, the testing of the theory by means of research designs, and the quantification of effectiveness. In addition, we began to fill in the framework by supplying some initial content to the idea of quantifying effectiveness. In the next two chapters, we proceed with the elaboration of the framework by considering in detail the primary elements of the program theory: the problem, outcomes, activities, and subobjectives.

Chapter Two

Outcomes and the Problem

The task of carrying out a sound evaluation presents two major challenges: asking the right questions and getting the right answers. Chapters Two and Three, as well as the final chapter, address the first of these two central issues—asking the right questions. This is an issue whose importance is widely recognized but whose accomplishment tends to be neglected in the methodology of evaluation. There is a tendency for program evaluation to focus on "objectives"—what the program is ostensibly meant to accomplish—and the activities that are apparently designed to achieve them. This preoccupation should not prevail, however, at the expense of the relative neglect of two other major elements, namely, subobjectives and the problem. The last two elements have the potential for greatly increasing the power and utility of an evaluation by helping it to focus properly or to ask the right questions.

THE PROBLEM

As noted in the previous chapter, there is little reason to have a program unless there is a problem. Accordingly, let us define a problem relative to a given program as *some predicted condition that will be unsatisfactory without the intervention of the program and satisfactory, or at least more acceptable, given the program's intervention* (Deniston 1972a, 1972b). The last stipulation (satisfactory) describes a relevance condition. There are many problems in the world, many things that would be unsatisfactory without this program. However, a state of the world should not be considered a problem relative to a given program unless the program can realistically be expected to do something about it. The definition has a subjective cast; not all parties need agree on what would be an unsatisfactory condition, and any individual or group might be interested in an evaluation based on its own determination of problems.

The problem, which corresponds directly to the outcome of interest, appears in impact analysis as the counterfactual. In other words, what would otherwise have been true (i.e., the counterfactual) is considered a priori to be unsatisfactory (i.e., a problem). It will be seen that a problem orientation can help to focus an evaluation on the kinds of outcomes that will lend it strength and influence in the policymaking process and that can aid materially in program planning even without the actual conduct of evaluation research.

To avoid serious challenges after its completion, an impact analysis should focus on an *inherently valued* outcome, which most commonly relates to an *inherent* problem. Let us now elaborate on these terms and provide a method for achieving the sort of focus suggested. Chapter One explained that the symbol C is used to represent the counterfactual and R to indicate the resulting state of the world on the relevant dimension in the evaluation. The impact of a program, we have seen, is indicated by $R - C$. Finally, an outcome of interest (e.g., a crime rate) was a dimension on which R and C are points or measured values—the resulting crime rate and the counterfactual crime rate.

Before continuing with the mainstream of the discussion of the problem in this context, it is well to acknowledge that the term itself is not always an apt one for the counterfactual in an analysis. We may note that anticipated program impacts may be (and this is again a subjective consideration) either beneficial or detrimental. It is the beneficial type to which the term *problem* is relevant since a problem is what would be experienced if the program did not have beneficial results. Most impact analyses *do* concern beneficial anticipated impacts, but some may concern the detrimental *side effects* of programs that were being conducted for other, presumably beneficial, purposes. For example, experimental evaluations of the negative income tax have been mainly concerned with work incentives, a side effect on which the program impact was feared detrimental. In this case, things are turned around. Without the program there would obviously be no problem of unwanted or adverse side effects. Here it is the *resulting* state of the world and not the counterfactual that actually represents the possible problem. Thus, when dealing with outcomes that one places in the category of detrimental program effects, the concept of the problem is not applicable in the same sense and, furthermore, does not serve the positive evaluation functions that will be elaborated below. It is enough to identify the particular detrimental side effect, consider it an outcome of interest, examine the simple impact of the program upon it, and, if desired, analyze the intermediate mechanisms through which the program had this effect. Effectiveness and adequacy ratios are not germane: just as the idea that there would be a problem without the program is inaccurate in this context, so the idea of the effectiveness or adequacy of the program in achieving a detrimental side effect has little meaning or utility.

THE OUTCOME LINE

Whether addressing beneficial or detrimental impacts, some concern outcome dimensions that are inherently valued, whereas others are merely instrumental to these. An impact analysis, as was stated earlier, should focus on an inherently valued outcome, and evaluation methodology should help to produce such a focus rather than leave it to common sense. Figure 2–1 illustrates the major concepts by showing a sample outcome line. The figure depicts a line of outcomes in the form of a causal chain (the arrows indicate causality). One of these is the outcome of interst, which must appear in every impact analysis. The outcomes to its left are instrumental to its attainment and are labeled subobjectives (the subject of Chapter Three). To its right may be one or more ultimate outcomes. Somewhere in the program there must be one or more activities designed to achieve either a subobjective or the outcome of interest. We will see momentarily, in examples of programs, that activities may affect the outcome of interest directly or they may produce one or more subobjectives that in turn lead to the outcome of interest. In many cases, activities may be necessary for both kinds of effect.

To take a concrete example, consider the outcome line for a wire-tapping program as part of drug-law enforcement in Figure 2–2. Here, the core activity is wiretapping to find out—a subobjective in this case—if suspects are indeed selling drugs and, perhaps, how to catch them in the act of dealing. This category of subobjective will appear very commonly in properly conducted evaluations and is labeled the discovery subobjective; the program discovers something, obtains information, that it needs for further operations. Other examples are discovering through screening procedures who might have a disease such as tuberculosis or cancer, discovering through inspections whether operators of restaurants are violating sanitation standards, discovering through energy audits the needs of residences for energy-saving measures, and so forth. Next in Figure 2–2, the information that is gleaned is turned over to the local police—the reporting activity—in order that arrests may be made. Arresting the "pushers" should lead in turn to decreases in drug sales, reduced consumption of drugs, and lower rates of addiction, which will then result in a variety of social and economic benefits.

It is extremely important for good impact analysis and for evaluation critique and appraisal (as well as for program planning) to make an outcome line explicit in this fashion. I hope to establish a case for this claim through examples in this and subsequent chapters. Here, I

FIGURE 2–1   Outcome line

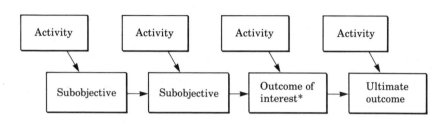

*Universal. Must appear in all evaluations.

FIGURE 2–2   Outcome line for a wiretapping program

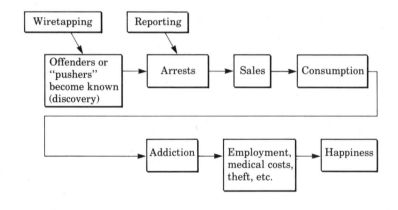

would simply emphasize my own view that the value of outcome-line analysis can hardly be overstated.

A critical idea in the construction of an outcome line is the distinction between outcomes and activities. An outcome is a *result* of activity by program personnel, generally a state of being or a state of the world that may be attained. Examples are the ignorance or awareness of certain information by program personnel (which relates to the discovery subobjective), the state of health of subjects, the degree of mastery of subject matter taught in class, the rate at which felonies are committed in a city, the level of an individual's motivation to perform some act, the degree of skill possessed, and any action of *subjects,* such as going to their doctor, and so forth. An activity is simply a kind of effort exerted *by program personnel,* without any inherent denotation of its results. Examples are screening for a disease, listening to information, treating patients, teaching a subject in a certain way, patrolling the streets, and so forth.

To construct an outcome line, one may start either near the beginning, with some notion of what program personnel are doing, or near the end, with some notion of a problem and the outcome that represents its amelioration. In either case, as we will see momentarily, one may complete the line by working forward, backward, or both, from one or more starting points. The completed outcome line represents the *program theory* insofar as one particular analysis of impact is concerned. It tells what is to be done in the program and why—what is to result from the program and how. It is, in short, a testable assertion that certain program activities and subobjectives will bring about specified results.

To complete and correct an outcome line from any starting point or points, two kinds of question are repeatedly asked. The first is, Why perform or accomplish X (an activity or an outcome), that is, what is expected to result from X? The answers to such questions help to extend the line as one moves from left to right. They help to determine the subobjectives and outcomes that will eventually lead to inherently valued outcomes toward the right-hand end. The second question is, How can Y be expected to follow from X, that is, what other things, if any, must be done or must occur to make the jump from X to Y believable? The answers here help to fill gaps in the line, to forge firmer links between outcomes and to find places where additional activities may be necessary. In health and welfare programs, for example, clients are frequently referred to another agency or to their private physician, but one cannot always simply assume that they will go. Follow-up contacts (an activity that might not have been thought of at first) may be necessary to give further encouragement or assistance. Or, consider the issuance of foster home standards (activity) that are designed to reduce delinquency (outcome) among teenagers assigned to foster homes. One can only expect the regulations to affect delinquency rates if the homes actually *meet the standards* (a subobjective that must be inserted between activity and outcome).

Finding the Outcome of Interest

Once the outcome line has been completed in this fashion (so that it runs from the basic program activities on the left to the ultimate benefits on the right), the critical issue of selecting the outcome of interest can be addressed systematically. Which outcome in the line shall be the particular outcome or variable on whose measurement the effectiveness of the program is to be judged? The core of the answer was suggested above with the assertion that the outcome of interest in the evaluation must be inherently valued. It remains, then, to define this critical category.

First, an inherently valued outcome is one in which there is interest for its own sake rather than for the sake of achieving something further. More specifically, outcome Y is said to be inherently valued if either one of two implications for the outcomes *to its right* is valid: (*a*) if Y is attained, the attainment of outcomes to the right is immaterial—one doesn't particularly care to learn whether they occurred or even what they are; or (*b*) if Y is attained, one is willing to *assume* that the specified outcomes further to the right will also be attained at a satisfactory level.

A good way to see the operation of the first consideration is by noting the word *happiness* at the end of the outcome line in Figure 2–2, and of almost any other proper outcome line that one might construct. In truth, the word *happiness* is just an indefinite substitute for the many complex benefits that are likely to be consequent on the achievement of higher employment levels, lower medical costs, lower crime rates, and so forth. One probably does not need to stipulate these additional consequences because they are probably immaterial. If the desired levels of employment, medical costs, and crime rates are attained, that is considered to be good enough, so these benefits in themselves are inherently valued outcomes. The meaning of consideration two is more straightforward; the simple assumption here is that one outcome surely leads to another.

The following is a scenario—very close to one that actually was played out in the early 1970s—that uses these considerations and Figure 2–2 to illustrate the way to determine the proper outcome of interest in the evaluation of the wiretapping program. The FBI and the Narcotics Bureau come to the appropriate congressional subcommittees with requests for authorization and funds to carry out the program. The committees, being somewhat skeptical and cautious, ask on what basis the success of such a program should be evaluated. The answer, supplied by evaluation methodology, is that *the proper outcome of interest is the first or leftmost inherently valued outcome on the line.* To find the first, it is best to start from the right-hand end to be sure that all of the links are tight, that is, that there are no tenuous causal assumptions about consequences. Surely, then, employment, medical costs, and theft constitute an inherently valued outcome; that is, both the agencies and the committees agree that the further consequences are immaterial if only the program can satisfactorily accomplish these things. But is it the *first* inherently valued outcome? Moving back to addiction, it is perhaps not immaterial what the results of decreases in addiction would be (although to some it may indeed be immaterial), but the agencies and committees can at least agree on consideration two—that if addiction levels are indeed substantially reduced, it is safe to assume based on other information that the benefits of employment and so on will follow. Addiction, then, is also an outcome dimension of inherent value. Going back a step further to the consumption outcome, the same reasoning applies. Going back to sales, the same reasoning again applies: reduced consumption can safely be assumed to follow reduced sales. We then move back to arrests. If many "pushers" are arrested, is that good enough in itself, so that achievement of the balance of the line to the right is immaterial? The congressional committees say that it is not; they are in fact quite interested in the next outcome—the consequent volume of illegal sales of narcotics. Can we then *assume* that adequately reduced sales will be the result of the expected number of arrests? The committees believe not. It is in fact widely accepted that if some drug dealers go to jail, others are quickly recruited to take their places. Arrests, therefore, which satisfy neither consideration one nor consideration two, cannot constitute an inherently valued outcome and therefore cannot properly be the outcome of interest for the evaluation. The effectiveness of the wiretapping program cannot be judged by arrests alone (although, as we will see later, arrests might well be measured and analyzed as a subobjective). This suggests that activities in addition to wiretapping would have to be carried out to affect the sales of drugs. On this basis, in fact, the continuing scenario finds that the request for the program is denied by the Congress; wiretapping is not expected to accomplish enough of what really needs to be accomplished. If the program were, however, to be carried out, sales, as the first inherently valued outcome from the left, would be the outcome of interest in the evaluation.

Let us consider one more example. Figure 2–3 shows the outcome line for a program of home energy audits. Total energy consumption is an inherently valued outcome. Residential energy conservation might possibly be considered an inherently valued outcome, although some might doubt the assumption that the next benefits will ensue because too much of the money saved on energy consumption in the home might simply be spent on extra car trips or other external activities that also consume energy.

Let us set this doubt aside for a moment and then return to it. If residential consumption may be accepted as an inherently valued outcome, can we move back to retrofitting? Instead of conserving energy in the home, retrofitting might simply induce people to "dial up," thereby increasing their comfort at no additional cost. This is indicated in the diagram as an acceptable alternative outcome, but if program personnel did not consider it acceptable, residential consumption, not retrofitting, must be the outcome of interest and additional activities

FIGURE 2–3 Outcome line for a program of home energy audits

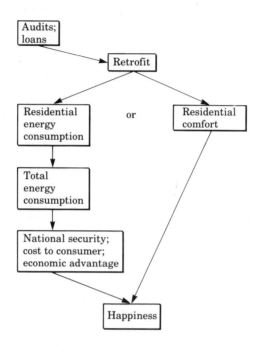

must be undertaken to convince people to conserve energy in the home rather than increase comfort. Similarly, if home energy savings cannot be assumed to result in net overall energy savings, then residential conservation is not an inherently valued outcome. One must move to the right and additional activities must be undertaken to curtail the expenditure of freed resources on car trips and other kinds of energy-consuming activity. If residential conservation and comfort together *do* satisfy the requirements, however, then so does retrofitting because other research has established that adequate amounts of energy definitely are saved by various weatherizing devices and conservation technologies. The proper outcome of interest could therefore well be the extent of retrofitting by home owners. (Data on the amount of energy actually conserved would no doubt be welcome for publicity or other uses. There is no reason except expense why one should not obtain data on rightward inherently valued outcomes.) Even if the data showed that adequate energy were not being conserved in the home, or in total, the program targeted on retrofitting could still be considered by some personnel to be worthwhile in its own right by condition one (further attainment is immaterial) and *other* programs could be undertaken, perhaps by other agencies or units entirely, to persuade people not to use their energy savings for further energy consumption.

Whether something is immaterial, or whether an assumption about consequences may be made, is therefore a *subjective* and not a logical consideration. These methods, however, do enable evaluators and program managers or financers, with some study and discussion, to select the outcome of interest to their own satisfaction. Also, experience shows that an awareness of what it will take to convince the necessary interested parties to support the program generally makes for broad agreement on where in the outcome line considerations one and two are indeed satisfactorily met.

RELATION OF THE PROBLEM TO THE OUTCOME LINE

Outcomes appear explicitly in the outcome line whereas problems do not. The correspondence between the two may seem almost one to one. Nevertheless, it is essential to supplement outcome-line construction and analysis with the question, What is the problem? What is the counterfactual? Doing so forces a more careful specification than, State an inherently valued outcome, as we will now see.

Distraction from the Problem

An outcome, for example, may represent only one possible channel for attacking a problem—perhaps an inadequate one—and its emphasis may distract one's attention from the problem itself in its larger scope. In a project whose major activity was physical therapy services for nursing home patients, for example, both program and evaluation personnel fixated on the physiological ability of patients to function (Kelman 1962). This led to an emphasis on the measurement of functional ability in the laboratory rather than the measurement of actual functioning in the home itself, which was recognized as the condition in the world that truly required change. Surely, physiological capability is a necessary condition, but if the problem had been stated explicitly as the failure of patients to care for themselves in the home (dressing, toileting, etc.), measurement is not likely to have been taken exclusively in the laboratory. Furthermore, supplemental treatment modalities aimed at changing motivation are not likely to have been totally neglected. It happens that far better results have been obtained in other projects simply by serving beer, cheese, and crackers socially to nursing home patients each afternoon (Volpe and Kastenbaum 1967). In the Kelman study, however, otherwise a laudable, pioneering impact analysis, the importance of the motivational component was truly recognized only at the end of the project. Attention to the problem together with thorough outcome-line analysis would have brought it in at the beginning.

Failure to Recognize Multiple Concerns

Second, the fixation on outcomes easily leads to the failure to recognize that what may seem to be one outcome actually represents several possible problems demanding alternative program activities. A good example is the outcome decreased juvenile delinquency. In one early study, the delinquency outcome was measured in four ways in what seemed on the surface a nice gesture toward capturing the concept in its entirety (Berleman and Steinburn 1967). The four ways were (1) average delinquency score per subject, (2) average delinquency score per delinquent subject, (3) average seriousness of acts of delinquency, and (4) percent of subjects who committed delinquent acts. A moment's thought shows that three different program emphases are actually suggested here, corresponding to three different problems: (*a*) working with all subjects to hold down the number who either become or continue to be delinquent (measures 1 and 4); (*b*) working with offenders to prevent further offenses (measure 2); and (*c*) working with a strategically selected subgroup or in strategically selected ways to prevent serious offenses while virtually ignoring the nonserious ones (measure 3). This kind of vagueness and confusion is not so likely to result if attention were given to stating the problem specifically and considering how to reduce it. One must state, in other words, that there would be, without the program, either too much serious delinquency, too much chronic delinquency, or too many delinquents. Even if one began with the loose but *explicit* statement, "too much delinquency," one is likely to realize quickly that there are, logically, several ways of bringing down the total and that an unconsidered set of program activities simply represents the selection of one strategy and the rejection of others by default. Failure to specify the problem in this sort of case can mean an ineffective and inefficient diffusion of energy by program personnel and evaluators.

Failure to Recognize the Targeted Problem

Third, there is a frequent tendency to state and measure the wrong outcomes, outcomes that are only incidental and that do not represent truly targeted problems. This again leads to confusion, poor program planning, and the dissipation of evaluation energy. An example is presented by a program that was considered able to kill two birds with one stone: (1) providing employment skills as home health aides to able elderly people who could not easily work otherwise, and (2) improving health status for individuals who needed such services in the home but could not pay for them through ordinary channels (Lyons and Steele 1977). In truth, however, the program was almost exclusively a training program. It was ill-equipped in skills, funds, or motivation to handle either employment services for the trainees or the potential clients' problems and outcomes. These issues, however, continued to draw attention that was incidental to the training efforts. It would probably have been far better to consider the client population a market to be developed (or at least researched) rather than a nebulous group assumed to be waiting for help. The demand for the service turned out to be weak. Moreover, evaluation personnel were able to conduct only a meager nonrigorous study on those aspects, such as the well-being of the clients, that were nominally objectives of the program but were in reality only the wish for a beneficial side effect. Still, evaluation energy and resources are always finite and generally quite restricted with the result that, as in this case, nonrigorous secondary studies may become a siphon in planning and implementation that detracts from the depth and conclusiveness of the main lines of research. On the other hand, if the evaluator or program manager were to consider such issues as unemployment and the health status of clients as true problems, one would almost inevitably realize the near *irrelevance* of a program consisting essentially of the training of a small number of home health aides. If aides were trained and little else were done, one should probably not expect to find much impact and, therefore, one would not see much wisdom in expending research resources to measure it.

Failure to Recognize Levels of Coverage

A fourth reason for attending to the problem as well as to outcomes is that it helps to bring in levels of coverage that might otherwise be unjustifiably neglected. The idea of coverage, introduced in Chapter One, means the inclusiveness of the population that is analyzed as the program's target. Consider the issue of employment for the potential home health aides in the previous example, or an ombudsman service, or a program of home energy audits. If one focuses only on outcomes, it is easy and common to orient the impact analysis toward the coverage level comprised by the treated population—employment for the aides who were trained, complaint solutions for the citizens who brought a matter to the ombudsman, or retrofitting by the residents who requested an audit. If one states the problem, however, the same orientation is highly unlikely to result. Surely, the problem in each case is not that only these volunteers would be in some undesirable state, but rather that some proportion of the community would be so. It is frequently inadequate to evaluate a program's impact on specific volunteers to the exclusion of its impact on some larger population, such as the community from which the treated subjects were drawn.

Failure to Acknowledge the Counterfactual

Finally, if one does not make a point of thinking about it, there is an all-too-common tendency to forget about the role of the counterfactual and to think about impact analysis (on beneficial outcomes) purely in terms of results. The counterfactual is generally a problem. Attending to the problem will ensure that the counterfactual will have the prominent role that it must have in program evaluation. If one conducted a voter registration drive, for example, one might present one's objective as signing up 1,000 new voters. If 850 were then registered, one might evaluate the program as 85 percent effective. But that statement does not reflect the effectiveness of the program; it neglects the issue of the number of potential new voters that would have signed up even without the registration drive. The true problem, presumably, is that some number would remain *unregistered without* the program, and the hoped-for results are that a much smaller number will remain unregistered after the drive.

JOINT USE OF COMPLETE OUTCOME LINE AND PROBLEM DEFINITION

I have offered five ways in which attention to the problem, in addition to outcomes, can be better than attention to outcomes alone. Many more examples could be provided. Let us continue by showing how the joint use of a complete outcome line and the definition of *problem* will produce the desired results. Thinking in outcomes is unquestionably better than trying to evaluate by counting activities (number of patients or clients seen, number of facilities inspected, number of pamphlets distributed, and so forth). Even an outcome orientation is not quite enough, however, because the concept is intentionally too broad—broad enough to cover the state of the world on almost any dimension. This may be quickly seen by considering the difference between the term *outcome* and the more common and narrower term *objective*. The second term connotes the goal or aim of the program's staff, or at least of someone with an interest in the program. The effectiveness of a program, however, need not be judged by criteria that represent conscious aims. One may be interested in the extent to which *any* particular phenomenon has been influenced by a particular program. There is no reason why evaluations should not be carried out to answer such questions when they arise, but it is unnecessary to consider the emergent criterion of appraisal as an "objective" if it were never any person's objective. For example, there apparently was an impact, totally unintended and unforeseen, of the U.S. military draft process in World War II (a program) on public health practice regarding school-children (an outcome) due to a heightened awareness of previously un-recognized physical problems in the potential recruits.

Almost anything might be a legitimate outcome; however, "just anything" cannot be a problem. A problem is a condition that from some perspective would be considered both unsatisfactory without the intervention of the program in question and satisfactory or at least more acceptable given that intervention. Thus, the sheer ability of the nursing home patients to care for themselves in certain respects—in spite of ability's being both an outcome and an actual objective—was not the problem; that ability could possibly have become quite *satis-factory*. But still there would have been a problem, namely, that the extent to which some patients did indeed care for themselves in the home would have been inadequate. Noting that there were some pa-tients who already were physiologically able to care for themselves but did not do so, program and evaluation personnel could then have seen the need to add services aimed at increasing patient motivation. That would have fashioned a fit between the program and the problem. The physiological outcome, in other words, was an unsatisfactory and dis-tracting one because it satisfied the definition of problem for only a small proportion of the patients. This kind if distinction, however, is not always intuitively obvious beforehand. In fact, it very often is not! It helps a great deal to remember to ask oneself, What is the problem? But it is also important both to lay out carefully the entire outcome line and to test each outcome on it by the definition of the problem. All should pass the test, for it would rarely be desirable to try to affect a factor that is either already satisfactory or that cannot be influenced by the methods contemplated. This device will almost invariably direct attention in the proper channels, point to the identification of the prob-lem, and ensure that the outcome of interest selected will prove satis-factory. In the nursing home case, a complete outcome line would quickly have been seen to require a link between the physiological ca-pability of the patients on one hand and such ultimate outcomes as the saving of staff time and greater attention to more important patient needs on the other: Why should enhanced physical capability save staff time? That missing link of course is greater self-care in the home. This inherently valued outcome (inherently valued because the freeing of staff time is virtually an automatic consequence), which also satisfies the definition of problem for many physically capable as well as inca-pable patients, must then have been selected as the outcome of inter-est.

The other examples offered above help to round out the point. It is not at all clear that each of the measures of delinquency cited earlier represented both a seriously deplored condition and one that was realistically remediable by the particular activities of the program. Additional self-questioning by program personnel would have been necessary to make that determination. Working with a complete outcome line and, particularly, applying the definition of problem, would maximize the likelihood that the appropriate self-questioning would be carried out in such a case. In the third case presented, it was not at all clear that levels of health or home care were inadequate without the intervention of the training program for home health aides, nor that possible inadequacies in health, home care, or employment levels were truly susceptible to amelioration due to the intervention of the *particular* program that was contemplated. The attempt to construct a complete outcome line, testing each outcome against the definition of problem, would have revealed a number of significant gaps in activities, information, and subobjectives, perhaps with the result of obviating the evaluation altogether. Considering the fourth example, it is easy to slip into the trap of evaluating a program only for its effects upon those it actually serves. Those effects do represent an outcome. When one specifies what would be inadequate without the program, however, the necessity for an outcome of broader scope will often become clear.

The fifth case, exemplified by a voter-registration outcome, is perhaps the most straightforward. There, failure to consider the problem leads to a fundamentally flawed evaluation—an evaluation without a counterfactual.

SUMMARY

In short, the method outlined in the previous sections, which features the relation of the problem to the outcome line, is a technical device for avoiding the many types of difficulties that are encountered—some noted here and some not—in trying to focus an evaluation on the right questions.

Finally, since the problem corresponds directly to the (beneficial) outcome of interest and the outcome of interest need not be a conscious objective, one may constitute the problem after the fact—from a side effect of the program, for example. Consider public health practice and the draft. It was noted earlier that although the upgrading of public health practice was never considered a problem in connection with initiating the draft, one may certainly assess the impact of the draft on subsequent public health programming. In doing so, one would construct the complete outcome line and no doubt be faced with deciding systematically whether the improvement of public health practice itself or the consequent health of American youth must be the outcome of interest. Although neither of these would have been seen as candidates for the problem in an evaluation at the time the draft was initiated, they could both be so now. Hence, to determine the proper outcome of interest, the concept of the problem would function in the same way as it does in an impact analysis dealing with conscious objectives.

This chapter has been devoted to an elaboration of the idea of outcomes (replacing the narrower notion of objectives) and the device of the outcome line, including an introduction to the meaning and function of the concept of the problem. We turn now toward completing the conceptualization of the outcome line with an initial discussion of the functions of subobjectives in a program evaluation.

Chapter Three

Subobjectives and Other Components

A subobjective is an outcome that, in the program theory, must be achieved before some further outcome may be achieved. When thinking of the attainment of certain outcomes as intentional, it is easy to conceptualize subobjectives as comprising the instrumental category, that is, intermediate achievements that are instrumental in reaching a desired goal. Technically, by this definition, all outcomes on the outcome line may be seen as subobjectives except the final one. The outcome of interest may be a subobjective, for example, when it is instrumental to the attainment of specified, important, further outcomes that are assumed to follow, as in the case of the street sales of narcotics and assumed levels of subsequent addiction in the targeted population. In practice, however, the term will be applied here to mean only those outcomes that are causally *before* the outcome of interest—those to the left of it on the outcome line.

Attention to subobjectives can serve two critical functions in program evaluation. One, which will be treated in Chapter Eleven, is in design: subobjectives can be used to lend strength and confidence to inferences about program impacts. The other, to be treated here, is in performance of the formative function.

FORMATIVE AND SUMMATIVE EVALUATIONS

Scriven (1972) has divided evaluations into the *formative* and the *summative*. The latter are studies that yield information only on bare simple impacts. They report a statistic such as a difference of means or proportions or a regression coefficient that quantifies the effect that has been caused on the outcome of interest, or perhaps they report a significance test that indicates whether the impact should be accepted as zero or nonzero. Such studies may necessarily be extensively elaborated and enormously complicated by measurement concerns, by the need for many or for ingenious control variables, by complex time series functions, and by the elaboration of treatment and control groups in the design, but the information they yield is limited fairly narrowly to quantifying the true impact of the program on the outcome of interest. In fact, one of the primary reasons why evaluations are not used more by program personnel is that this kind of information is not enough for their purposes. They frequently deplore being told that their efforts are or are not having much effect, especially the last. What they want to know is *why*—how to make a weak program stronger or an effective program even more effective, or perhaps more efficient. Subobjectives are a means to that end. It is fairly astounding, in view of such needs, that subobjective analysis has not become common; yet, it is extremely rare (for examples, see Deniston 1969; Lee 1986; Hawthorne 1988).

In contrast to the summative evaluation, the formative evaluation gives additional guidance, namely, it helps to improve or "form" the program itself. It can do this by two methods. The first gives no additional type of information, but it provides periodic or even continuous summative feedback rather than providing it only once. If program personnel feel they know what combinations of things to do to affect the outcome under varying circumstances, they can adjust their activities accordingly. This is commonly done in both the public and private sectors through the use of performance indicators such as changes in the money supply, sales figures, and so on.

The other type of formative evaluation, and the one that concerns us here, provides additional information of a different type (and may do so continuously, periodically, or only once). If the program turns out to have failed or fallen short in the summative sense, formative evaluation may attempt to answer the question why. If the program succeeds in some measure, formative evaluation may attempt to answer the question, Were all of the activities necessary, or were some dispensable? These responsive functions are accomplished by observing subobjectives and activities, as well as the outcome of interest. The subobjectives, it will be remembered, are outcomes that must be achieved so that the outcome of interest may be achieved. If it is known that one or more subobjectives were *not* achieved, a weakness may thereby be pinpointed or, perhaps, some waste motion may be identified. In this fashion, the program theory is tested and, if necessary, amended. Rarely will the audience for an evaluation consider the only options either to terminate the program or continue to run it as in the past. Yet a summative evaluation, which is by far the most common type, does not provide the kind of information that would directly support any other alternatives. The formative evaluation, which rests on the measurement and analysis of subobjectives and activities, on the other hand, operates to suggest actions to change the program in certain ways to make it more successful (Judd and Kenny 1981, p. 603). In addition, as Judd and Kenny (1981) also point out, information on the mechanisms by which a treatment has its impact can help in generalizing the results, that is, in applying the program to different populations or to similar populations in other settings.

THE FORMATIVE ANALYSIS OF SUBOBJECTIVES

The matrix in Figure 3–1 is a simplified paradigm that sets out some of the basic possible combinations of results on a subobjective and the outcome of interest. The implications of each set of results are then outlined in the text. In reviewing the matrix, let us have an illustrative program in mind, a program to provide job-seeking and job-keeping skills to the hard-core unemployed. T is the treatment variable, measured as treatment and comparison groups—those receiving the training program and those not. S is the subobjective, measured, let us say, as ratings by independent observers regarding the extent to which each enrollee has absorbed job-seeking and job-keeping skills. Y is the outcome of interest, for example, number of days employed over a six-month period following the training. Three relations are of concern: (*a*) that between T and S, treatment and subobjective; (*b*) that between S and Y, subobjective and outcome; and (*c*) that between T and Y. The last is the standard summative relation; it seeks to answer the question, Has the treatment affected the outcome? The first two are the two component links of this relation, operating as a causal chain in which the subobjective appears as the intervening or linking variable. In the figure, each of these three relations is referred to as either strong or weak (it should be understood that strong means strong enough to be satisfactory to the program people). In reality, each relation might take on any magnitude from very weak to very strong. Correspondingly, since only the implications of the outcomes weak and strong are discussed below, these must be understood to be shaded and modified appropriately to reflect other locations on the continuum.

In reviewing Figure 3–1, let us begin with cell a at the upper left of the data cells in the matrix. This represents an impact analysis in which both component links appear strong; that is, the treatment seems to be accomplishing the subobjective of imparting skills and that in turn seems to lead to more employment. Under such conditions, if the program theory is precisely correct, the summative relation between T and Y will also be strong, but not as strong as either of the components (if the associations are all given by Pearson correlations, for example, and causality is as specified in the outcome line, then the

FIGURE 3–1   Formative results

Subobjective–outcome link T→ S → Y	Treatment – subobjective link T → S → Y	
	Strong	Weak
Strong	a. T-Y link strong ――――――― a*. T-Y link strong+	b. T-Y link weak ――――――― b*. T-Y link strong
Weak	c. T-Y link weak ――――――― c*. T-Y link strong	d. T-Y link weak ――――――― d*. T-Y link strong

T-Y correlation may be expected to equal the product of the two component correlations). If the T-Y outcome is strong, as expected, what is
learned about the program theory from the results and what are the
action implications? The program theory states that if the program is
carried out properly and the subobjectives are attained, then the outcome of interest will be attained. The cell-a result would seem to corroborate the theory because both were indeed attained. It does not constitute a proof because the relations observed in the data are not
necessarily causal relations; the remainder of this book is heavily concerned with just that issue. However, the results certainly do not contradict the theory, and since what happened is exactly what was predicted, one's belief in the theory may be maintained and even
strengthened. The action implications are, presumably, to carry on exactly as before; the program seems to be going quite well.

On the other hand, it is possible that the T-Y relation might
emerge as even stronger than would be expected from the magnitude
of the two component links alone, the condition noted as a* in Figure
3–1. (Regression analysis for program evaluation will be introduced in
Chapter Five. It may be noted briefly here, however, that there is a

simple test for the condition just noted, namely, a nonzero coefficient on T when Y is regressed on T and S.) If that occurs, it means that the treatment is affecting the outcome through an additional channel. The program theory actually was incorrect, then, because the subobjective specified is apparently not the only mechanism through which the training program is affecting the outcome. The evaluators and program personnel can think together about what the additional operating channel or channels might be. If the resources are available, program personnel might want to try to capitalize on this discovery by strengthening attainment through these unexpected channels and obtaining even better results. Otherwise, one may choose to leave well enough alone and carry on as in the past. Before moving on from a*, we should note the possibility that the relation between T and Y might be *weaker* than expected. If that occurs, it is a clue that there may be less than perfect causality in the subordinate links. The implications of such results are discussed in Chapter Ten. Briefly, however, any hint that the links are, to some noteworthy extent, not truly causal must clearly and seriously undermine the formative analysis.

In cell b, the S-Y link is strong but the T-S link is weak. Thus, the summative or T-Y link will probably be even weaker. If one were to look at the summative outcome alone, it would be apparent that the treatment was not working, but by considering the subordinate links a good deal is also revealed about the probable reasons. The subobjective is fine; one may apparently count on raising employment levels if only one can improve job-seeking and job-keeping skills. The problem seems to be that the training program is not doing a good job of upgrading these skills. The implication would clearly be, first, to make sure that activities are being carried out properly, and second, to make some modifications in the program, or perhaps simply to try harder. In b*, the T-Y association is stronger than would be expected from knowledge of the two component links alone. The analyst knows quite a bit more, however, than the simple T-Y observation that the training program seems to be satisfactory. We observe that it is satisfactory *in spite of* its not imparting the important skills! Do not abandon the training. One may not know precisely why it works, but it does appear to work. If the mystery can be solved, one might modify it a little to get even better results. But do not abandon the subobjective, either, for it too seems to work. The problem, however, is that the training is not resulting in upgraded skills, as hoped. If appropriate modifications can be made to yield better attainment on this specified subobjective, the results on employment are likely to be even more satisfying.

In cell c, the T-S association is strong, but the S-Y link is weak so that the overall T-Y association will again probably be quite weak. Although the summative outcome is the same here as in cell b, the message is very different. The treatment is doing a good job of attaining the subobjective, but in vain; either the subobjective is useless or, perhaps, it may be necessary but inadequate, needing another subobjective in conjunction before the desired results may be expected. The current training program may be retained or not, but in either case it will be necessary to add further activities and attain another subobjective. One might, for example, seek to impart actual job skills for employment opportunities known to be available in the area, or one might introduce an employment service to help enrollees make connections with employers who have vacancies. In any case, it will not be sufficient, as in cell b, to try harder at the same kind of program. Now consider c*; the summative relation is stronger than is to be expected from the results on the components. As in a* and b*, the treatment clearly has another channel. In this case, however, deemphasize the subobjective of augmenting job-seeking and job-keeping skills, or perhaps give up on it altogether. It is apparently superfluous. Try to figure out why the training works anyway; if that can be done, more accurately aimed effort might achieve even better results.

Last, consider cell d: all associations weak. The treatment is not attaining the subobjective, but no matter, since the subobjective doesn't do the required job anyway. The program theory is apparently quite thoroughly incorrect. It may possibly be necessary to attain this subobjective, but it clearly is not sufficient. A new subobjective must be sought, such as teaching actual job skills, perhaps, and if it appears necessary to retain the subobjective of improving job-seeking and job-keeping skills as well, a new or revised method of pursuing that subgoal must also be found. If the summative association is strong anyway (d*), the training works somehow, but through a mysterious channel, just as in c*.

In short, if the outcome of the program seems satisfactory, a summative evaluation can only indicate that it should be continued as before, whereas the analysis of subobjectives is likely to yield suggestions for improvement, particularly in the case of b*. If the outcome is unsatisfactory, a summative evaluation in itself can suggest little other than abandonment, whereas formative evaluation may show the efficacy of carrying on, but with a few modifications, as in cell b, or with an additional necessary activity, as may frequently be indicated by a cell-c result.

Moreover, Figure 3–1 contemplates only one subobjective. When there are several, as will often be the case, and the outcome is satisfactory, some subobjectives may be contributing to the result (cell a) and some not (cells b* and c*). The activities concerned in the c* category might well be abandoned, thus saving money with little or no decrease in effectiveness (or, one might be able to add subobjectives that are necessary conditions for effecting those in c*). The activities in b* might be modified a bit for greater subobjective attainment and thereby even more satisfying results on the outcome of interest. Formative analysis is especially constructive when the results of running the program are *less* favorable than desired and there are several subobjectives, for then the analyst may be able to pinpoint the critical weaknesses. These would be one or more cases of b*, where the subobjective does indeed appear to be important but it is just not being achieved. There is no reason to doubt the entire program theory in such an event since one would expect failure unless all of the subobjectives were attained. Moreover, one knows where one has failed, and the action implications are clear: modify activities or work harder to attain the apparently critical subobjectives that were not attained earlier.

In sum, subobjectives are a specification of the rationality of a program, and their observation and analysis represent a powerful means of understanding the program's impact, or lack thereof, and guiding it toward greater efficiency and effectiveness. As of this writing, however, subobjectives have rarely been used in evaluations in the formative manner just outlined. Modification of evaluation practice in this direction could substantially increase the power and utility of the studies that are conducted.

ACTIVITIES: IMPLEMENTATION ANALYSIS

Not very much was said above about *activities,* although it was indicated that they too need to be considered for formative purposes. In the program theory, it is essential that the activities be carried out, and done so properly—adequately—for all instrumental and inherently valued outcomes to be achieved. Sometimes, after preliminary activities, one outcome will lead to another without any additional activities (as reduced addiction to drugs leads quite directly to reduced drug related theft, for example) but there must have been some original program effort to bring about the reduced addiction. Sometimes, each new outcome requires additional activities even though the previous subobjectives have been attained (as self-care in the home appeared to need patient-motivating effort even after adequate physiological capability was induced by the physical therapy program). Activities therefore have fundamental importance and it may frequently be necessary to make specific observations about the *implementation* of a program as part of the formative evaluation. Often activities simply are not carried out; thus it is no wonder that the program does not succeed. Posters that were supposed to persuade, for example, were left in railroad depots and never distributed for display (Hyman and Wright 1971, p. 187); health center personnel actively worked so few hours daily that only a fraction of the targeted health goals for the area could be met (Hyman and Wright 1971, p. 188); a summative evaluation report showed that a program had failed, but an implementation analysis quickly revealed that it had never begun to be carried out (Patton 1979). In the early years of the federal affirmative action program, the goals could hardly have been achieved because the policy was barely implemented in the form of modified agency personnel practices (Rosenbloom 1980).

Nevertheless, it is not necessary to make a special point of observing systematically each type of program activity in every impact analysis. In fact, only a small proportion of total evaluation resources need be devoted to implementation analysis. For the most part, unlike subobjectives and the outcome of interest, the performance of activities tends to be open, evident, convenient to observe, and well known, as opposed to subtle, obscure, and tricky to measure. The extent to which and the manner in which activities are carried out are usually—with exceptions, to be sure—not problematic items of information.

Attention to implementation should be an invariable component of all formative evaluation. There must always be a point at which the evaluation team stops, considers the activities on the outcome line, and asks, Should we look further? Is there any possibility that the quantity or quality of effort may be a factor in understanding the record of this program? Further observation of activities will sometimes be indicated, sometimes not; when it is, it can often be done quickly and without elaborate or complex instrumentation.

THE OPERATION OF SUBOBJECTIVES

Most subobjectives are specialized instruments for the attainment of a particular further outcome within a given program. If, for example, one wishes to evaluate the impact on deaths from lung cancer of an antismoking campaign, the curtailment of smoking is clearly a subobjective, and it is relevant in its own unique way to the activity and outcome concerned (Warner 1984). Because of this kind of specialization, subobjectives do not fall readily into a small group of conceptual categories. There are, however, two general types of subobjective that crop up again and again and so deserve special mention.

The Discovery Subobjective

The first type, already alluded to in Chapter Two, is the discovery subobjective. It is extremely common that program personnel must find out something about the condition of the targeted part of the world before operating on it. Frequently, this means learning something about the problem—where and to what extent it exists. A few examples of discovery subobjectives are finding out which people have or are susceptible to a health condition, what is the nature and extent of pollutants in the air or water, where pests are breeding or infesting, which houses have code violations or need energy-saving measures, and who does or is likely to commit certain crimes or other undesirable acts. By its nature, the discovery subobjective would rarely if ever be expected to lead directly to further outcomes; there must generally be additional activities to bring those about.

Behavior Prerequisites

The other category of recurring subobjective may be called the behavior prerequisites. As the label suggests, they become important considerations for a program and a formative evaluation whenever the behavior of people appears as an outcome on the outcome line. The program, for example, might be trying to get farmers to maintain sanitation standards in temporary camps for migrant workers (Deniston 1969). In all such cases, there is a set of three subobjectives worth considering, any or all of which may be problematic to attain: the targeted individuals (1) must know what is to be done, (2) must be motivated or have the incentive to do it, and (3) must have the ability and other resources necessary to carry it out. These are referred to as the knowledge, motivation, and resources subobjectives, respectively. In the migrant-camp program, for example, the farmers must understand what needs to be installed or repaired, must have an incentive to maintain a camp that meets the standards, and must be able to purchase, install, or repair the facilities in question. The behavior prerequisites, if more than one of them is problematic, would appear in stacked form on the outcome line, as in Figure 3–2. Note that there are no activities specifically designed to attain the resources subobjective. Presumably, the farmers need no help in furnishing the required materials and skills, i.e., the resources subobjective is not considered problematic to attain in this instance.

Note also that the farmers' behavior is not included explicitly on the outcome line, although it might well be. In the present illustration, it is simply assumed that if the necessary knowledge, motivation, and resources are attained, the behavior of installation or repair will ensue. When, in fact, in an actual analysis of impact, these subobjectives were attained but the facilities in question were not in proper condition at the time-2 inspection, it was not assumed that the repairs had been neglected, but that after the repairs there had been recurrent breakdowns through misuse of the facilities (Deniston 1969).

The behavior prerequisites are pertinent whenever behavior is an outcome, although they need not always be measured or even pondered. Behavior, of course, is an important outcome in a host of programs that are subject to evaluation, sometimes as the outcome of interest, sometimes as a subobjective. Examples of behaviors as outcomes in programs are preventive health measures (cancer tests,

**FIGURE 3–2   An example of the discovery subobjective and the
behavior prerequisites**

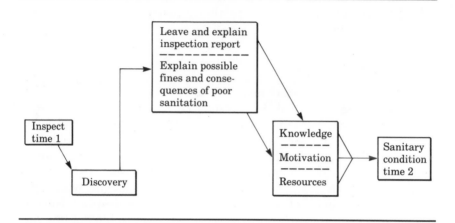

etc.), birth control, alcohol and drug use, discrimination, driving
speeds, seat-belt use, minority hiring, use of public transportation, energy conservation, quality of medical care, adoption of innovations, exports by small businesses, and high school drop-out rates.

The Omission of Subobjectives

We have concluded the discussion of special categories of subobjectives,
but let us return for a moment to the observation that the farmers'
behavior was not included on the outcome line in Figure 3–2. All types
of subobjectives might sometimes be omitted. In fact, if all were to be
included, the outcome line would be densely packed and far too detailed. It is important to exclude subobjectives for the sake of parsi-
mony unless they will be measured and potentially used for formative
purposes, or there is some ad hoc reason for documenting them or en-
suring that they receive attention from program personnel, interested
publics, or the evaluators themselves. Subobjectives whose attainment
is not problematic are good candidates for exclusion; much detail may
be omitted from any outcome line on the assumption that values on
certain intervening variables are nearly completely predictable from
what has come before. Furthermore, in some programs an intervening
step does not even seem to exist between the core activity and the outcome of interest. An example that is common in program evaluation is
education, where the core activity is often some teaching technique and
the outcome is simply learning. In other kinds of programs, an inter-

FIGURE 3–3   Direct and indirect effects

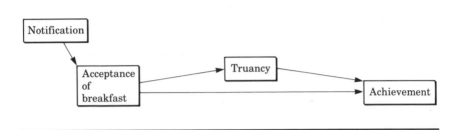

vening step may sometimes be imaginable, but too obscure to consider measuring. An example is the serving of beer to nursing home patients; some motivational and attitudinal changes no doubt do intervene between the activity and outcomes, such as self-care and need for tranquilizers, but, given the measurement difficulties, it may well seem unprofitable to pursue them. Last, it will frequently occur that an activity or subobjective affects an outcome indirectly—through the medium of another important and specified subobjective, but also in other ways that do not seem to merit special attention, so that the link appears both indirect and direct. One example is a program in which a nutritious and appealing breakfast was proposed to be offered to disadvantaged junior high school students (Figure 3–3). The outcome of interest was school achievement. The mechanisms of attainment were two: first, coming to school for breakfast would generally mean staying, thereby increasing school attendance (reducing truancy). Second, being full and nourished rather than hungry would increase the inclination and ability to learn, but the subobjectives on this path—hunger, inclination to learn—are perhaps not worth pursuing specifically.

Example: The Kirtland's Warbler

Having reviewed the various ways in which subobjectives appear in formative evaluations, it remains to consider how they are used. It may be difficult to appraise the kind of difference it makes to have subobjective data in hand without at least one concrete example. There is a problem, however, in that few published evaluations give specific attention to the formative use of subobjectives. This may be one of the most surprising and puzzling observations to be made about the current state of the art and science of program evaluation. To fill the gap for the present, I will illustrate with a project on which a good quantity of data is available, but not in the form of a published evaluation. The data were gathered from an unnumbered pamphlet issued by Region 3 of the U.S. Fish and Wildlife Service and from numerous articles appearing over the years in Michigan newspapers.

The program under analysis is a cowbird control program undertaken to save the Kirtland's warbler from extinction. This warbler, which winters in the Bahama Islands, now nests only under young jack pine trees, about eight to eighteen feet tall, in three counties in Michigan, although its summer habitat was considerably broader when jack pine forest was more widespread. Some of the habitat was lost to agriculture and human settlement, but much of the loss was paradoxically caused by excellent forest fire prevention and control: the Kirtland's depended on randomly recurring fire to burn over mature stands, pop the seed cones, and start new jack pine forest that would reach suitable nesting size in about eight years.

In the spring of 1961, a special census indicated that there were only about 1,000 Kirtland's warblers in existence, an alarmingly small number. In response, the U.S. Forest Service and the Michigan Department of Natural Resources began and still maintain an annual program of controlled burning of mature jack pine forest to provide increased habitat over the long term. Ten years later, however, in the spring of 1971, the census showed that only 402 Kirtland's warblers remained, despite the increase in suitable nesting territory. Clearly, factors other than nesting sites were at work to reduce the population.

One of these factors was strongly presumed to be cowbird parasitism, so the cowbird control program, to be evaluated here, was begun in the spring of 1972. At that time, about 400 birds were again counted, with an increase expected in 1973 as a result of the new program. Cowbirds lay their eggs in warblers' nests and rely on the warbler parent to feed their young. Furthermore, newly hatched cowbirds push warbler eggs out of the nest so that frequently it is the cowbird hatchlings alone who are fed by the hoodwinked warblers. The authorities therefore began setting large traps in the spring of 1972 and removing cowbirds on a very large scale, repeating the operation every year to the present. If the program were successful, an immediate population increase of about 100 percent could fairly conservatively have been expected, taking into account that some birds are inevitably lost on the migration to and from the Bahamas, or over the winter, and that suitable nesting habitat was not yet as extensive as it would eventually be. In the spring of 1973, the anxiously awaited bird count (which is highly accurate for these birds) showed 432 Kirtland's in existence— an increase of about 8 percent. The increase was heartening because it was at least positive, but discouraging and puzzling because it was so small. The summative results of the cowbird control program are shown in Table 3–1. While the program continued, the warbler population showed an alarming decline in 1974, returned to an encouraging

TABLE 3–1   Summative evaluation of the cowbird control program

Program status	Year (spring)	Number of Kirtland's warblers
Before	1961	1002
	1971	402
	1972	400
After	1973	432
	1974	334
	1975	358
	1976	400
	1979	422
	1980	486
	1981	460
	1982	400

size in 1980, and receded again in 1982 to its level when the program first began. Clearly, the cowbird control program (added to the controlled burning) was not enough to produce the desired results.

Although the summative evaluation indicates an inadequate program, it is not a very good policy guide. What is to be done with the program? Does it do any good at all? Should it be abandoned, perhaps because it inevitably leaves too many cowbirds? Should it be redoubled because not quite enough cowbirds are being trapped, but more could be removed with greater effort and expense? Should it be continued at the same level because it is successful but something else is killing off the increased population? This policy choice dilemma is most difficult to solve, and tinkering with the magnitude of the program is not likely to reduce the ambiguity. In the meanwhile, the bird population remains in great danger of dwindling to extinction.

Let us now see how data on subobjectives may improve the policymaking perspective. The outcome line in Figure 3–4 represents the program theory, with a formative evaluation in mind. It is believed that trapping the cowbirds will greatly reduce their numbers in the nesting areas. This in turn—without any further activities—will reduce the number of warbler nests parasitized. Thus, the number of young fledged each summer should increase and one hopes that the number of Kirtland's that successfully make the round trip to the Bahamas and return in the spring will increase as well. The outcome of interest is the number of warblers in the spring. That outcome would be judged by most to be an inherently valued one, whereas the number of young fledged in the summer would not: one cannot simply assume

FIGURE 3–4   Outcome line for the cowbird control program

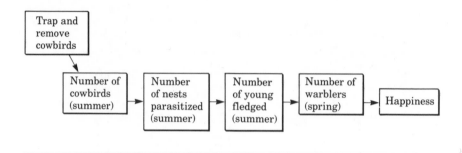

from successful fledging that the spring population will consequently increase, nor be uninterested in whether it does or not.

The subobjective and outcome data for the formative evaluation are shown in Table 3–2. There are more gaps than one would wish, but a picture does emerge in which one can have a fair degree of confidence. Before the program, it appears that cowbirds were contributing substantially to population decline since the level of parasitism was very high and less than one warbler was being fledged per nest. Once the program got under way, parasitism was reduced to negligible proportions and, in apparent response, the number of birds fledged rose to a high enough level to produce substantial population expansion. As we have seen, however, the population did not expand. This is therefore a case of cell c in Figure 3–1, in which the T-S link is very strong, but the S-Y and T-Y links are weak. The results tell us that the program theory was wrong, but perhaps not completely wrong: cowbird control is not sufficient to bring the Kirtland's warbler population back to safe levels, but it may be saving it from complete and rapid extinction, allowing it just barely to hold its own since without the program the birds may not nearly have replaced their numbers across generations. The action implications now are fairly clear: maintain cowbird control activities at their current level; it would be unwise to decrease the effort and a waste of money to increase it. At the same time, look for additional activities and subobjectives that will permit the gains made in the summer to carry over to the following spring; it appears almost certain that something in the migration or the wintering grounds is killing off an alarming number of warblers.

Having data on the subobjectives thus makes the job of the decision maker a far more comfortable one. It does not, of course, solve all of the problems of program management. In the present case, the right combination of money and ideas has not yet been put together to de-

TABLE 3–2 **Formative evaluation of the cowbird control program***

Year	Season	Percent of nests parasitized	Average number of young fledged per nest	Number of nesting warblers
1971	Spring			402
	Summer	65	.81	
	Spring			400
	Summer	6	2.84	
1973	Spring			432
	Summer	0		
1974	Spring			334
	Summer			
1975	Spring			358
	Summer			
1976	Spring			400
	Summer	3.4	2.74	
1979	Spring			422

*The dashed line indicates the start of the program.

termine what the additional deleterious factor(s) might be. For now, the Kirtland's warbler population remains stable, but at a dangerously low level.

TYPES OF DIVERSITY WITHIN PROGRAMS

When an evaluator contemplates a program, and talks about it with sponsors or staff, it is generally a complicated affair. The evaluator's aim is to break it down neatly into the form of the outcome line, but there often seem to be so many different kinds of elements to consider that doing so is no easy task. With the help of a few additional important categories, however, the multifaceted nature of the ordinary program can be readily and parsimoniously organized for research. We have already seen that the basic components of a program for impact analysis purposes are activities, outcomes, and subobjectives. To these there may be added multiple outcomes, parts, comparative methods, and multichannel treatments.

Multiple Outcomes and Parts

The first two of the new categories, multiple outcomes and parts, are quite similar to one another functionally. Each consists in a group or set of outcomes that are not serially ranged; that is, one member of the

set is not a step in the attainment of another, but rather are *independent ends that may be accomplished, where the means are intertwined
in a common program.* The term *parts* is used instead of *multiple outcomes* when the set of outcomes can conveniently be organized either
verbally or numerically into a common integrated whole. Parts are
thus *components of an outcome such that if any component is achieved
some portion of the outcome is thereby achieved, and if all components
are achieved, then the whole outcome is considered by definition to be
achieved* (Deniston 1972a).

Let us take some examples of parts to make the concept clear. In
the field of medical care, Professional Standards Review Organizations
(PSROs) had as a primary outcome of interest the *utilization rate* of
hospitals. Utilization, however, can be divided into three independent
parts: number of admissions, length of stay, and intensity of service
use while in the hospital. If any of these decreases, we say that utilization has decreased. None is really a subobjective of the other, but the
means to achieve them all are intertwined in the publicity and record
review activities of the PSRO. Another example would be an inspection
and enforcement program to enhance compliance with regulations
against discrimination in the workplace. The program may actually
aim simultaneously at discrimination by race and by sex, as well as
discrimination in promotion and in hiring. Thus, the program has four
independent parts. Many of the program's activities, however, are instrumental in achieving two or more of the parts, and the achievement
of any part is, by definition, a reduction in discrimination.

Multiple outcomes are the same as parts except that they are not
considered together under a common verbal heading or as numerical
contributors to a common quantitative index. The Outward Bound program, for example, is one in which participants undergo a gruelling
and challenging wilderness experience. In an evaluation of the program, four outcomes of interest were considered rather than only one.
They were self-esteem, self-awareness, self-assertion, and acceptance
of others (Smith et al. 1976). Similarly, the federal government's food-
stamp program may be considered for its impact on the nutrition of the
poor and the economic status of farmers. A dam may have the multiple
outcomes of irrigation benefits, recreation, flood control, and power
generation. Sometimes the multiple outcomes may be considered to
work against or offset one another. At least in the short run, for example, a program that makes decision making in the workplace more
democratic may increase morale but decrease efficiency. Any program
may conceivably have an infinite number of effects, but an impact
analysis frequently considers only one outcome of interest; when it considers more than one, we will apply the term *multiple outcomes* to be
able to organize the elements with which the evaluation deals. Chapter
Twelve will be devoted entirely to this general subject matter.

With both parts and multiple outcomes, each part and each outcome may be and often should be considered as occupying the focal position on its own outcome line. In a strong sense, there are as many programs as there are parts or outcomes of interest. Many of the activities and subobjectives on the different outcome lines may be exactly the same, but some will be unique, and these differences can be extremely important to a formative evaluation. Reducing discrimination by sex, for example, will take some different activities from reducing racial discrimination, and increasing the acceptance of others will need some activities that are different from those involved in increasing self-esteem.

Comparative Methods

The third of the new categories of diverse elements within programs is called comparative methods. These are *different programs on different subjects, but considered common or unified because each treats the same problem and the same outcome of interest.* Comparative methods are common in national or other large-scale programs that are implemented by different personnel at different sites (Hyman and Wright 1971, pp. 189–192). The CETA program, for example, was not one program. It was implemented differently in different cities, although all accepted the objective of upgrading the employability and employment levels of the disadvantaged. It would be extremely difficult to carry out a formative evaluation of the CETA program. A summative evaluation could be accomplished but it would say next to nothing, especially if a close look at the data were to show that the programs were far more successful in some cities than in others. The same is true of many counseling programs, where the true program lies in the nature of the counseling, which differs from one counselor to another. Similarly, the success of a work release program in preventing recidivism, or a foster home program for delinquents, may depend on the kind of experience the prisoners have with their employers or the delinquents have with their foster parents. Comparative methods often go unrecognized as such as long as no evaluation or only a summative evaluation is contemplated. As soon as one begins to think in terms of formative evaluation, however, and to lay out subobjectives, one may realize that some rather simple-minded assumptions have been made right along. At the same time, one may put oneself on the track of some truly constructive breakthroughs in program design. When a comparative-methods program is at issue, so much more is generally to be gained from formative than from summative evaluation that looking at only a few sites, but with the benefit of careful subobjective analysis, will be preferable to national studies that consider the outcome of interest alone.

The Multichannel Treatment

The final category of multiplicity is the multichannel treatment. This consists in *a variety of means or activities, considered either jointly contributory or alternative, all used at once on the same subjects toward a single outcome.* The problem and confusion evoked by the multichannel treatment is that it seems to defy evaluation. Programs expend effort, and the ultimate purpose of all evaluation is to determine how best to expend such effort or whether to expend it at all. We are interested in what is being accomplished by activities. That is possible to discover most of the time because certain activities are so specifically and uniquely associated with certain subobjectives or outcomes of interest that assessing these outcomes gives a direct reading of the value of the activities. If the program people are doing twenty things at once to achieve a certain end, however, and the end is reasonably well achieved, how do we know what was essential and what, if anything, was superfluous? The channels are all experienced together and become hopelessly confounded with one another. Consider the following program to promote popular support for the United Nations in one city.

> 12,868 people were reached through the Parent-Teachers Associations which devoted programs to the topic of world understanding; 14,000 children in the Weekday Church Schools held a World Community Day Program; 10,000 members of the Catholic Parent-Teachers Association were exhorted by their archbishop to support the United Nations; the radio stations broadcast facts about the United Nations, one of them scheduling spot programs 150 times a week; 225 meetings were served with literature and special speakers; in all, 59,588 pieces of literature were distributed and 2,800 clubs were reached by speakers; hundreds of documentary films were shown; and the slogan "Peace Begins with the United Nations—the United Nations Begins with You" was exhibited everywhere, in every imaginable form—on blotters, matchbooks, streetcar cards, and so on. (Hyman and Wright 1971, p. 189)

One common request of evaluators is that they analyze a political campaign. Considerable energy and money are necessary to do the TV ads, the coffees, the press releases, the speeches to organizations, the door-to-door canvassing, and so forth. Candidates want to know what works and what does not. They are asking for the evaluation of a multichannel treatment and it is true that they are, in fact, asking for the nearly impossible. When the target audience is subjected to several potential influences, it is difficult indeed to distinguish the efficacy of each. If the target audience is composed of human beings, one can ask them what they saw or heard or read and what influenced them most, but the information obtained will rarely be considered with confidence to be reliable. The best solution, rarely available, is to randomly assign subjects to each possible combination of activities. Such a factorial experiment permits the complete analysis of separate effects. Sometimes one can find subsets of the audience that have been selectively exposed to only one channel, or not exposed at all to one given channel. Sometimes, as in a long-term continuing sales campaign, one may withdraw channels selectively and see if achievement is reduced. These are some of the main tricks for getting around the problem, but basically, it is indeed a problem. Evaluators should advise the implementers of multichannel treatments as follows: Try to reduce the channels to which any segment of the audience is exposed to one or a very few; otherwise, if you must have a full-blown multichannel treatment and it works, you must be prepared to pay for the whole thing again if the program is to be continued or repeated.

In dealing with any type of multiplicity of elements, the basic mechanism of analysis is still the outcome line, whose focus is a single outcome of interest. A multichannel treatment is simply a number of activities stacked up in one location above the line, with a single collective arrow to one subobjective or to the outcome of interest. Multiple outcomes and parts demand several outcome lines instead of one, even though there are many common subobjectives and activities, because the several outcomes are not all in one causal chain. Comparative methods also demand several outcome lines even though each contains the same outcome of interest; each will feature a somewhat different set of mechanisms for achieving it. In this way, programs containing a great deal of diversity and multiplicity may either be reduced to terms that are conducive to organized and informative evaluation or will show that such evaluation is not practical.

Chapter Four

The Quality of Design:
Experiments and the
Elementary Quasi
Experiments

INTRODUCTION TO THE ISSUES

In this chapter, we begin the extended discussion of design that will occupy much of the remainder of the book. The kind of design that authorities tend to agree is best is the randomized experiment (Campbell and Stanley 1966; Gilbert, Light, and Mosteller 1975), of which there are many variants. Such designs, however, may often be extremely difficult—even impossible—to arrange and implement. To appreciate why it is desirable to bother with them nevertheless, it will be essential to begin with some simpler, nonexperimental designs—those that are generally relatively easy to arrange and implement and that therefore tend to be used most frequently—and proceed by contrasting these with randomized experiments according to their respective advantages and disadvantages.

In considering the quality of designs, the primary criteria employed are usually internal and external validity (Campbell and Stanley 1966).[1] The group to whom conclusions based on an evaluation design technically refer is the set of subjects actually studied. The time

---

[1]Cook and Campbell (1979) add statistical conclusion validity and construct validity. The first refers to sampling from larger populations and is not a basis for distinguishing among the various experimental and quasi-experimental designs. Construct validity issues can be considered issues of internal or external validity and will be so treated here. Judd and Kenny (1981) add the important consideration of conclusion validity, which is essentially captured by the concept of sensitivity, discussed in the next section.

and context implicated are only those that were actually observed. Internal validity refers to those conclusions. A threat to internal validity is a charge that the design that is used allows the causal link between treatment and outcome to remain obscure; the design is weak in some way and does not enable one to have confidence in one's conclusions about what the program actually did accomplish regarding the subjects, time, and context observed. External validity, on the other hand, refers to the generalizability of the study's results. A threat to external validity is a problem that casts doubt on the extent to which the results of the evaluation as conducted would be duplicated with the same program at a different time or place, or with different subjects, or with other indicators of the main conceptual variables.

THE BASIC EXPERIMENTAL DESIGNS

Evaluation designs will be divided into three basic types: experimental, quasi-experimental, and ex-post-facto. There are two characteristics that distinguish experimental designs from those in the other two categories. First, in true experiments, the locus of "selection," that is, the locus of decision regarding which treatment a given subject will have, is centralized (where the subjects may be people, cities, rivers, court cases, time periods, work groups, streets, or any other entity that is the target of some program). Either the program's management, evaluator, or some other central authority sets up one or more subjects to receive the treatment (the program) and one or more different subjects not to receive it, or to receive something else. Second, in experimental designs, the manner in which the selection decision is made, that is, the mechanism of assignment, is a random process, usually called randomization. Most often, a fairly large group of subjects is identified as the set of subjects to be observed. This set is then subdivided into experimental and control groups (or assigned to whatever treatments the experiment will investigate) by some random process, such as picking names out of a hat or employing a table of random numbers. More rarely, but equivalently for practical purposes, a population is identified and, to represent that population, the experimental and control groups are derived from it by random sampling in such a way that the whole of the larger population is not used up; much of it is not actually observed in the study. The two distinguishing characteristics of true experiments, then, are *centralized selection and random assignment*. It should be noted that if assignment is by randomization, selection essentially has to be centralized. Thus, only one criterion would seem to be needed. We will see, however, that the criterion of selection serves to distinguish nonexperimental designs from one another, and that a dependence between selection and assignment does not exist for nonexperimental as it does for experimental designs.

Design 12, the R-comparative-change design (where the R is for Randomized), may be considered the classic experimental design. It is diagrammed as follows:

(12)
$$\frac{R \quad X_E \quad\quad T \quad\quad Y_E}{R \quad X_C \quad\quad\quad\quad\quad Y_C}$$

where R means randomly determined or selected, X and Y are the pretest and posttest, respectively, E and C represent the experimental and control groups, respectively, and T stands for receiving the treatment. The diagram is a time line in that randomization comes first, then the pretest, and so on.

Another basic experimental design—lean, simple, and still powerful—is design 11, the R-comparative-posttest design:

(11)
$$\frac{R \quad\quad\quad T \quad\quad Y_E}{R \quad\quad\quad\quad\quad\quad Y_C}.$$

It is clear that design 11 is the same as design 12 but without the pretest.

Let us take a moment to scan some of the relative advantages of these two experimental designs. Since Y is the outcome of interest and X is a measure of Y at a point in time before the administering of the program or treatment, the mean of X is often referred to as the location at which a group starts out. An advantage of design 12 is that the pretest provides a check on the randomization process. We presume that randomization causes the two groups to start out at approximately the same place, but we are never sure. That is why the difference between their ending points, $\bar{Y}_E - \bar{Y}_C$ (where $\bar{Y}$ is the mean of Y), is generally tested for statistical significance: to determine whether a difference that large could have been with us from the beginning through "unhappy" randomization. In the R-comparative-posttest design, that is the best we can do: run a significance test to determine whether a difference in $\bar{Y}$ could be due to an initial difference in $\bar{X}$ (unmeasured) caused by unhappy randomization. If the result is statistically significant, then at least some of the difference $\bar{Y}_E - \bar{Y}_C$ may be inferred to have been caused by the treatment (with certain reservations—the subject of the balance of this chapter).

In the R-comparative-change design, however, X is measured. One need not wonder whether the groups might have started out unevenly; one need only look and see. The great advantage is that if they did start out in different places on the dimension of interest, one can control for that in the analysis. Including X as a control variable greatly increases the *sensitivity* of the design (see the concept of conclusion validity in Judd and Kenny 1981), and that is one of the most important concepts in the analysis of program evaluations. The sensitivity of a design is a measure of how small the difference can be between the observed experimental group outcome and the "null-case" outcome (the counterfactual—the outcome predicted on the assumption of no treatment effect whatever) while still permitting us to infer that the treatment has had some causal impact. If one design permits an inference of treatment effect when the difference between the actual and null-case outcomes is small while another demands a very large departure, then the first is much more sensitive. Or, stated differently, the first design is more sensitive if it permits an inference of treatment effect while the second one does not when the difference between result and counterfactual has been the same in both cases. One way to increase sensitivity is by using larger experimental and control groups; otherwise, the key to sensitivity is that it depends on the amount of unexplained variation in the Y scores of individuals that is left by the design (statistically, it depends on the variance of the error remaining when predicting Y). If we can explain the Y scores of subjects perfectly in the normal course of things, and we subsequently apply a certain treatment, then, clearly, any tiny departure of the outcome from the perfectly estimated counterfactual must be due to the treatment. If, on the other hand, our predictions are known to be error filled, then even a large departure from the estimated counterfactual cannot necessarily be ascribed to the treatment; that design is relatively insensitive. (It is important to say *relatively* because such is the power of statistical sampling theory involving means that even design 11 is quite sensitive.) The critical factor, then, is the reduction of error variance. The best way by far to accomplish this is by adding good predictors of Y into our analytic equations. Design 11 has no such predictor at all so that it demands moderately sizable departures for a causal inference. Design 12 has what in most cases is the best single predictor known, namely, the pretest—what the subjects were like just a little while ago. If more good variables are added as predictors, the design can be made even more sensitive.

Furthermore, a pretest can prevent false conclusions of program effect that are actually traceable to unhappy randomization. Or, more generally speaking, it enables a more accurate estimate of the precise magnitude of the true effect. Let us say that the R-comparative-posttest design were employed and unhappy randomization led to the experimental group's being significantly lower on X than the control group. This difference may well show up in Y, then, leading to an erroneous conclusion that the program was effective, or effective to a certain quantitative degree. After all, unhappy randomization does regularly occur although its frequency is low. If the R-comparative-change design were employed, however, no such mistake would be made. We would *see* that the experimental group was lower than the control group on X and allow for this fact in the analysis; that is, we would *expect* the treatment group to be a certain amount lower on Y than the control group in case the treatment were completely ineffective. Of course, unhappy randomization might still have produced a difference on some unmeasured cause of Y, but for the pretest and other measured variables, this sort of error would be obviated.

The advantages of entering X as a control variable are therefore great, but there are also some advantages of design 11 over design 12. One is that the pretest may spoil the naturalness of the experiment. One must fear that the results obtained might have been different had the subjects not been sensitized or otherwise contaminated by the pretest. Internal validity (see the following section) is not threatened: since the control group also had the pretest, the difference between the two mean Y scores cannot be due to X instead of the treatment. External validity, however, is affected. One might not, with confidence, be able to generalize results based on the R-comparative-change design to situations in which a pretest was not given. Another advantage of the R-comparative-posttest design is that a pretest cannot always be given, that is, design 11 has more potential applications because design 12 is often essentially impossible. In one study, for example, the outcomes of interest were fever and other ill effects after a tonsillectomy (Skipper and Leonard 1968). Fever before the operation is clearly irrelevant as a pretest. Previous employment may also be irrelevant as a pretest in a training program for the hard-core unemployed. Similarly, there is no relevant pretest for an education program in which all subjects are ignorant of the material at the beginning, and so forth.

In sum, there are advantages to both designs. The R-comparative-change design is the more powerful of the two, however, and should be used whenever a pretest can be given, unless a serious problem is posed by the resulting limitations on generalizability. A design in which a pretest is not administered but *other* predictor variables are entered is intermediate between designs 11 and 12. Usually, it may be considered closer to design 12 in that the major significance of a pretest is the provision of a predictor that constricts the error standard deviation in Y and provides a check on unequal randomization.

THE THREATS TO INTERNAL VALIDITY

Any threat to internal validity means a threat to the validity of an inference or conclusion about a program impact based on a certain design. A threat to validity is another way of saying an inadequacy of design. The term *design,* or *evaluation design,* in the framework of impact analysis, also has a special meaning. It connotes a method for arriving both at a result and a counterfactual, the two elements needed for assessing a program impact. There can be no design in program evaluation if there is no counterfactual. The counterfactual always comes from one of two sources or their combination: (*a*) the same subjects at one or more previous time periods, and (*b*) a group of comparable subjects.

Referring to Figure 4–1 (on the next two pages), of the several threats to internal validity that we will eventually consider, the three primary ones are *history, selection, and contamination*. We will see momentarily that the threat of history is relevant when there is a before measure but no comparison group and the threat of selection is relevant whenever there is a comparison group. Contamination is a mixed category, but primarily a threat to comparison-group designs.

Campbell and Stanley (1966) begin with a design that they call the "One-shot Case Study." It is diagrammed as follows:

(1)   T   Y

Since there is no before measure and no comparison group, design 1 is in fact not a design at all for impact analysis. Its primary threat to validity is that there is no counterfactual and therefore no basis, technically, for inferring the impact of the treatment. A threat to internal validity may be thought of as a question of the following nature: Could not something else besides the treatment, such as history, selection, and so on account for the difference between the actual results and the counterfactual? Without a counterfactual at all, design 1 is simply not advanced enough for the idea of internal validity to be a pertinent one.

History and Related Threats: The Before-After Design

Let us take a step forward, then, to an elementary quasi-experimental design, design 3, which we will call the before-after design. It will be remembered that true experiments are distinguished by the characteristics of centralized selection and randomization. Quasi-experiments are also characterized by centralized selection but the assignment process in this case is nonrandom: the categories on the two classification traits for quasi-experiments are, therefore, *centralized selection and nonrandom assignment* (see Figure 4–1).

If one could have a tally of all of the impact analysis that is done in this world, the before-after design would no doubt emerge as the most heavily used; one simply compares the relevant state of the world after the program with its state beforehand and attributes the difference to the effects of the intervention. Design 3 would be diagrammed as follows:

(3)   X   T   Y

The classifying traits that distinguish quasi-experimental designs—centralized selection and nonrandom assignment—may appear inapplicable to design 3 because only one group seems to be involved

FIGURE 4–1   Characteristics of design

		Design		
No.	Chapter	Name	Diagram	Selection/ assignment type
1	4	One-shot case study	T Y	Either/none
2	10	Ex-post facto	Assorted	Decentralized/ nonrandom
Elementary quasi-experimental designs				
3	4	Before-after	X T Y	Centralized/ nonrandom
4	4	Comparative posttest	$\dfrac{\text{T}\;\;\text{Y}_E}{\text{Y}_C}$	Centralized/ nonrandom
Quasi-experimental designs				
5	7	Comparative change	$\dfrac{\text{X}_E\;\;\text{T}\;\;\text{Y}_E}{\text{X}_C\;\;\;\;\;\;\;\text{Y}_C}$	Centralized/ nonrandom
6	9	Interrupted time series	X.... T Y....	Centralized/ nonrandom
7	9	Comparative time series	$\dfrac{\text{X}_{E}...\;\;\text{T}\;\;\;\;\;\text{Y}_{E}...}{\text{X}_{C}...\;\;\;\;\;\;\;\;\;\text{Y}_{C}...}$	Centralized/ nonrandom
8	11	Subobjective	Assorted	Centralized/ nonrandom
Mixed designs				
9	8	Random comparison group	$\dfrac{\text{X}_E\;\;\text{T}\;\;\text{Y}_E}{\text{R}\;\;\text{X}_C\;\;\;\;\;\text{Y}_C}$	Centralized/ part random
10	6	Regression discontinuity	$\dfrac{\text{A}_E\;\;\text{T}\;\;\text{Y}_E}{\text{A}_C\;\;\;\;\;\;\;\text{Y}_C}$	Centralized/ near random
Experimental designs				
11	4	R-comparative posttest	$\dfrac{\text{R}\;\;\;\;\;\text{T}\;\;\text{Y}_E}{\text{R}\;\;\;\;\;\;\;\;\;\text{Y}_C}$	Centralized/ randomized
12	4	R-comparative change	$\dfrac{\text{R}\;\;\text{X}_E\;\;\text{T}\;\;\text{Y}_E}{\text{R}\;\;\text{X}_C\;\;\;\;\;\;\text{Y}_C}$	Centralized/ randomized

				Threats to internal validity			

					Contamination		
Spurious-ness/time order	History	Selection P	Q	Assignment	Treat-ment	Controls
NA	NA	NA		NA	NA	NA
X	NA	X	X	X	X	X
NA	X	NA		NA	X	(X)
NA	—	X	X	X:div. events, div. attr.	X	X
NA	—	—	X	X:div. events, mat.,attr.,regr.	X	X
NA	X	NA		NA	X	X
NA	—	—	X	X:div. events, matr., regr.	X	X
NA	—	— (At best)	—	— (At best)	X	— (At best)
NA	—	—	—	—	X	X
NA	—	—	—	—	X	X
NA	—	—	—	—	X	X
NA	—	—	—	—	X	X

rather than two. There are indeed two groups, however, the time periods before and the time periods after. In design 3, a central authority decides by fixing the time of the intervention that all of the scores chronologically preceding the program shall be counterfactual and all the later ones results. There is no set of several, mutually independent choosers each of whom assigns a time period or two either to the results group or the counterfactual group at whim. It is in this sense that the selection process is centralized. At the same time, the central authority does not make the assignment randomly; the results group surely does not end up with about half of its scores being before measures and the other half taken from after measures, with a similar mixture for the counterfactual group. Rather, all of the before period measures are sweepingly assigned to the counterfactual group, and all of the after to results. It is in this sense that the assignment process is nonrandom.

Design 3, having a counterfactual, is a great improvement over design 1. It is, however, quite vulnerable to threats to internal validity—particularly the threat of history. We will see that contamination may also be a problem, but history is the threat that is uniquely pertinent to designs in which the counterfactual is derived by this first method, that is, by observing at previous points in time the element(s) that the program is considered potentially to affect.

The general threat of history is the threat, or possibility, that *something else besides T accounts for all or part of an observed change over time.* Moreover, it is important to note that the observed change over time may be zero—before and after measures are the same—but that this may be accounted for by some change-producing force of history that exactly counteracted a true impact of the treatment.

The threat of history may be divided into several subcategories, prominent among which are external events, testing, maturation, regression, and attrition. Let us consider these one at a time.

In prior treatments (e.g., Campbell and Stanley 1966; Cook and Campbell 1979), the above threats to internal validity were considered independent concepts and were not grouped together as they have been here. There, the threat of *external events* was called the threat of history. Here, external events refers to just one kind of history, namely, the threat that some outside occurrence, not a property of the program, the study, or the subjects, has intervened to affect outcome scores. This might be the weather, a political or economic event, another program, a newspaper article, an accident, and so on. For example, an evaluation of the Bay Area Rapid Transit System (BART) showed that highway traffic decreased in 1974 when BART's Transbay Tunnel was opened. External events posed a threat of history, however, because at about the same time there was both a gasoline shortage and higher gas prices, occasioned by the Arab oil embargo. These, rather than increasing BART ridership, may have accounted at least in part for the change in highway traffic (Webber 1980, p. 419). The threat of external events can be extremely troublesome for over-time designs; it is usually quite impossible to be confident that no extraneous forces or occurrences have been at work. It is primarily for this reason that design 3 is weak and undesirable. Since it is commonly employed, especially in informal or nonprofessional evaluations, the implication is that a substantial proportion of all evaluative conclusions are suspect.

The threat of external events, and indeed all threats of history, would seem at first glance to be irrelevant to the R-comparative-post-test design because there are no before measures in that design and thus no opportunity to observe any change over time. That is not quite true, however. At the moment of randomization, both groups in a design 11 study are considered to be essentially equal; if at the posttest they are observed to be unequal, one may question whether the change over time was caused by the treatment or by something else. In a design 12 experiment, there is a true pretest and therefore clearly an opportunity to observe change over time. In neither of these experimental designs, however, are external events a threat to validity. The reason is not the randomization process, but simply the existence of a comparison group. The comparison group is considered in principle to be a recorder of history; whatever happens to one group also happens to the other so that any differences emerging between them must be due to the treatment, or perhaps to some other threat to internal validity.

A comparison group nullifies the threat of external events essentially by definition. Clearly, it is still possible for the two groups concerned to be subject to different external events, but the threat to validity posed by this eventuality is in a different category. It will be called divergent events (in previous treatments it has had other labels, such as intrasession history and local history). In a single-group design, the focus is on the difference between before and after; the counterfactual comes from the before measures. Whenever there is a comparison group as well as a before measure, however, the focus shifts to the difference between changes over time (usually, statistically adjusted changes, as we will see), and the counterfactual comes from the *change* in the *comparison* group rather than simply from a before measure. If the treatment group is found to change over time, we are not left in uncertainty about whether the observed change might have been caused by external events. Rather we look at the comparison group. A similar change in that group documents the effects of history and leads to a conclusion that there was indeed no treatment effect. However, we might still wonder whether there has been a *difference* in change over time due to a *difference* in external events between the two groups—the problem of divergent events. Thus, we abandon the idea of history as a threat to validity whenever there is a comparison group and turn to a threat that captures the differences between groups rather than a simple change over time. External events, then, is a threat to the internal validity of a single-group design in which the counterfactual is derived from before measures; it is not pertinent to comparison-group designs at all. The true experiments are thus clearly superior to the before-after design in susceptibility to the threat of external events.

Any divergent history, such as divergent events, is a form of contamination of comparison-group designs and, as such, might be thought to pose a serious threat to true experiments as well as to less well-controlled designs. We will consider its precise implications below, when contamination is treated in full.

A second form of the basic threat of history is *testing* (Campbell and Stanley 1966). The term refers to the pretest and the threat consists in the possibility that scores on the posttest may be different from what they otherwise would have been, not just because of the treatment, but because the subjects were subjected to previous measurements—the pretest. One clear example is in achievement or attitude measurement, where the pretest sensitizes the subjects to certain forms of information or simply starts them thinking about something that they otherwise would have given no attention. Other forms of behavior may be affected by measurement operations as well. For example, if the police are conspicuous in gathering baseline information on traffic violations, the rate of violations is likely to be lower afterward than it otherwise would have been.

Design 3 is in principle quite vulnerable to testing effects. It may be impossible to have confidence that the pretest itself did not affect the outcome so that the separate impact of the program may be in serious doubt. This threat, unlike the threat of external events, finds Design 11 to be totally immune; there can be no testing effects if there has been no pretest. In the case of design 12, the control group is a recorder of the effects of testing; that is, since both groups are pretested, any differences between them will necessarily be due either to the treatment or to other threats to validity, but not to the measurement of X. Note that there still may be testing effects in design 12 in that the program, although it may clearly have had an impact, might not have had such an impact unless the pretest had been administered first. This kind of phenomenon has been referred to as an interaction between the treatment and the pretest (Campbell and Stanley 1966). It is not a threat to internal validity because the program effect that shows up in the difference between the experimental and control groups is real enough. It is, however, a threat to external validity; the program effects observed may not be generalizable to groups that are not pretested beforehand. With design 3 this issue is not as relevant because the only effect that can be generalized is in fact the difference between a pretest and a posttest. In sum, particularly with respect to internal validity, the true experimental designs are far superior to the before-after design as a defense against the threat of testing.

A third form of history is the threat of *maturation.* It refers to a null-case difference between before and after that results purely from the process of aging or natural development. It is quite pertinent in connection with outcomes which themselves commonly change with age, such as knowledge, intelligence, political attitudes, and physiological condition, but in addition, virtually any outcome may be affected later by unmeasured factors that were present in the subjects at pretest time. For example, a pharmaceutical may be administered to patients and they may get better, but it is possible that many would have gotten better anyway from natural causes—factors already present. Getting better is then a maturation process. Or many couples who receive marriage counseling might stay together, but it is possible that some would have worked it out anyway, not because of the treatment or external events, but mostly on the strength of their initial commitment. Or a polluted lake might be treated and might not show positive results, but it is possible that without the treatment it would have continued to degrade over time as a result of the process set in motion by the earlier pollution. Any time a maturation process in the subjects can affect the outcome of interest, design 3 is weak and vulnerable; there may be no way to discern the extent to which a before-after difference is due to maturation and the extent to which it is due to the program being evaluated.

The threat is relevant in the context of design 11, even though there is no pretest, because one can think of maturation that may have taken place since the groups were equalized at the time of randomization. It is also relevant in the context of design 12, where the change from pretest to posttest may be due in whole or in part to a maturation process. Although relevant, however, maturation is not a threat to validity within either of these true experimental designs. Again, the reason is the existence of a comparison group. The control group (or any comparison group) is a recorder of the maturation process; any observed difference between the two groups must not be caused by maturation effects and must therefore be due either to the treatment or other threats to internal validity. With this threat, moreover, there can be no divergent maturation in experimental designs (except for the effects of unhappy randomization) because the potential for this kind of change inheres in the subjects at the time of randomization. The randomization then equalizes the two groups (within sampling error) for their potential for maturation. Divergent maturation would, however, be a threat to internal validity if the treatment and comparison groups were not created by randomization. At any rate, as was true with external events and testing, design 3 is far weaker given the maturation threat than are designs 11 and 12.

Closely related to maturation is the threat of *regression*. Whereas maturation connotes a linear sort of development, regression refers to cyclical or episodic change. For many phenomena, subjects scoring toward an extreme are likely to drift naturally toward a less extreme norm over time. In test taking, for example, many extreme high and low scores are due to transient conditions rather than innate ability and a retest after some time passes is likely to produce a less extreme score. Some forms of arthritis have cyclical effects; a patient suffering severe loss of physical function at one point in time is likely to feel a lot better after a month or two (see the evaluation by Deniston and Rosenstock 1973). Not all outcomes, however, are subject to regression effects. Dental caries, for example, cannot be expected to act like arthritis; once the tooth begins to decay, it does not regenerate. There is debate about whether serious juvenile offenders would get worse or better if not incarcerated (McCleary et al. 1979; Murray and Cox 1979). Whenever regression effects are at all plausible, the results of a design 3 analysis must be in serious doubt since any change observed over time may be due at least in part to regression rather than the treatment. For the two experimental designs we have been considering, regression fares exactly as maturation. It is relevant to both design 12 and design 11, but it is neutralized in both because of the comparison group, which is a recorder of the regression. Moreover, divergent regression is not a potential problem in these designs because the randomization process ensures that regression will be the same in both groups (within sampling error). Again, experimental design is far superior to design 3.

The concept of the threat of regression is truly simple and straightforward. Ultimately, it needs no more space than it has already received. However, the subject of regression effects has been magnified in much previous literature on program evaluation and made into one of the most difficult ideas in the entire technology. To skip the additional concerns completely would be to puzzle many experienced readers at this time. To undo the difficulties, however, demands a complex discussion in itself, resting on the earlier presentation of the putative problem, which is not at all straightforward. Since this subject constitutes a necessary digression, it has been appended to the end of the chapter.

The last form of history to be considered is *attrition*. The threat of attrition refers to the possibility that subjects may leave the group between time one and time two or, more precisely, that the Y scores of some subjects become unavailable or irrelevant. Bias is introduced if the subjects who drop out are not average or mutually cancelling in their Y scores, but since such information is by definition unavailable, any attrition of subjects presents a serious problem. In a preschool education program for disadvantaged children, for example, some may leave the area before it is time to take Y scores in the second or third grade. Or in a juvenile crime prevention program in which Y is measured by numbers of offenses over an extended period, those who are incarcerated because of a serious offense will have Y scores that are artificially low, and therefore irrelevant. In such cases, the validity of an inference based on design 3 becomes highly problematic. In the experimental designs, we need not be concerned about attrition itself; the existence of a comparison group shifts concern to the problem of divergent attrition. But this problem can be a serious one indeed, even for true experiments. We will see that it is true that randomization neutralizes certain of the potential for divergent attrition, but some remains. Experimental design is not strong in the face of a threat to validity from divergent attrition.

In sum, none of the threats to internal validity under the rubric of history is technically problematic in experimental design because all experimental design is based on control groups. The issue shifts to *divergent* history—divergence in experience concerning these threats. Randomization manages divergent regression and maturation quite well. It was suggested earlier that although randomization also goes far toward neutralizing the threats of divergent events and divergent attrition, it is not completely successful. Experimental design is therefore not perfect, even apart from the possibility of unhappy randomization. The details of this imperfection will be addressed as we consider the basic threat of contamination. First, however, after an important closing note on validity in connection with evaluation designs in general, we will turn to a consideration of the threat of selection.

It is extremely important to note that although, technically speaking, the before-after design is almost pathetically vulnerable to threats to validity, it can at times be quite adequate. No design gives absolutely unassailable information on a program's extent of impact; in the end, a certain amount of subjective presumption is always involved in accepting the assessment of effectiveness. Even with the randomized experiment, which, when applicable, is generally the very best that we can do, the threats of divergent events, divergent attrition, and other forms of contamination remain quite active, not to mention the ever-dangerous possibility of unhappy randomization. The other side of this same coin, however, is that even with weaker designs, the situation in which they are applied may be such that the evaluators and essentially all of the audience for the evaluation may feel safe in making the presumption that no threat to validity is truly a problem—as safe as they might feel, let us say, in the case of a true experiment. One basis for such a presumption is of course specific information about or just general experience with the world outside of the study, sometimes accompanied by a careful process of reasoning. But this information generally must interact with one of two primary factors connected with the study itself: *(1) a very surprising, large or dramatic apparent impact, and (2) a very direct, close causal connection between treatment and outcome.* Even with design 3, there are times when, because of one or both of these factors, all are willing to accept that no force other than the treatment can realistically account for the observed difference between results and counterfactual. For example, the extent of dog litter in an urban neighborhood was measured and then a program was initiated in which people walking dogs were given pooper scoopers, plastic bags, and an explanation and asked to cooperate. Immediately after the intervention, posttest measurements were taken that revealed very little dog litter at all in the neighborhood (Jason et al. 1981). The design in this case is merely design 3, yet few would doubt that the program was responsible for the decrease in litter; the results were too dramatic and the connection between those results, on one hand, and handing out the pooper scoopers and observing their use, on the other, was too obvious to allow any other interpretation. Some fraction of the results may have been due to some fortuitous element, but it was clearly the program that produced the before-after difference. Thus, the appraisal of each design relative to threats to internal validity in this and all subsequent sections has strong general significance, but there are always special cases when the threats are simply not a problem and a weaker (and cheaper) design will serve as well as a stronger one. No impact analysis may be dismissed out of hand because the design is weak in principle, just as none can be automatically accepted as valid because the design is generally strong.

The Threat of Selection:
The Comparative-Posttest Design

We have found that true experimental designs shine as a means of overcoming the basic threat of history that plagues an elementary quasi-experimental design, design 3. We have also seen, however, that they do so not because of the classification characteristics that set them apart—centralized selection and randomized assignment—but simply because their structure calls for a comparison group and the threat of history becomes irrelevant whenever the counterfactual derives from a comparison group. The question therefore naturally arises whether the control of history might not be attained without encountering the operational problems of true experiments by using a comparison group without resort to randomization. The answer is yes, but in so doing one encounters other equally troublesome ills.

Let us explore this issue by considering the simplest alternative that provides a comparison group, the comparative-posttest design. It is the second and last elementary quasi-experimental design that we will consider. In subsequent chapters we will explore more sophisticated alternatives to the strong but commonly unavailable true experiment. The comparative-posttest design is diagrammed as follows:

$$(4) \qquad \frac{T \quad Y_E}{Y_C}.$$

Design 4 is exactly like design 11 with one exception: although the selection process is still centralized, there is no randomization. The two groups are selected by some process that may be careful and systematic or may perhaps be arbitrary, but is not connected with powerful probability and statistics theorems such as those that are related to random sampling. This is noted by the absence of the R beginning each line of the diagram. Otherwise, the notation is the same and has the same significance here as in the diagram for design 11, the R-comparative-posttest design.

The threat of history is truly nullified. The comparison group is considered to record regression, external events, and so on so that any differences observed in the mean posttest scores of the two groups must be due either to the treatment or perhaps to some threat to internal validity other than history. It is immediately clear that, as was the case with the R-comparative-posttest design, one must become concerned with divergent events and divergent attrition. Moreover, we will see when we consider the basic threat of contamination under which they fall that these are more serious in design 4 than in design 11 and that divergent maturation and regression now become threats to validity as well. Let us continue to postpone these issues, however, as we proceed with the threat of selection, which is logically prior in the classification scheme.

Selection is the basic threat to internal validity that is uniquely connected to quasi-experimental designs in which the counterfactual is derived from a comparison group. Selection is not a problem with single-group, over-time designs, just as history is not a problem with comparison-group designs. Selection bias is sometimes used in connection with over-time designs in the sense of selecting subjects who would have improved even without the treatment or, perhaps, who are particularly likely to be helped by it. In the former case, the use would seem to be legitimate, but for the sake of technical expedience and purity of definition, we will avoid mixing categories and use only maturation and regression, as previously explained, to denote that sort of threat to over-time designs. In selecting just one group, you have selected whomever you have selected; there is no bias so far. The true problem is that the maturation or regression process in those subjects may turn out not to be neutral with respect to Y. Thus, the basic categorical threat to internal validity there remains the threat of history.

In the case of subjects who are particularly likely to be helped, the concept of selection bias is being used as a proxy synonym for the idea of poor external validity; the concern is that not everybody would respond in the same way to the treatment. Again, for clarity, we will use each term to satisfy a narrow technical function, recognizing that ordinary linguistic practice may be more permissive. Selection, then, refers only to a *difference* on Y between two observed groups due to differences that exist between them at the time of selection.

We will speak both of selection *effects* and selection *bias*. A selection effect occurs whenever the two (or more) groups differ on some variable (other than the treatment) that causes a difference in Y scores. Selection effects, however, need not necessarily imply selection bias. The latter occurs when the selection effects go undetected and so may in principle be confounded with treatment effects. If the variables causing selection effects are measured in the evaluation study, they may be controlled by one means or another in the analysis so that selection bias does not become a problem at all.

For convenience, we will also speak of two *sources* of selection effects, P and Q, where P refers to a pretest and Q refers to all other possible sources of difference in outcome. Thus, selection-P bias means bias that results because the two groups started out in different places on the outcome-of-interest dimension when this initial difference is not accounted for in the analysis. When there is selection-Q bias, a pretest may or may not be measured and accounted for in the analysis, but one or more additional causes of Y are omitted and are confounded with the treatment. The deadly problem posed by selection-Q bias for quasi-experimental designs is that its sources are potentially infinite, so that no matter how many control variables are included, others may have been omitted.

In connection with the comparative-posttest design, it is clear that both types of selection bias can occur; that is, if the mean Y score is different for the two groups it may not be because of the treatment, but because they started out in different places on the pretest (if a pretest had only been administered) or on some other cause of the outcome of interest. Furthermore, if the two posttest scores are exactly the same, so that the treatment seems to have had no effect whatever, the threat of selection implies that one group may have started out behind the other and it is only because of the effective treatment that their respective levels are now equal. The threat of selection is so devastating for design 4 that it is classified here, like design 3, as an elementary quasi-experimental design, in contrast with those described in later chapters.

Designs 4 and 11 stand in marked contrast to one another concerning the threat of selection. The only difference between them is randomization, but that difference is great indeed. Randomization means that the groups are equalized (within statistical sampling error) on *all* variables, measured and unmeasured. The number of sources of possible selection bias goes from infinity to zero with this one operation; the only remaining source of substantial initial difference between the experimental and control groups is unhappy randomization. The sharpness of this contrast between the two designs makes quite a difference in one's willingness to accept an inference of program effect.

Design 12, the R-comparative-change design, is even better, unless problems of external validity are introduced by pretesting. As noted above, when the true experiments were first compared, substantial estimating efficiency is obtained in design 12 because of its relatively great sensitivity. A much smaller treatment effect will be detectable (i.e., will yield a statistically significant result) through design 12 than design 11. Moreover, in the case of no treatment effect, if there happened to be unhappy randomization of influential initial conditions, then the selection problem so produced would lead to a large outcome difference between the groups, and design 11 would lead to the incorrect conclusion that the treatment was effective. If design 12 were employed, however, and if the responsible initial conditions were the pretest and other measured variables, one would *expect* the two groups to end in different places and make no false attributions of program effect.

Clearly then experimental design is far superior to design 4 from the threat-of-selection standpoint. One might well ask at this point why a manager or evaluator would ever opt for anything but an experimental design for the analysis of impact. True experiments have their own technical problems, which will be reviewed momentarily. It must be remembered, however, that one of the primary reasons for rejecting experimental design is that it demands a measure of control over assignment to treatments that may be either impractical or undesirable. It has long been found difficult, for example, to withhold selectively certain remedies or procedures thought beneficial instead of making them available to all who care to apply. But further, it is politically or practically infeasible to randomize subjects for some programs rather than use program-relevant criteria. Imagine asking the government to assign military aid to countries at random in order that its effects might be properly evaluated! Many claim that experimental designs might be used more often than one would think—that there is a tendency to give up too soon (Gilbert, Light, and Mosteller 1975)—but all agree that substitutes must be available for many cases. When randomization is not possible but centralized selection still is, design 4 is a reasonable first thought; if it is not good enough, one must simply seek a better quasi-experimental design.

As we have noted frequently, even true experiments are not immune to serious threats to validity, so that it is possible that a good quasi-experimental design might be preferable in some instances even though it is not preferable in general. External validity issues, for example, might at times put experimental design at a disadvantage. Regarding internal validity, all of the threats to experimental design lie in the basic category of contamination, to which we now turn.

The Threat of Contamination

The thing that is contaminated here is the implementation or unfolding of the design. *Contamination* means rendering impure, or rendering different from the pure state that is assumed when an inference of program-effect is made based on the study. The term *design* in the phrase "implementation or unfolding of the design" refers to three elements: assignment of subjects to treatments, delivery of the treatments, and controls. Thus, *bias due to contamination occurs whenever an impurity enters into the unfolding of the assignment, treatment delivery, or controls.* Like history and selection bias, contamination means that something other than the treatment, as defined and understood, has managed to have an undetected effect on the outcome. Let us specify some of the kinds of interference that would be classified under the contamination threat to internal validity (many but not all were called reactive arrangements by Campbell and Stanley 1966).

The assignment aspect becomes contaminated in its unfolding when certain types of divergent history occur—divergent maturation or regression or specific types (but not all types) of divergent attrition or events. As these terms are elaborated and exemplified, it will become clear that they are forms of selection-Q bias: a divergence due to assignment must logically mean that the seeds of the divergence were there to begin with. In that sense, the threat to validity that we now treat under the heading of contamination is precisely the same as the one we have already treated under selection. However, it might be extremely difficult if not impossible (*a*) to measure these seeds of divergence, or (*b*) to separate them from the treatment and by these means to control them in the analysis. For these two reasons, it is desirable to consider them under contamination, where the *unfolding* of assignment factors is highlighted rather than the previous existence of the assignment factors as identifiable entities. Furthermore, it is convenient to group divergent history due to preexisting characteristics with other kinds of divergent history—those having to do with experimental controls and not connected with the processes of selection and assignment.

The first two types of divergent history due to assignment—divergent maturation and regression—mean simply that the subjects develop in different ways; the groups mature at different rates or one group regresses toward a norm while the other does not. It is clear that this cannot occur in a true experiment, except within the limits of random sampling error, because the groups are equalized in their potential for maturation and regression by the randomization. Contamination from these two sources, however, is definitely a threat in quasi-experimental designs. Furthermore, the seeds of divergence may easily be too obscure, multifaceted, and complex to hope to measure and control. What, after all, is responsible for one group's learning a bit faster, or experiencing a greater decrease in accident rates when both started out the same: or for one group's regressing from an extreme standardized achievement test score toward the population mean while another group with the same initial score does not regress? The causes of such development frequently cannot be specified; their possible existence is simply inferred from their apparent effects.

Divergent attrition and divergent events might also occur as the result of assignment in some designs. The a priori characteristics of some subjects may cause them to drop out early—their economic and family situations cause them to move from the city, for example—and those subjects may be more heavily represented in one group than the other. Bias would occur if the subjects who drop out were not average or somehow mutually canceling. Concerning divergent events, if the treatment group is taken from one or two geographic areas, for example, and the comparison group from a few others, which frequently occurs in impact analyses (e.g., Smith 1976; Farquhar et al. 1978; Freeman et al. 1981), they may have quite different experiences in ways other than the treatment. One area may have a crime wave, heat wave, publicity wave, or a wave of budget austerity, and so on, and these, singly or in combination, may affect the outcome of interest at issue. This may seem the threat of history—of external events. Indeed as we have noted, it is history that causes the change (in one group), but it is *divergent* history that causes the incorrect inference. Note the difficulty of controlling such contamination, particularly in the last sort of example where it is impossible to separate the geographic factors from the treatment itself: even if heat wave, crime wave, and so on, were measured, one could not distinguish their effects either from each other or from the effects of the program because they do not vary independently of one another.

Divergent events and divergent attrition due to assignment are, like divergent maturation and regression, threats to quasi-experimental but not to experimental designs since randomization makes all initial propensities subject to statistical inference. This is perhaps non-intuitive and therefore particularly noteworthy in divergent events. It means that if two groups are formed by randomization (and especially if the groups are large), one can expect them to experience, on the average, exactly the same futures—the same weather, divorce rates, assaults, disappointments, capital gains, and so on—as long as there is no unnatural interference. Essentially, their futures will differ only by random sampling error (chance) or because of the experiment itself.

Last, it may be noted that the assignment type of contamination is pertinent only to comparison-group designs. Divergences of maturation, regression, attrition, and events in context of a one-group, over-time design is meaningless; divergence necessarily involves at least two units of analysis (e.g., two groups) as well as two points in time.

Contamination within the treatment-delivery element means that the treatment has not been administered properly. It may simply be done incorrectly, for example, as when medical personnel administer the wrong drug. A frequent occurrence is that some subjects in the comparison group get the treatment that only the experimental group was supposed to get, either by mistake or because program personnel were induced by friendships, politics, the sight of suffering, or similar pressures. More subtly, delivery is well known to be capable of having psychological effects not considered part of the essence of the treatment itself. The Hawthorne effect is an example, where subjects identify with the experimenter to some extent and behave in a way they believe may be expected of them. Teachers can cause differential performance by their differential expectations for students as well as by their teaching methods (e.g., Rist 1970). Double-blind experiments in medicine (where neither patients nor doctors know the status of the patient within the experiment) were created to prevent both the treatment and its administration from having a psychological effect. All of these are ways in which contamination of delivery can bias an inference of program effect. We may note that contamination from this source is a threat to the before-after design, as well as to comparison-group designs since the treatment might be delivered improperly in any sort of program. Last, we may note that true experiments are not immune to the threat to internal validity from this source. It occurs after randomization has taken place and is integrally bound to the treatment itself so that it may easily affect the experimental and control groups differentially.

Quite apart from the a priori characteristics of the subjects and the delivery of the treatment, the subjects must be kept free of all impurities once the study has begun to unfold. The final type of contamination thus takes the form of incomplete or improper experimental controls. This means that there is a failure to insulate the subjects properly from fortuitous characteristics of the treatment, which in social programs frequently involves the necessity of insulating them from each other. This threat is precisely the usual sense of the need for laboratory controls, although the implications are a bit different when there is no true laboratory. Programs, even if they are delivered properly, come packaged with all sorts of trappings and implications that are not integral to the treatment itself but that may somehow affect outcomes. Because it is known that they have received a certain program, for example, subjects may be contacted by businesses or interest groups. Or consider a program to curb crime that is carried out in selected parts of the city. The subjects in such an evaluation would be the various geographic sections. If criminals began to be wary of the experimental sections and gravitate toward the conveniently nearby control sections, the design would have been contaminated by reactions to an unnatural variation in the city's neighborhoods (some not having as much policing as others), which is not at all integral to the treatment.

As noted, faulty controls may be due to relations of the subjects or groups with each other as well as with the outside world. Thus, even if the treatment is administered purely, there is still a danger that the other group, or just information about the other group, might influence the results. Comparison-group subjects may behave differently because of rivalry, for example, as public school teachers might in any program that experiments with a different method of delivering public education (see Gramlich and Koshel 1975; Weiler 1976). Or, those in one group may resent the treatment given to the other group and not to themselves, and therefore behave unnaturally. Or one group may pressure the other, as is a danger when the time of some young people is used in a program to prevent juvenile delinquency, while their friends go on with life as usual (e.g., Berleman and Steinburn 1967), or when some but not all medical students at one school are taught to treat "the whole patient" (Hammond and Kern 1959; Gilbert, Light, and Mosteller 1975). A frequent danger is that information that is given to one group as part of the treatment will diffuse to the other, as in any program designed to instruct, educate, or persuade. (All of these types of contamination resulting from relations among subjects or treatment groups are listed by Cook and Campbell 1979.) Divergent attrition may be brought about by these same sorts of failure to insulate; they would in that case simply affect duration in the program (e.g., some delinquents quit coming to the counseling or recreation sessions) rather than scores on the outcome dimension.

Controls contamination is not applicable to single-group, over-time designs because bias from faulty control in that case is simply a matter of not having prevented *external events* from affecting the subjects. The threat is the threat of history. It is, however, applicable to all comparison-group designs, both experimental and quasi-experimental. Frequently, then, it is a form of divergent events. True experiments, however, are not immune to this type of contamination because it is bound to the implementation phase of the study rather than to the assignment phase so that randomization affords no protection whatever.

Summary of Threats to Internal Validity

The above completes the treatment of threats to internal validity. Having undertaken it in the context of a comparison of experimental with elementary quasi-experimental designs, we may now see in summary that: (1) The threat of history affects a design only to the extent that the counterfactual is derived from previous observation of the same group that is later observed in order to obtain the results; it therefore does not affect true experiments since the randomization process implies that the counterfactual will be derived from a comparison group. (2) The threat of selection does affect comparison-group designs, and only those. Still, it does not affect experiments because it is neutralized by the randomization process. Selection is therefore quite specifically a threat to quasi-experimental, comparison-group designs. (We will see in Chapter Ten that it also has an interpretive sort of relevance for ex-post-facto designs.) (3) The threat of contamination is mixed in its application. Contamination through assignment, like the threat of selection, affects only quasi-experimental, comparison-group designs. Contamination through controls affects only comparison-group designs (in single-group, over-time designs, it is simply external events). Contamination through treatment delivery can affect all designs (these distinctions are schematized in Figure 4–1, which is repeated on pages vi–vii for your convenience).

We see therefore that experimental designs are immune to all threats to internal validity except improper delivery of the treatment and imperfect controls. These threats, however, should not be minimized; they can be quite damaging. The point will be elaborated after external validity has been treated, when all of the threats to the validity of inferences from experimental designs may be considered together in review.

EXTERNAL VALIDITY

The issue of external validity refers to the extent to which one may safely generalize the conclusions derived from an evaluation. There may well be a doubt about whether the results would be valid for other subjects, other times, other settings, or other operationalizations of the treatment (T) or outcome dimension (Y). Let us briefly consider these categories one at a time.

The program may or may not have worked on the subjects actually observed, but it is almost always questionable whether it will produce the same results on other subjects. The prominent exception where this problem is of little concern occurs when the subjects observed were selected as a random sample from a larger population; all results are then generalizable to the larger population, with the appropriate statistical reservations. Note that the random sample may in turn be randomized into two or more subgroups for the sake of employing true experimental design. One then gains all of the advantages of experimental over quasi-experimental or ex-post-facto design and attains generalizability to a definite larger population besides. This exception has not been of substantial importance in program evaluation, however, both because program managers and evaluators rarely seem in a position to select subjects by random sampling from a large population (regardless of how they would then assign the subjects to treatments), and because one must often wonder whether the results on the population itself are generalizable, which may be an issue unless the population sampled is quite large and important. A good example of the issue of generalizability to other subjects is reported by Haefner (1965). One experiment found that inducing fear through threatening communications did not improve tooth-brushing regularity in schoolchildren. A replication, however, found a moderate effect. The mystery was substantially cleared up when, at the data-analysis stage, the children in the second study were subdivided into two groups based on social class. It was then revealed that fear inducement apparently produced a substantial effect on the working-class but not the middle-class children. In the first study, the children had been almost entirely middle class. There is, in short, almost always a doubt whether an impact is generalizable to subjects of different age groups, social classes, regions, and, certainly, to other cultures.

A program may produce substantial effects in one time period, but there may often be a concern whether it will continue to do so if retained, or will do so again if introduced anew in another time period. Social, political, demographic, and economic conditions change, and these may interact with the treatment. For example, the national fifty-five-mph speed limit appeared to have a substantial impact on driving practice when it was introduced in the mid-1970s, but it is well known that driving speeds have crept upward over time, even though the same limit is still in effect.

Third, the setting in which a program is administered may be important. In particular, studies carried out on human subjects or animals in a laboratory may not produce the same results when replicated in natural settings. Kelman and his colleagues (1962) were able to get nursing home patients to dress themselves at the rehabilitation center, but the behavior did not carry over to daily living in the home. Since much of evaluation is concerned with programs that are to be applied in natural settings, the pilots, trials, and demonstrations must usually also be in the natural setting to be convincing. Unfortunately, this raises difficult questions about what the natural setting really is, and challenges the evaluator to control out the aspects of the field setting used that are not common to most others in which the program would be applied.

Last, in any given study, the treatment is operationalized in one way, or a given set of ways, and so is Y, the outcome of interest (in some impact analyses, the operationalization of subobjectives may easily be a concern as well). The question arises whether the operationalizations will always be the same and, if not, whether the results would be duplicated with other operationalizations (Cook and Campbell 1979, consider this issue under the heading of construct validity). The issue arises in three prominent ways. For one, it occurs all too frequently that the precise nature of the treatment is not even known—not even approximately known. The problem occurs particularly when the treatment delivery is highly decentralized and scattered over many sites rather than being administered by the same personnel to all subjects. Consider a work-release program where prisoners are released during daytime hours to work for employers in the community for some months before their total release from prison. If the program is to have a favorable effect on recidivism, the individual work-release employment experience may have a great deal to do with it, but this varies for the many prisoners in any given program and is generally unknown to program and evaluation personnel. Similarly, one might conduct a summative evaluation of the impact of an international student-exchange program on attitudes toward other countries and peoples, but the experience of each student is different, even among those who attend the same foreign university, so that one does not really know what the treatment has been. National programs for underprivileged children or the structurally unemployed may also be implemented differently at different sites. When one evaluates such a program, one assesses only the average impact of the different things that were done. That is reasonable only if there is some element that is fairly common to the various applications and that constitutes the core of the concept of the treatment (e.g., one might consider employment or community connectedness of any sort to lower the probability of recidivism, or any experience in a foreign country to improve one's attitudes toward the outside world). Furthermore, in ignorance of what actually was done, it could be hard to predict whether a replication would produce approximately the same results. If one knew what the treatment was truly supposed to be, one might call this a concern about contamination, but with vague treatments one can only question external validity.

A second kind of operationalization problem occurs when the treatment is implemented in a known manner, but could well be implemented differently. One might try to frighten people into preventive health habits with words, for example, or with pictures. When this is a conscious concern, one must either be content to generalize to the one operationalization used or employ several in a factorial type of design (see Kerlinger 1967, pp. 325–332).

A more frequent problem lies in the operationalization of the outcome dimension. It is not uncommon for this dimension to be an attitude or some other concept that could be operationalized in several different ways. Different measurements of the general concept might yield different results for a given treatment. Toothbrushing, for example, is but one operationalization of preventive health behavior. Do theoretically based programs designed to improve preventive health behavior have the same effect on getting chest X-rays or quitting smoking as they do on toothbrushing regularity (Rosenstock 1966)? Is the impact of a counselling program on juvenile delinquency the same for serious offenses as for all offenses (Berleman and Steinburn 1967)? When a concern for this aspect of validity is conscious, a good remedy, often available, though by no means always, is to use several operationalizations of the concept at issue (Cook and Campbell 1979, pp. 59–64; Campbell and Fiske 1959). With good effect, for example, and without too much trouble, Waldo and Chiricos (1977) report fifteen measures of recidivism—each a slightly different interpretation—as outcomes of a work-release program. When multiple measures cannot be employed, external validity is correspondingly restricted.

Finally, if a pretest is administered, one must often be concerned that it may interact with the treatment, that is, the treatment may have had the (large or small) effect that it did only because the pretest was administered first. The pretest, in essence, becomes part of the treatment and the program results are not generalizable with validity to any application in which the pretest is omitted. We noted this problem previously, in comparing design 11 with design 12. A pretest is extremely useful in impact analysis but it does in principle constitute a threat to internal validity in a before-after design and, unless it is considered a part of the treatment itself, a threat to external validity in *any* comparison-group design in which it might appear.

Several of the above issues may be illustrated—with a twist—by Goldman's (1979) study of appellate litigation. The burden of such litigation on the court system is considered undesirably heavy; Goldman's well-planned and executed experiment was designed to assess the impact of a technique for reducing it. There is a tendency to think of external validity primarily in connection with generalizing the results of a successful intervention to other subjects, times, and so forth. As Gilbert, Light, and Mosteller (1975) have demonstrated, however, most social programs that are evaluated emerge as not having worked very well. In this case, it may be true either that the intervention is essentially inefficacious or, perhaps, that the negative results are not necessarily widely generalizable. Concluding that the procedure of court-supervised conferences and judicial orders did not bring about the desired improvements, Goldman notes that the treatment was operationalized using an attorney rather than a judge as supervisor of the conferences—and one particular attorney, at that—and that there is some reason to believe that the setting, New York, may not be typical. One way to try to resolve such an issue is by replication in varied operationalizations and settings. Another method, or at least a supporting one, is to use subobjectives. Pinpointing the strengths and weaknesses in the causal chain can suggest whether variations in method, subjects, or setting are needed.

At this point it is well to ask whether internal or external validity is more important. The answer is that they are both critical. It is perhaps more evident in the case of internal validity: an impact analysis is worthless if the results are highly generalizable, but wrong. But at the same time, evaluation is a policy tool; as such, it is never carried out for the sake of the past. Our interest is not in knowing whether the program *was* effective, given the context of subjects, time, setting, and operationalizations in which it was observed to operate in the evaluation study. Rather, we are interested only in how effective it *would be* if continued, modified, or repeated—and why. For that reason, the retrospective evaluation of a program is essentially worthless if its external validity is poor, no matter how valid it is internally, that is, concerning the past. From the standpoint of design, therefore, the best must combine excellent internal and external validity.

Experimental design has been shown to be extremely strong in internal validity. Does it fare as well in external validity? The answer for any design lies in the extent to which it permits the subjects, setting, time, and operationalizations observed to be equivalent to those to which one would like to generalize. In this respect, experimental designs are at a slight disadvantage. Because they demand enough control to be able to assign subjects to treatments at random, they make it more difficult to employ typical subjects and natural or representative settings. The need to randomize is one additional constraint that must be satisfied in one's quest for broad generalizability. This clearly does not mean that external validity is necessarily lower in an experimental than in a quasi-experimental study, but only that the probability of strong external validity is somewhat reduced.

SUMMARY

We have explored the idea of quality of design in this chapter, where quality has been rendered primarily as internal and external validity. In doing so, we relied heavily on a comparison between experimental and elementary quasi-experimental studies. Relatively speaking, the first were found extremely powerful from the standpoint of internal validity, but they have three kinds of weakness, nevertheless. One is that, because they demand a comparison group and randomization, experimental designs are often impossible or highly impractical to execute. It is hardly possible to apply true experimentation to the Oregon or Michigan bottle bills, the impact of foreign aid, the national fifty-five-mph speed limit, or the impact of high school graduation on income. Second, experiments are subject to the threat of contamination due to the treatment or the implementation of the study: in particular, randomization often sets up an artificial little world in which subjects are in close proximity but are nevertheless being treated differently. Last, the need to randomize makes it more difficult than it might otherwise be to carry out a study with strong external validity.

For the many occasions when experimental design is not an option or is apparently less desirable than one would wish because of these particular vulnerabilities, one would hope that other designs were available whose general strengths were greater than the before-after or comparative-posttest designs. We turn now to an exploration of such possibilities.

Appendix

THE REGRESSION ARTIFACT

The text for this chapter notes a threat to internal validity called regression and describes it in quite uncomplicated terms. This treatment is unusual. Often, the threat, or an aspect of it, is referred to as regression artifacts, instead of regression, and the explanation is lengthy and complex (e.g., Campbell and Erlebacher 1970; Campbell and Boruch 1975; Hoole 1978; McCleary et al. 1979). When considered in such terms, the point of the threat is that an artifact of statistical relations implies that the score of a group on the outcome of interest almost inevitably moves over time to a more middling position:

> If, for example, in a remediation experiment, students are picked for a special experimental treatment because they do particularly poorly on an achievement test (which becomes for them the O_1), then on a subse-

quent testing using a parallel form or repeating the same test, O_2 for this group will almost surely average higher than did O_1. This dependable result is not due to any genuine effect of X, any test-retest practice effect, etc. It is rather a tautological aspect of the imperfect correlation between O_1 and O_2. (Campbell and Stanley, 1966, p. 10, where O_1 and O_2 refer to pretest and posttest, respectively, and X refers to the treatment).

Or again,

For example, when intelligence tests are given one year apart in an orphan asylum, the children brightest on the first test are, on the average, somewhat duller on the second (though of course, still above average), while the dullest now average brighter than they did initially. This is an inevitable finding if the test-retest correlation is less than unity, but it has been frequently misinterpreted as evidence of a "leveling" effect of the homogeneous environment. (Campbell and Clayton 1961).

The primary thrust of the warnings in treatments of the regression artifact is not incorrect; at bottom, it means simply that changes over time in a group's mean score may have hidden and unsuspected causes. However, many treatments of the subject have overemphasized the role of statistics (statistics in fact have no power over the movement of scores) and the idea of inevitability (there is in fact nothing inevitable about the movement of group mean scores over time).

There is not the slightest doubt that, in the absence of any treatment effects, extreme scorers nevertheless do frequently show movement toward a more moderate value over time. Why might this be? The answer when it is put in regression artifacts language is that because the correlation between pretest and posttest is less than 1.0 (which of course it must nearly always be), such movement must inevitably take place. That answer, however, is not a satisfactory one both because it is essentially incorrect and because it is not an explanation; it is not a proper response to the question that was posed: Why might this be? Indeed, the statistically oriented response throws consideration of the entire issue fundamentally off the track. There are three things wrong with it: First, it is incorrect if it is meant to suggest that the average raw score of a group must inevitably move in this fashion. Second, it is backward; it is the particular criss-crossing and nonuniform movement of the scores of the subjects over time that causes the correlation to be less than 1.0, and not the other way around. Third, the particular changes in scores have real-life reasons, not artifactual ones, and these are neither addressed nor even recognized by this response. The answer to the why question should be put in these real-life terms instead of in the obscure language of statistical artifacts. To understand these difficulties, let us briefly review the logic behind regression artifacts and the reasons that make the logic irrelevant for impact analysis in program evaluations.

THE BASIS UNDERLYING
THE STANDARD ACCOUNT

The generally recognized statement on which the idea of regression artifacts is based is the following: If the correlation between any variables X and Y is less than 1.0 in absolute magnitude, then, for any X score other than the population mean, *the predicted standard score on Y is closer to zero than the standard score on X for the same subject.* A standard score, on X, for example, is the number of standard deviations from the mean of the distribution. Symbolizing a standard score with z, as is common, we have $z_X = (X - \mu_X)/\sigma_X$, where μ and σ are the population mean and standard deviation, respectively. In symbolic notation, the above statement relating the standard scores on Y and X becomes, for the ith individual:

$$(4A-1) \qquad |z_{\hat{Y}}| < |z_X|, \text{ given } X \neq \mu_X, |\rho_{XY}| < 1.0.$$

(If $X = \mu_X$, then it is well known that the corresponding predicted Y is μ_Y and both standard scores, having numerators of zero, would therefore be equal to zero and to each other; if the correlation ρ_{XY} is exactly 1.0 or -1.0, then again the two standard scores will be equal.) The proof of statement 4A–1 is quite uncomplicated when the regression of Y on X is considered. In standard score form, the regression would be written as

$$(4A-2) \qquad\qquad z_Y = \beta^* Z_X + u,$$

where β^* is the standardized coefficient and u is the disturbance term. Using predicted Y, that is, the point on the regression line above X (still for the ith individual), the same equation is written

$$(4A-3) \qquad\qquad z_{\hat{Y}} = \beta^* Z_X.$$

Since the standardized beta coefficient in the bivariate case is equal to the correlation coefficient, ρ_{XY}, it is always less than or equal to 1.0 in absolute magnitude. One readily sees from the above equation, then, that the predicted standard score on Y is always less than or equal to the corresponding standard score on X in any bivariate regression, which is the burden of statement 4A–1.

In analyses of impact, we are generally concerned with groups of subjects rather than individuals. Statement 4A–1 for groups becomes,

$$(4A-1') \qquad |z_{\hat{Y}}| < |z_{\bar{X}}|, \text{ given } \bar{X} \neq \mu_X, |\rho_{XY}| < 1.0,$$

where $\hat{Y}$ is the predicted mean Y score and $\bar{X}$ is the subgroup mean of X.

The above has been general in that X and Y may stand for any variables. If X is a pretest and Y the posttest, statement 4A–1′ means that a group's predicted standard score on the posttest will be closer to zero (which is the mean of any population of standard scores) than was its mean standard score on the pretest. In essence, the group's score on the dimension of interest will move closer to the population mean over time, provided that the population correlation is other than 1.0 in absolute value.

THE WEAKNESSES OF THE STANDARD ACCOUNT

To this point, we have spoken only of standard scores, but impact analyses deal primarily with raw scores. The regression-artifact statement may be converted to raw-score form only by stipulating that the population mean and standard deviation of Y are equal to the population mean and standard deviation of X, respectively; otherwise, statements 4A–1 and 4A–1' become invalid inequalities. For our case, in other words, the regression artifact applies to ordinary or raw scores of a subgroup if the mean and standard deviation of the population remain the same over time, that is, from pretest to posttest. However, if, for example, the grand mean should decrease markedly over time, the predicted posttest value for a group of extreme low scorers on the pretest may be even lower than it was to begin with and further away from the original pretest mean, not higher and closer. The *standardized* mean posttest score of the group will still be closer to the mean (zero), but because of the general population drop, the group's *raw* score will have gone downward, perhaps by quite a bit.

Given all of this, there are two properties of regression artifacts that tend to invalidate the idea as a relevant notion for impact assessment. They are:

1. *The regression artifact applies only to standard scores or to populations in which the mean and standard deviation do not change over the time period involved.* We generally do not care about standard scores in program evaluation because we generally cannot calculate them. Doing so demands a knowledge of the population parameters μ and σ. Not only are these values generally unknown, but so is the identity of the population itself. A group that is observed in an evaluation is in fact a member of infinitely many populations, and which one we take to be *the* population is generally unspecified and unmeasured. By the same token, we cannot generally know if the population mean and standard deviation have remained stable from pretest to posttest, not only because we do not happen to have these measurements but because in general we have not even identified the population. (Note that it is not a solution to throw the treatment and comparison groups together and call that combination the population of interest; the posttest mean and standard deviation for the combined group would then be contaminated by the treatment. What we would wish to know in the evaluation instance is whether or how much the population mean and standard deviation on Y would have moved in the absence of the treatment. Then one might assess the extent of regression artifacts. That becomes impossible to judge, however, once the treatment has been introduced.)

In general, we are simply confronted with a group whose mean raw score has changed somewhat over time. We truly cannot say with confidence that this is a regression artifact in a given case because we do not know whether the mean and standard deviation of the relevant population have changed. Even if we knew that they had not changed, however, we still could not say that the observed movement was the inevitable result of a regression artifact. The reason is that scores may move, but they do not move because of statistical procedures. There are in fact two prominent explanations for such movement when it is observed in an analysis of impact: one is the treatment and the other is an ordinary regression effect or any other threat to internal validity—maturation, external events, and so forth. Thus, it does not help at all to be warned about a possible regression artifact. Assuming a stable mean and standard deviation in some unidentified population, that warning, at bottom, does nothing more than alert one to the possible confounding of ordinary threats to internal validity with the apparent effects of a treatment.

2. *The statistical statement applies to the predicted mean posttest score only for a complete or a randomly selected population subgroup.* Remember that statements 4A–1 and 4A–1' refer to *predicted* scores. For any given value of X or X̄, some subjects and some groups of subjects do perhaps score at the predicted posttest value (i.e., right on the regression line), but, as is indicated by an imperfect correlation, some subgroups score above the line and some below. Thus, whereas the mean predicted (standard) score for *all* members of the population with a given start on X is as given in 4A–1', *the prediction is not the same for just any subgroup, but only for one that has been randomly chosen from all those in the population with that beginning X value.* This constraint carries the topic far from program evaluation. We do not ordinarily start with a group of subjects all having the same value on X. If we did, we still do not ordinarily select them at random from all in the population having that X score. Indeed, as we have seen, the population from which to select is usually quite undefined. What we do generally begin with is a group with a certain *average* value on X, but not selected at random. Whether these subjects are typical of those in the (generally undefined) population *with that X score* is anybody's guess. If they are not, the regression artifact notion does not apply to them; *their* average Y score may just as well be expected to fall above the regression line or below it as to be right on.

This last fact is frequently recognized in writings on the regression artifact, but its full implications may not be taken into account by the reader. In a critique of an evaluation of the Head Start program, for example, Campbell and Erlebacher (1970) clearly show that one subgroup with an extremely low pretest score (the comparison group) regresses toward the presumably higher population mean whereas another with the same average pretest score (the treatment group) does not; it continues to have essentially the same low score over time in the absence of treatment effects. How should we have predicted for both of these groups? In light of the foregoing discussion, we need to give two kinds of answer to this question. The first is that *we cannot predict differentially based on statement 4A–1'*. That statement applies, or actually fails to apply, equally to both groups; there is no mathematical or statistical way of differentiating between them. This should make the idea of regression artifacts immediately suspect. The second response is that we can, however, predict or guess or fear based on ordinary regression effects (not artifacts), and that is truly the point of the critique, although it is not given as such. The authors correctly and innovatively show that it is dangerous to form a comparison group by matching new subjects to a treatment group of extreme scorers. The comparison group may have been (not must have been) extreme for temporary reasons; many of its members may well regress toward the population mean because they are on a cyclical trend, as in arthritis (the example noted earlier in this chapter), or have episodically departed from a stable score that is truly closer in. It is this kind of behavior, among others, that tends to cause the correlation between pretest and posttest to be less than 1.0. The treatment group, however, may not regress at all. There is nothing inevitable about the ordinary regression effect; this nonrandom subgroup of extreme low scorers may be quite permanently extreme for the population unless the treatment helps them, which is why one wishes to apply the treatment to them in the first place. Thus, one group may be temporarily extreme and the other, without help, permanently extreme. The point about matching is thus well taken, but not because of statistics or artifacts. It is rather because of possible differential real-life properties of the subjects in the two groups—a selection-Q effect—that one cannot understand without pondering the individual program, evaluation, and subjects.

Consider two normal everyday programs that should be comparable by regression-artifact logic and yet are not, showing that the logic is faulty for the reasons outlined above. Assume that one were contemplating a program and an evaluation in connection with mine safety (Moran 1985). Certain mines have had quite high accident records and are about to be the subjects of an intensive bout of special government inspections. Surely, one would seriously entertain the possibility of regression *effects* here, since it is very possible that this extreme score would right itself before very long without outside interference. Similarly, if we were to worry about a regression *artifact*, we would say that, by statistical necessity, the situation would be found to have improved upon further observation after a reasonable length of time. If the world turned out actually to conform to these expectations, we know now that the manner in which it probably came about is something like the following.

There is a population of similar mines (probably unmeasured, even unknown), most with better recent safety records than those in the target group, but records that do tend to fluctuate. In the time period between observations on the target mines, the mean and standard deviation of accidents and injuries in the population will have remained about the same, but mines will have shifted about in their individual scores. Some who were a bit higher are now a bit lower, and so on. That is why the correlation between pretest and posttest in the population would presumably not be perfect. The mean raw score of our target group will have improved (for whatever reasons make some accident records in a group improve when they become extreme) as part of this shifting about and so will its standard score (since the mean and standard deviation of the population have remained the same while the target group's raw score improved). Another group of mines, but no doubt with some overlap, will now have the poorest record.

Next, assume that one were considering a program and an evaluation in connection with housing rehabilitation. Certain parts of the city have deteriorated seriously and are about to be the subjects of a program of loans and grants to improve the condition of the housing stock. It is likely that one would not worry too much about regression *effects* as a threat to validity in this case; one would not count on conditions improving on their own because one knows that, with substantial probability, once city housing begins to deteriorate, it keeps on going in that direction until it becomes worthless as property and costly in crime and expense of city services. By the logic of regression *artifacts,* however, we should be able to count on some improvement! These have become the worst areas in the population (city) and therefore they *will* regress toward the mean of better condition over a reasonable period of time. What is wrong with this logic? First of all, we are making the mistake of believing unreflectively in regression artifacts, and second, if we are to think about an artifact at all, we are making the mistake of thinking about it in raw scores. Assume that there turns out to be no regression effect here, as is certainly probable, and that, on the contrary, the housing does continue to deteriorate in raw-score form. What has happened to the technical regression artifact of statement 4–A1'? To visualize it, consider the population of all housing stock in the city (which probably remains unmeasured). To take the toughest case, assume that the mean condition of the population of houses has remained the same over the subject period of time. (If the whole city deteriorated substantially instead, then the target areas can easily have deteriorated to some degree also, while still becoming closer to the new lower mean; the regression artifact therefore occurs, even though it doesn't look that way at all.) That means, since our target group has deteriorated, that other housing must have improved enough to counterbalance the deterioration and keep the mean the same. Furthermore, there has probably been a certain amount of criss-crossing of scores; some houses in the city that formerly were better than others are now worse. These changes, brought about by whatever natural behaviors do bring about such outcomes, are the reason why the population correlation is presumably less than perfect. They also mean that the standard deviation of housing conditions in the population has necessarily increased, since our lows got lower and some highs got higher. Thus, our target group has deteriorated in raw-score form but has actually improved (regressed) in standard-score form because the population standard deviation has become so large that our group is no longer quite as many standard deviations away from the mean as it formerly was, even with its deterioration. The operation of the regression artifact is preserved intact, but it surely has nothing whatever to do with our problem, our program, or our evaluation.

Can we be confident in our presumptions about regression *effects* in these two cases? No, for it is certainly possible that the mine safety record would stay the same or get worse in the null case and that the housing conditions might possibly improve. The point is that as long as we are thinking about such issues and the reasons behind the probable developments, we are thinking constructively about the seriousness of the regression threat to validity concerning the evaluations we might undertake. If we expended our mental energy on regression *artifacts,* we might in fact come out quite well in the first case, but drown in the second. Pragmatically speaking, evaluators do not do that. They tend rather to speak of the regression artifact as a general phenomenon and then ignore it when it seems not to apply.

CONCLUSION

In sum, it is clear that the regression artifact idea is not a helpful one in impact analysis for program evaluation. It is a hindrance because it distracts attention from considering carefully the ordinary threats to internal validity that might or might not be seriously confounded with the treatment. To take one example of analysis, McCleary et al. (1979) present a simulation that purportedly demonstrates a regression artifact. The simulation *assumes* a regression *effect* and, in so doing, omits consideration of the heart of the issue—whether that regression effect does occur in real life. The artifact, in other words, is demonstrated by assuming the effect, but the issue of the validity of that assumption, which is the most critical point for the entire discussion, slips by unnoted. The question that should have been addressed was the following: To what extent do juveniles who commit serious crimes improve thereafter on their own, without incarceration? At present, that question is still unanswered. Note that it is a question about regression effects and it cannot be answered by the idea of regression artifacts. Regression effects are the real issue. Regression artifacts cannot settle it and should not be used to prejudge it.

In addition to being unhelpful and to being a distraction from important issues, the notion of a regression artifact and how it affects program evaluations tends to throw a good deal of confusion into the subject. It is difficult to grasp the idea itself, but all the more so when the explanation comprises an attempt to apply the inapplicable. The subject has been explained many times, but there seems to be a continuing perception that it is not well understood and needs to be explained yet again. It is recommended, therefore, that the subject be dropped entirely both from methodological treatments and from evaluation analyses.

Chapter Five

The Regression Framework for Impact Analysis

We have thus far referred extensively to certain technical elements of evaluations and to the designs that use them. Relatively little has been said about analysis of the data obtained. This book is not a manual on creative data analysis and since every piece of research is so different, it has always been difficult in social science to treat such a topic systematically. It is important, however, to make clear the mutually illuminating relation that exists between multiple regression and other aspects of impact analysis for program evaluation. We will therefore examine the relation between elements of the program theory and the designs that might be used, on one hand, and the basic regression framework in which analyses would generally best be carried out on the other. The chapters covering individual designs will each be somewhat more specific than the present one in relating multiple regression analysis to the application of the design in question; this small introductory treatment is offered to outline the basic ideas and common notions that will be used later in building more individualized models.

We treat techniques of analysis primarily for two reasons. The first is that the knowledge of the structure of the data analysis is a helpful, an indispensable aid to designing an evaluation properly. It is inadvisable to plan the use of one design or another without understanding how the observations would be analyzed in each case to provide an inference of program effect and, one would hope, to reach appropriate formative conclusions. Knowledge of the structure and procedures of the analysis enables one to know that a design will be workable, especially when such complicating factors as control variables and subobjectives are introduced. The second reason for presenting this and later material on regression analysis is that it helps in the understanding of the different designs themselves. It will become evident that the differences between the comparative-change design and the regression-discontinuity design cannot be understood either as readily or as well in strictly verbal presentation as they can in the regression models that underpin the respective analyses. The essence of the need for and contribution of the random-comparison-group design could hardly be communicated without reference to underlying regression models. Thus, assuming at least an elementary knowledge of multiple regression by the reader, a sketch is presented in the following pages of the basic regression technique and the key concepts involved in its application to impact analysis for program evaluation.

THE BASIC BIVARIATE EQUATION

Consider income as a function of education. The bivariate linear regression equation ordinarily used to express the relation between them, which we will presume to be causal, is as follows:

$$(5\text{--}1) \qquad Y_i = \alpha + \beta X_i + u_i,$$

where Y is the dependent or effect or result variable (income, in this example), X is the independent or causal variable (education), i refers to the ith individual (that is, any individual), α is the Y intercept (the height at which the regression line crosses the vertical axis, or the value of Y when X = 0), β is the slope of the regression line (the change in height on the vertical axis, or Y, when X increases by one—and therefore, in causal terms, the *effect* of X on Y), and u is the disturbance term—a term assumed to have a mean of zero and to be randomly distributed across subjects. The term u gives the scatter of data points above and below the regression line. See Figure 5–1.

Equation 5–1 may be written in a few other ways that are important for impact analysis:

$$(5\text{--}1a) \qquad \hat{Y}_i = \alpha + \beta X_i$$

$$(5\text{--}1b) \qquad E(Y_i) = \alpha + \beta X_i,$$

where $\hat{Y}$ and E(Y) mean the expected or predicted value of Y, that is, the value exactly on the regression line above the X value for the same subject, or the value at which the disturbance is zero; and

$$(5\text{--}1c) \qquad \bar{Y} = \alpha + \beta \bar{X},$$

where $\bar{Y}$ and $\bar{X}$ are the respective means, showing the well-known relation in linear regression that, for any set of data, the predicted value of Y for the mean of X is the mean of Y.

FIGURE 5–1   The basic regression equation

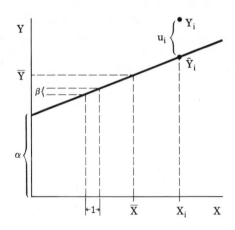

REGRESSION AS AN IMPACT STATEMENT

Equation 5–2 is exactly the same as Equation 5–1, except that the causal variable is specialized to be a treatment or program:

$$(5\text{–}2) \qquad\qquad Y_i = \alpha + \beta_T T_i + u_i,$$

where Y is now the outcome of interest or posttest and T is the treatment variable—the variable whose categories denote the different treatment groups in which the subjects are found. Generally, T is a dummy variable, that is, a variable whose only two values are 1 and 0, with 1 denoting the treatment group and 0 denoting the control or comparison group or the "before" measure. Regression on a single dummy variable is shown in Figure 5–2.

When the basic bivariate regression equation is used in this way to model a treatment, the two regression parameters, α and β_T, take on important special meanings for program evaluation. When there are only two categories or scores on the causal variable (T)—0 and 1 in this case—the regression line always passes through the empirical mean of the Y scores in each category. Thus, it is clear in Figure 5–2 that α is the mean Y score for the comparison group, denoted $\bar{Y}_C$, which would be taken in an analysis of impact to be the *counterfactual*. Since β_T denotes the causal effect of its associated variable on Y, and since the associated variable in this case is T (the treatment), then β_T is clearly the *treatment effect* (subject, of course, to possible threats to validity)—the information whose discovery is the purpose of a sum-

FIGURE 5–2   Bivariate regression for program evaluation

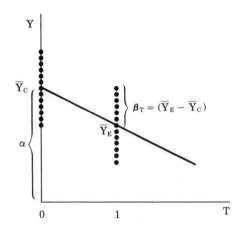

mative evaluation. Furthermore, since β_T is also defined as the change in Y when T increases by one, then β_T is simply $\bar{Y}_E - \bar{Y}_C$, so that, in the bivariate case, the regression coefficient and the difference-of-means are equivalent modes of expressing the treatment's impact. In Figure 5–2, it is seen that β_T is negative, indicating the results of an effective treatment when Y is scaled so that higher scores represent more of a problem, as should in general be the practice.

EXTENDING THE REGRESSION TO INCLUDE CONTROL VARIABLES

A skeletal overview of regression as a framework for evaluation design and impact analysis is complete when the above foundation is extended to include a third and further variables. Since the third variable makes the key difference, we will treat that case and note on occasion that the fourth, fifth, and further variables are straightforward extensions of the reasoning regarding the third. The regression equation with a third variable added is written as follows:

$$(5–3) \qquad Y_i = \alpha + \beta_1 X_{1i} + \beta_T T_i + u_i.$$

The variable added has been symbolized by X_1, so that additional variables may conveniently be labeled X_2, X_3, and so forth. Most often by far, the variable that is used in this position in an analysis as well as in the exposition of important evaluation designs is the pretest. The notation of Equation 5–3 is thus consistent with the use in previous chapters of the symbol X to indicate a pretest. It should be understood, however, that X could stand for socioeconomic status, time, or any other factor that, in addition to T, is a possible determinant of scores on the outcome, Y. For clarity, let us continue to use the symbol X_1 alone to mean pretest, that is, previous measurement of the outcome of interest in impact-analysis equations.

The primary function of third and further variables in evaluation designs is to make up either for imperfect randomization or for the lack of randomization altogether. In other words, one must be concerned that there may be influential differences between the treatment groups other than the treatment itself, but to the extent that such differences have been measured, they may be entered into the analysis in such a way as to avoid confounding their effects with the treatment effects. The pretest is of course one important control variable of this type, since the treatment groups may simply have started out at different levels on the outcome of interest. All variables in this functional category are preexisting, that is, they affect or inhere in the subjects before their assignment to treatment groups. Another category would contain variables that occur after assignment. Here, the function is not to make up for vagaries in assignment but for factors that may arise afterward. Some factors in this category would also be control variables; for example, exposure of the subjects to other treatments for the same condition or receipt of sensitizing information in the mail. We will see in a later chapter that another kind of factor in the after-assignment category is the attainment of subobjectives. In sum, third and further variables may function either as controls or as subobjectives (whose analytic treatment is postponed for now) and may be active either before or after assignment.

With the addition of a third variable, a second regression slope coefficient is also added. Not only must the meaning of β_1 therefore be considered, but the inclusion of that parameter also changes the meaning of both α and β_T so that they too must be reconsidered.

We saw in Equation 5–2 that β_T was the presumed effect of the treatment. It retains the same meaning in Equation 5–3. Now, however, it also reflects the application of a control. Instead of being simply the difference in means between the treatment groups on Y, it is now the difference between the groups on Y with X_1 held constant. Considering X_1 a pretest, for example, β_T answers the question, What is the difference in average (or, more technically, in expected) Y score for subjects in the different treatment groups having *the same* pretest score? That is, given the subjects' starting point, what is the effect of the treatment? Even if the pretest scores of the groups do not overlap at all, still, by a projection of the relation between pretest and posttest, the regression algorithm can supply the predicted difference between the groups on Y judging from the effects of X_1 alone. This difference would not be ascribed to the treatment, but to the discrepancy in starting points. Any departures from this predicted difference, however, may be inferred as due to the treatment (with appropriate caveats regarding internal validity). In this fashion, the difference between the groups in average pretest score will not be confounded with the effects of the treatment. Of course, the groups may also have differed initially on variables other than the pretest that partially determine Y scores and these *will* be confounded with treatment effects—unless such variables also happen to be measured and incorporated into the regression analysis as X_2, X_3, and so forth.

In Equation 5–2, we were able to interpret β_T as the difference between the two group means. That interpretation is too simple for Equation 5–3, where the posttest means could differ (because of different starting points) *without* our wanting to infer a treatment effect. There is, however, an analogous interpretation for β_T in Equation 5–3, which will be more readily understood after a consideration of β_1.

The new parameter, the coefficient β_1, gives the effect of the variable X_1—the pretest, for example—with T held constant. To hold T constant is to confine it either to the value 0 or the value 1, assuming the usual number of two treatment groups for simplicity. That is, holding T constant means to speak of the treatment groups separately rather than as all subjects in all groups mixed up together. Thus, this new coefficient, which must somehow be interpretable as the slope of Y on X_1, is clearly the *within-group* slope of Y on X_1; it gives the simple bivariate relation between pretest and posttest within each of the treatment groups. (This assumes that the relation is the same in both groups and provides a weighted average of the two if it is not. An appreciable difference in within-group slopes is one example of an interaction effect in the evaluation, an issue to be addressed as it arises on several occasions in the ensuing chapters.)

The idea of within-group slopes of Y on X_1 provides a most welcome, convenient, and powerful geometric interpretation of Equation 5–3, which could otherwise be extremely cumbersome. The general geometric diagram for Equation 5–3 is a plane, slanting through three-dimensional space. That is most awkward to work with on a two-dimensional piece of paper, especially given the need to show and label many data points, projections, and relations. If we presume the case of two treatment groups, however, so that one causal variable is the treatment-comparison dummy, the diagram may be represented as just two lines rather than a plane. In Figure 5–3, the difference may be seen by imagining that there is depth behind the page and that the bottom

FIGURE 5–3   The control-variable regression

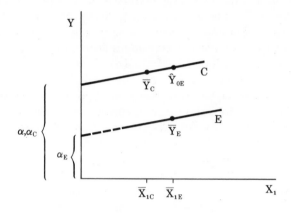

regression line is recessed back into the distance. The imagined plane thus slants upward from left to right—the X_1 dimension—and also downward from front to back (or from the page surface toward the book cover behind it)—the T dimension. Since there are no intermediate T values between 0 and 1, however, there is no need to show the depth of space between the two lines and we merely move the bottom one forward to the surface of the page.

We may now consider α in Equation 5–3 and also return as promised to the interpretation of the treatment effect, β_T. The parameter α is defined as the Y intercept. Considering Y as the vertical axis, the Y intercept is the height of the regression surface above the point at which all causal variables—X_1 and T in this case—are set at zero. It is clear in Figure 5–3 that this intercept is the same as the comparison-group intercept, α_C, since that occurs above the point where both X_1 and T are zero (remember that the treatment-group line—marked E— is really recessed some distance behind the page so that it is above the point T = 1 rather than the point T = 0). Turning to β_T, it now becomes evident as well that since β_T is the expected difference in Y scores for subjects with the same X_1 score, it is simply the vertical distance between the two lines. Thus, whereas in the bivariate case of Equation 5–2 the treatment effect was interpretable as the difference in means $(\bar{Y}_E - \bar{Y}_C)$, it is interpreted in the control-variable case of Equation 5–3 as the difference in subgroup intercepts $(\alpha_E - \alpha_C)$. This use of α with subscripts is figurative rather than literal because the analysis is based on only one equation, Equation 5–3, representing only one regression plane and containing only one α. With the help of Figure 5–3, however, it serves to communicate the idea of the treatment effect as the difference between two parallel lines. Whenever the control-variable case is diagrammed in the manner of Figure 5–3, as it will almost always be, any difference in height between the two regression lines is taken as a possible treatment effect—a difference in height is the "picture" of a treatment effect.

We also now have a different, and quite general, statistical interpretation of the counterfactual. Thinking in group means, the counterfactual for the treatment group was simply the comparison-group outcome $\bar{Y}_C$ in the simple bivariate Equation 5–2. Since the conceptual meaning of the counterfactual, however, is the treatment-group score that "would have been," $\bar{Y}_C$ is not satisfactory in principle when there is a control variable, as in Equation 5–3. Clearly, if the treatment group started out in a different place ($\bar{X}_{1E} \neq \bar{X}_{1C}$), it should not be expected to end in the same place ($\bar{Y}_C$) as the comparison group. Let us symbolize the counterfactual, or the null-case outcome, more generally, then, as $\hat{Y}_{0E}$—the predicted score for the experimental group in the case of 0 treatment effect, or the null case. It is obtained directly from Equation 5–3, using the experimental group pretest mean ($\bar{X}_{1E}$) as the starting point, simply by assuming that $\beta_T = 0$ (i.e., no treatment effect); that is,

$$(5\text{–}4) \qquad \hat{Y}_{0E} = \alpha + \beta_1\bar{X}_{1E}$$

(see Figure 5–3). This measure of the counterfactual, $\hat{Y}_{0E}$, will be employed extensively in subsequent chapters.

Last, given our general statistical interpretation of β_T as the impact of the treatment, and of $\hat{Y}_{0E}$ as the null-case outcome or counterfactual, we may return to the *adequacy* measure of Chapter One. The simple notation used there was, Adequacy = $1 - (R/C)$, or 1 minus the result over the counterfactual. But that is equivalent to $(C/C) - (R/C)$, or simply $(C - R)/C$, that is, *the negative of the program impact divided by the counterfactual*. In our new, more general conceptual notation, this precise idea may now be symbolized as:

$$(5\text{–}5) \qquad \text{Adequacy} = -\beta_T/\hat{Y}_{0E}.$$

Since both the numerator and the denominator remain conceptually the same no matter how many variables are added to the equation as additional controls, the adequacy measure is thus readily calculated for almost any analysis of impact. One must remember, however, that the adequacy ratio is a meaningful quantity only when the measurement of Y is such that higher equals worse, and only when the device of the gap is appropriately employed.

THE RELATION BETWEEN β_T AND GAIN SCORES

Several evaluation designs employ before and after measures on both a treatment and a comparison group. There is in that case a mode of analysis, one that is in fact very commonly used, that is far simpler in concept and calculations than the regression of Equation 5–3. The analysis would proceed by comparing gain scores; if the experimental group gained (or lost) more from pretest to posttest than the comparison group, the difference in gain could be ascribed to the treatment. This model would seem to account adequately for differences between the groups in starting point. The purpose of this brief section will be to examine whether the gain-score approach is sound and to note its relation to the regression approach outlined above.

To take a concrete example, consider a very early evaluation of the impact of the movie "Gentleman's Agreement" (Glock 1955). The issue was whether the movie had the effect of decreasing anti-Semitism in those who saw it. Suppose that anti-Semitism were measured by a psychological scale on a group that saw the film and a comparison group of subjects that did not, both before and after the movie ran in Baltimore. Suppose further that the comparison group dropped 2 points from $\bar{X}_{1C} = 9$ to $\bar{Y}_C = 7$ on the anti-Semitism scale and the treatment group—those who saw the movie—dropped 2.5 points from $\bar{X}_{1E} = 11$ to $\bar{Y}_E = 8.5$. The conclusion from a gain-score analysis would be that the movie was effective in reducing anti-Semitism by a half point since the treatment group lost a half point more than the comparison group. Provided that the comparison group is a sound one, so that there is no selection-Q bias, the conclusion would seem valid.

Let us interpret the analysis, however, in terms of Equation 5–3, where Y is the posttest, X_1 is the pretest, and T is seeing the movie. It would appear at first glance from the comparison-group data that in the normal course of things, everybody dropped two points over this period of time. This might be attributable to news events, TV shows, and so forth. In terms of Equation 5–3, this suggests that $\alpha = -2$ and $\beta_1 = 1$. For the comparison group, Equation 5–3 then gives

$$\bar{Y}_C = -2 + 1(9) + 0 = 7.$$

Since the treatment group started out at $\bar{X}_{1E} = 11$, one would expect to find—if the treatment were totally ineffective,

$$\hat{Y}_E = -2 + 1(11) + 0 = 9.$$

Since the actual finding was $\bar{Y}_E = 8.5$, one concludes that the program was effective by half a point.

The problem is that the analysis has assumed the magnitude of parameters. *It has assumed, in particular, that $\beta_1 = 1$, and this is always the case in gain-score analysis.* In truth, infinite other possibilities for the magnitude of this slope will also explain the comparison-group data perfectly but lead to different predictions for the treatment group. Let us suppose, for example, that $\beta_1 = 7/9 = 0.77$, so that α must equal zero to make the comparison-group data come out right. That is,

$$\tilde{Y}_C = 0 + .77(9) + 0 = 7.$$

Why might this occur? It simply means that instead of an average *uniform* loss of two points, there has been an average *proportional* loss down to 77 percent of the pretest score; how much anti-Semitism you lost depended on how much you had to begin with. Both explanations are reasonable, as are infinitely many mixtures of the two. Furthermore, there is no way to discern which is correct from the information that $\tilde{X}_C = 9$ and $\tilde{Y}_C = 7$.

If there is no treatment effect, one then (under this second assumption) expects, for the group that saw the film:

$$\hat{Y}_E = 0 + .77(11) + 0 = 8.5$$

which is exactly what occurred. Thus, the conclusion must be that the treatment had no effect whatever—quite the opposite of the conclusion that was reached under the first assumption for β_1.

There is rarely if ever good reason simply to assume that $\beta_1 = 1$ when the data are available subject by subject (an excellent demonstration of the importance of getting this slope right is provided by Reichardt 1979, p. 158). The clearly preferable alternative is to use the individual-level data to find out just what magnitude β_1 truly takes in the study population observed. That is, one should run the regression of Equation 5–3. It is true that this entails its own assumptions, such as that of linear relationships, but one can avoid some of these by fitting curves and by other statistical stratagems, and in any case, these assumptions are quite a bit less extreme than simply grabbing for the arbitrary parameter value, $\beta_1 = 1$.

There is a procedure that is closely related to gain-score analysis, also commonly employed, and equally suspect. It is to use the pretest as a denominator. The logic goes: If the comparison group changed by 77 percent, it is to be expected in the null case (no treatment effect) that the treatment group should change by 77 percent as well; if not, there has been a treatment effect. It is clear that this is simply employing the assumption in the second illustration above instead of the first, namely, the assumption that $\alpha = 0$. That is no more justifiable than assuming that $\beta_1 = 1$.

It is therefore recommended that neither gain-score analysis nor proportional-gain expectation ever be used when the individual-level data are at hand. If the assumption that $\beta_1 = 1$ or $\alpha = 0$ is correct, that will emerge from the regression analysis, but if either is incorrect, one is on much more justifiable ground in inferring the magnitude of the treatment effect from the calculated values, whatever they may be.

SIGNIFICANCE TESTING OF THE IMPACT PARAMETER

It is extremely common to run a significance test on the parameter indicating the degree of program impact, whether this is a regression coefficient, a difference between two means, or any other statistic. Is this procedure informative? In fact, it is sometimes informative and sometimes not. The purpose of the present section is to clarify the application of tests of significance in the various contexts of impact analysis for program evaluation.

By the function of a test, we will mean the kind of information that the significance test gives when interpreted in conjunction with the design and data-analysis operations employed. There are four basic and common functions of tests of statistical significance that have some relevance to the needs of impact analysis, although only one is central to the inference of a program effect (another is central to the inference of program effect in one design, only; see Chapter Six). There are scattered, legitimate functions of significance tests beyond these four since their use by researchers is to some extent an individual affair, but none that I know of that would modify in any way the elaboration that follows.

In order to discuss the functions of significance tests, it is important to keep in mind the meaning of the term *sampling distribution.* A sampling distribution is the probability distribution of a statistic—the probability of occurrence of each possible value of the statistic such that the sum of all the probabilities is equal to one. A statistic is a quantitative characteristic of a sample—but for this purpose only a random sample—such as the sample mean, standard deviation, median, range, or the correlation between two of the sample variables, or the difference between the means of two random subsamples, or a regression coefficient, and so forth. Thus, the sampling distribution of mean IQ in a random sample of one hundred individuals from a certain population, for example, is the probability of occurrence of each possible numerical value of the mean IQ. In most cases, only one sample of one hundred is drawn. However, when it is about to be drawn, the mean IQ that will result could at that moment take on any one of a large or perhaps infinite number of values, some of which have a higher probability of occurrence than others. The numerical value of the mean depends on the particular one hundred subjects that might fall together in the sample. The sampling distribution is thus the probability distribution of all these possibilities. Some possible means have a high probability of being picked, some quite low. The sampling distribution is valuable to know about because, under a given set of assumptions about the population, it tells what the probabilities are of getting any specific value (or set of values) when sampling from that population. It is important to bear in mind that the idea of known sampling distributions applies only under conditions of random sampling; statisticians have essentially nothing to say about the probability of one value or another when the sampling is not fundamentally random.

The first function of significance testing might be called the *survey design* function. It gives the probability of getting a sample statistic, a difference between two means, let us say, above or below a certain magnitude when sampling at random from a population in which the comparable value (difference of means) is zero. For example, if we assume that the difference in mean cognitive development is zero between those children in the population who have had good nutrition and those who have had poor nutrition, the significance test informs us about the probability of getting a large difference of means even so in a random sample. If we do get an improbably large difference, we would then tentatively reject the notion that the population value is truly zero since this was only an assumption and not an observation. We would not be in a position to say that the nutrition was *responsible for* the cognitive development since many other explanations for the difference in means are possible; we can, however, infer that nutrition and cognitive development show a nonzero relationship in the unobserved population as well as in the observed random sample. This function, connected with the idea of random-sample surveys, is not commonly applicable in program evaluation because impact-analysis designs rarely involve sampling from an unobserved large population to find out something about that specific population.

The second function of significance testing may be called the *experimental design* or the *causal inference* function. Whereas one is not able to infer a causal connection in the first kind of case (that nutrition is responsible for cognitive development), one can do so in this one. Here one selects a group all of which is to be observed, and randomly subdivides it into subgroups. This, as we have seen, is the randomization process. Let us assume for simplicity that the randomization subdivides the group into two subgroups, although one might randomize into more groups as well. Note that, still thinking of nutrition and cognitive development, the mean cognitive development in the population from which each of the subsamples was drawn is clearly the same because each subsample was drawn at random from the same population, namely, the combined set of subjects before the randomization took place. Thus, the two subgroups can differ in cognitive development at the outset only by the vagaries, generally quite small, of the randomization process. One then administers an experimental treatment to one of the two groups. Assume, for example, that one group is given good nutrition whereas the other, the control group, is allowed for the time being to follow the natural course for the population, which is poor nutrition. Knowing the details of the sampling distribution of the difference of means of two random samples from the same population, one is now able to say how probable a difference of means of a certain magnitude is as a result of the vagaries of the randomization alone. That is precisely the information communicated by a significance test. Note that the difference could be in initial cognitive development or in any other preexisting cause of later cognitive development; all such traits are randomized. If the significance test tells us that the difference actually observed is improbably large for a randomization vagary, then some of that difference, at least, may with substantial confidence be attributed to the treatment since that is the only nonrandomized difference between the two groups (assuming no contamination due to the implementation of the study—see Chapter Four). Note as well that the conclusion is possible only if there has been randomization, or let us say, only if there has been an assignment procedure so close to random sampling that the statistical model becomes essentially relevant. The sampling distribution is known only for the case of random sampling, not for the selection of groups or subgroups in any old way. Thus, the combination of randomization, a postrandomization administration of the treatment conditions, and a known sampling distribution allows a causal inference to be made on the basis of the results of a significance test. This function of significance testing, the experimental-design function, is the only one that is valid and major for impact analysis in the sense of playing a critical role in the inference of a program effect.

The third function might loosely be called the *econometric modeling* function. It gives the probability that a parameter of a certain magnitude might be attributable to the random-disturbance component of a model rather than indicating a true causal effect. Consider, for example, that one has assumed that the cognitive development of children is caused only by a certain set of specified variables, including nutrition, plus a random-disturbance component. When one collects data on the variables and analyzes them, there will be a coefficient on nutrition of a certain magnitude. When one tests this coefficient for significance, one learns whether it (*a*) is so large that it probably could not be entirely the misleading result of the action of the random disturbance but indicates rather a true causal impact; or (*b*) is so small that it might be due to the random-disturbance component so that nutrition may no longer be assumed to be causal. Thus, there is a causal inference connected with this function. Moreover, no random sampling is necessary except for the assumption that the disturbance term for each subject is in essence drawn at random from the set of all disturbance terms. However, the validity of the causal inference based on the significance test does depend on the validity of the model. That is, if the assumption about the specified set of causes is wrong and there is a cause of cognitive development that, for example, is not included in the specified set of causal variables and in the analysis, the basis for the causal inference evaporates. If that omitted variable is related to nutrition, then *its* causal impact will show up in the coefficient on nutrition, making a causal inference about nutrition quite incorrect. This mandatory reservation or assumption or contingency regarding the necessary validity of the model is extremely important for the analysis of impacts in program evaluation because the primary kinds of causes that concern the analyst in that context as being possibly omitted are threats to validity such as history or selection. In impact analysis, where the whole point is to *demonstrate* the causal nature of one particular coefficient, one *must* generally worry that variables connected with history or selection bias have gone unmeasured and are omitted; one cannot get around this worry simply by assuming it away—by assuming, in other words, that all such factors have been included in the model and the analysis.

The fourth function is the *strength of relationship* function. It gives the probability that one *would have* obtained a statistic in a certain range of magnitudes if one *had* gone through the randomization or random sampling procedure (given the sample size and variance estimates that obtain). It may sound strange that anyone would want to speculate in this manner, but this function is useful in a great number of ways in research of all kinds. In impact analysis, a nonsignificant result means that the coefficient on a treatment variable, for example, is so small (no matter what its raw magnitude happens to be) that it could fairly easily occur through the vagaries of a randomization process. It therefore may be too small to bother with even if it were truly causal (caution is necessary because the treatment may actually have had a powerful effect that was almost canceled by some countereffect of history, selection, or contamination). In fact, any time, in any research, that a relationship turns out to be nonsignificant statistically, one might, with some caution, interpret it as indicating lack of importance. The basis for such a conclusion would be that if the magnitude of a relationship is such that it could easily occur by a random selection process, it is too puny to repay the time and effort necessary to think about or research it further (Blalock 1960, pp. 270–271). On the other hand, if the treatment coefficient in a program evaluation is statistically significant, it means that the observed relation between treatment and outcome is so large that it could not easily have occurred as the result of random forces. Why, then, did it occur? If the design is experimental, one may conclude that the cause, not being contained in random forces, was either the treatment or contamination; all else has been randomized. The test then is actually performing the experimental-design function. If the design is not experimental, however, one is not really concerned with random forces; one is concerned with history and selection bias. Since the test only communicates, "so large that the relation could not easily be due to random forces," it is almost useless. It tells one nothing about whether the relation might have been caused by the treatment, history, or selection, which is by far the most important information one must have in order to say something about a treatment effect with reasonable confidence in validity. (The foregoing has involved comparing one's actual results with the hypothetical results of a random procedure. By extension, one actual result may be compared with another: Strength of relationship is one element among several that determine the level of significance—the stronger the relationship, the more highly significant. Other elements being roughly equal then, greater significance indicates a stronger relationship, so that two results may be compared.)

The uses of significance testing in impact analysis for program evaluation may now be briefly summarized by organizing the above material in the design perspective rather than the function perspective.

If one has drawn one's subjects as a random sample from a specific larger population, the results of the analysis may, by the appropriate statistical procedures, be generalized to that same larger population (the survey-design function). This conclusion is a matter of external validity only; it has nothing to do with causal inference and internal validity. It simply means that whatever one found in one's sample is likely to be found in the population as a whole; if one's conclusion about the observed sample must be hedged in deference to threats to internal validity, one's inference about the population must be hedged in the same way.

If one has been able to employ experimental design, one may use statistical procedures to test whether the treatment has had a causal impact on the outcome of interest or not (the experimental-design function). There would still be reservations, however, regarding possible causes of the outcome that were not randomized (certain categories of contamination) and regarding unhappy randomization (that is, the rare randomization that does leave causal traits distributed unevenly across treatment groups).

For quasi-experimental designs, significance testing is nearly irrelevant. (1) The survey-design function is not applicable unless there has been random sampling from a specific larger population, which is rare. Even where such sampling has been implemented, the test has implications for external but not internal validity, as noted above. (2) The experimental-design function is not applicable in the ordinary way (although more will be said about this function in Chapter Ten) because there has been no randomization, no procedure, in other words, that justifies invoking the statistical model. The absence of proper random procedures means that the sampling distribution of the statistic is utterly unknown; that fact, in turn, means that sound probability statements about results cannot be made. In essence, the test would be ruling out the effects of a randomization that did not take place. (3) The econometric-modeling function is applicable but it is critically weak in the context of quasi experimentation. The causal inference it permits depends fully on the accuracy of the model. The model may stipulate that the outcome of interest in the study depends only on the treatment, the random disturbance factor, and other included variables, but that assumption does not have the power to make threats to validity evaporate; they will be there regardless of our assumptions. If the threats are indeed operating, they are confounded with the significant treatment coefficient and make the causal inference incorrect. (4) The strength-of-relationship function is similarly hobbled. If the treatment coefficient is nonsignificant it means that the treatment-outcome relation is small, but it may be small because the treatment and selection effects, for example, have offset one another, as well as because the treatment has accomplished little. If the coefficient is significant, it means that the relation is large, but its magnitude may as easily be due to the effects of history or selection as to the treatment. Thus, no function of testing would seem to help very much with quasi-experimental designs.

This conclusion is important because the reader will encounter significance tests frequently in connection with quasi-experimental designs. The tests show that the results "are not due to chance." That interpretation is valid enough in that the results are unlikely to be due to random measurement error, sheer coincidence, or other random forces, but it is at the same time fundamentally unhelpful. As we have noted, the true concern is not with chance but with the effects of history or selection, which clearly cannot be assumed to be distributed in a random fashion. If significance tests are carried out and reported, readers will be well served if analysts interpret the tests explicitly and carefully, showing which extraneous causes are effectively ruled out by the tests (i.e., those known or assumed to be randomly distributed to the groups observed) and which still remain as possible threats to the validity of a causal inference (e.g., history or selection). Surely, it is a disservice to the reader to report the significance test results *alone*. The magnitude of the effect statistic—the regression coefficient, difference of means, and so on—which contains more pertinent and useful information by far than the significance test, should always be included, together with a discussion of the possibility that each relevant threat to internal validity may be in part responsible for that magnitude.

Significance testing in the context of ex-post-facto designs has not been explicitly treated here because the definition of the design itself needs extensive previous discussion. When we do turn our attention to that case, it will be clear that a constructive role for significance testing there simply does not, in principle, exist; the tests have little relevance and, in general, can hardly be anything but misleading.

The conclusion we have reached on the lack of connection between significance testing and quasi experiments will be, to many, both surprising and disappointing. Why emphasize a category called quasi-experimental design if that category is not characterized by any connection with rigorous causal inference as in true experimental design? In fact, there is a genius to quasi-experimental design, and its emphasis by Campbell and Stanley (1966) was a major contribution. It is connected with statistical testing in principle, although actual test results, as has just been explained, are not directly meaningful. The primary message for the reader should be the one elaborated above. Significance tests do not have their ordinary meaning in the context of a quasi experiment; they may easily be misunderstood and should be used only with great caution and careful attention. Yet, there are some kinds of cases in which something can be said about quasi-experimental treatment effects based on inferential statistics; significance tests are not totally irrelevant in principle. That discussion, however, presented in Chapter Ten, must await an elaboration both of quasi-experimental design and, for comparison, the ex-post-facto study.

Chapter Six

The Regression-Discontinuity Design

The regression-discontinuity design is a special case that stands between experimental and quasi-experimental designs. Recall that the two bases we use for classifying designs are (*a*) whether selection into treatment groups is centralized or decentralized, and (*b*) if centralized, whether assignment is randomized or nonrandomized. Neither of these two dimensions is a pure dichotomy. We will see in Chapter Eight that selection may be mixed—neither completely centralized nor completely decentralized. Here we will consider an unconventional basis of assignment to treatments that is neither randomized nor nonrandomized in the ordinary sense of those terms. Experimental, regression-discontinuity, and quasi-experimental designs all represent centralized selection; the program or evaluation authorities decide which subjects are to receive each treatment or no treatment. In experimental designs, assignment is by a randomization process. In quasi-experimental designs, it is by some nonrandom process, and it is that fact that renders those designs vulnerable to the threats of history and selection. In the regression-discontinuity design, assignment is determined based on some measured quantitative variable, A, such that one treatment group is comprised of subjects with a score below some cutpoint on A and the other group has those subjects whose score on A is above that cutpoint.

Since the regression-discontinuity design was first introduced (Campbell and Stanley 1966), those who have written about it have emphasized some of the esoteric problems involved in its application and interpretation while devoting quite a bit less attention to the basic logic of the design, which is not straightforward. I will do the opposite here. I will try to emphasize the basic logical mechanism, not only to permit a thorough understanding of the foundations and to provide a good basis for working with the more technical problems, but also to contribute to an understanding of other designs. As indicated by its title, regression analysis is integral to this design, with the implication that the design deals in a critically important way with the framework we are using for the conceptualization of all designs. To date, the design has been used extensively in the evaluation of compensatory education programs (see Trochim 1984) but not at all extensively outside of that area. It is worth studying then, both because its potential value and applicability are greater than its previous use would indicate and because it contributes to an understanding of evaluation designs in general. We will note the more technical difficulties with which scholars have grappled, but only briefly. A deeper treatment of the technical issues would be out of place in the present context and, furthermore, a reasonable case can be made that if the ordinary evaluation practitioner were to ignore some of these problems, more good might be done than harm.

Assignment procedures in impact analyses are good to the extent that they tend to leave the treatment variable, T, unrelated to the outcome variable Y, except for the effects of the program. Another way to say this is that the treatment groups must be as nearly identical as possible in characteristics other than the treatment itself that can affect Y. A second and related criterion is whether one can know the probability that a certain degree of nonuniformity, or null-case relationship with Y, has nevertheless crept in. Randomization fulfills these two criteria admirably. The process tends to leave the groups nearly uniform, and the likelihood of a departure from uniformity of any particular size is given by statistical theory. The quasi-experimental designs treated in subsequent chapters fail these criteria rather resoundingly and must therefore be bolstered more than experimental designs by presumptive reasoning, at least in principle. The regression-discontinuity design operates as follows: Assignment of subjects to treatments—to a score on T—is based on their score on some assignment variable, A, such that those who are higher on A go into one group and those who are lower go into another. The variable A may well be related to Y. That would automatically make T be related to Y as well, even without the treatment's being causal. That feature would clearly seem to be *detrimental* to the design by the first of the two criteria stipulated above. We will see, however, that this relation may be accounted for statistically so that the *residual* relation of A to Y, and therefore the null-case relation of T to Y when controlled for A, tends to zero (see Judd and Kenny 1981, pp. 11–12). Moreover, considering the second criterion, significance testing is applicable, much as with experimental design, to assess the probability of a gratuitous relationship of a given magnitude. In these critical respects then, the regression-discontinuity design is very strong. Its major weaknesses are: (*a*) it demands enough control to be able to subdivide a group into treatment groups purely based on their scores on some measured variable, and (*b*) one must make an unavoidable and critical assumption about the functional form of the relation between A and Y in the absence of the program.

THE LOGIC OF THE REGRESSION-DISCONTINUITY DESIGN

Let us assume that a program was carried out in which there was an attempt to decrease the shortfall in the cognitive development of four-year-old, economically disadvantaged children in City B by giving them nutrition supplements. Assume further that there were not enough resources to administer the program to all eligible children and that it was determined to give it to the most needy, using the balance of the eligible group for comparison purposes. (Some might not believe that such circumstances could ever genuinely arise, or that the program would be ethical or politically feasible in denying the treatment to some citizens while permitting it to others. The circumstances do arise from time to time. See, for example, Campbell and Stanley 1966; Berk and Rauma 1983; Trochim 1984. But to the extent that such political or ethical considerations are influential, the regression-discontinuity design is simply not applicable.) Suppose, finally, that selection into the treatment groups was determined by a height-weight assignment index A—height in inches plus weight in pounds—with a cutpoint at A = 70. Those with a combined height and weight below 70 received the nutrition supplement while those at 70 or above did not. Figure 6–1 shows one possible outcome in an evaluation of the program, a very typical illustrative outcome of the regression-discontinuity design.

In this design, the Y-counterfactual for all individuals whose scores on A place them in the treatment, or E group, is given by a simple extension of the comparison or C group line to the other side of the cutpoint. This extension is shown as the dashed line in Figure 6–1. Note that, since the lines are assumed to be straight and to have the same slope, the distance between the dashed extension—the counterfactual—and the actual treatment-group outcome is everywhere the same. The equation of the comparison-group line, including its extension, is estimated by regression analysis and is given by Equation 6–1 (where A is measured at assignment time and Y at posttest time):

$$(6\text{--}1) \qquad Y_i = \alpha + \beta_A A_i + u_i.$$

It will be recalled from the previous chapter that the counterfactual Y score for the treatment group—the Y counterfactual at the treatment group's mean score on the pretest X_1—is symbolized as $\hat{Y}_{0E}$, the

FIGURE 6–1 The regression-discontinuity design shows that the treatment has lowered the E-group scores

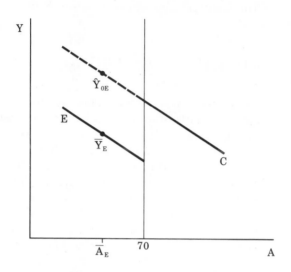

"null-case" mean posttest score for the E group. In the present case, we may consider the null-case outcome to be predictable from A instead of X_1, that is,

(6–2) $$\hat{Y}_{0E} = a + b_A \bar{A}_E,$$

where b_A is the regression estimate of β_A in Equation 6–1. Thus, the treatment effect is given by

(6–3) $$\text{Treatment Effect} = \hat{Y}_E - \hat{Y}_{0E}.$$

It is worth noting this relation because it clearly represents the treatment effect as the difference between the actual outcome and the counterfactual or null-case outcome. No matter how complicated the analysis—no matter how complicated the equation(s) needed to supply the counterfactual—this relation will always accurately represent the estimated treatment effect. In the present case, however, essentially the same quantity may be found more straightforwardly as β_T in the standard comparative-change evaluation equation, Equation 5–3, with the predictor A substituted for the predictor X_1:

(6–4) $$Y_i = \alpha + \beta_A A_i + \beta_T T_i + u_i.$$

Additional predictors $X_1, \ldots, X_k$ may be entered as control variables; they will function to increase the sensitivity of the design in exactly the same way as the pretest and other control variables increase the sensitivity of design 12, the R-comparative-change design, over design 11, the R-comparative-posttest design.

As long as the treatment-group line in Figure 6–1 has approximately the same slope as the comparison-group line, the estimates of that slope based on Equations 6–1 and 6–4 will also be nearly the same. The treatment effect derived by the two methods, then, will hardly differ. The small difference that does emerge would be occasioned by the fact that Equation 6–1 provides an estimate of β_A from the comparison-group data alone, whereas the standard multivariate regression equation, Equation 6–4, directs a pooling of the data from the two groups to provide this estimate. If the two within-group slopes are quite different, a complication is introduced that we will consider toward the end of the chapter. At this point, we need rather to consider why, in the uncomplicated case in which the two within-group slopes are the same or nearly so, the assignment and analysis processes represented in Equation 6–4 become almost as good as randomization.

The task of a comparison-group design of any sort is to provide a counterfactual while avoiding selection bias. This is accomplished in the regression-discontinuity design by the combination of rigid assignment procedures and the proper use of the regression model. Rigid assignment means assignment on a known, accurately measured variable with no exceptions. We will see that the key to the efficacy of this procedure is that, for any given score on A, all subjects with that score must be in the same treatment group. Since each subject i represents a disturbance term μ_i, this means that all disturbance terms associated with a given score on A are in the same treatment group.

If it were somehow known that the height-weight index A were linearly related to cognitive development—whether causally or not—and if the treatment groups were selected to differ on A *and nothing else that matters,* one would be in an excellent position to determine a true treatment effect. That is so because one can always adjust or control for the effects of A in a regression analysis, as is routinely done with a pretest, for example—thereby deriving the effects of nutrition without confounding from A—and under these assumptions there would be nothing else to worry about. The question then is how one can know that one has gotten rid of everything besides A that "matters," that is, that is a cause of Y. This wonder is accomplished by the regression algorithm, although before becoming overawed with the power of statistical analysis it must be remembered that the achievement depends also on a rigid assignment procedure and a valid assumption of the functional form relating A to Y (which we take for the time being to be linear).

To see how it turns out that everything else that matters has been eliminated as a source of selection bias and therefore as a threat to validity, let us trace the fortunes, in this analysis, of yet another variable, mother's IQ. It will be assigned the notation X_2 (reserving X_1 for the pretest, even though no pretest will be used here). The analysis is, by Equation 6–4, where X_2 remains omitted. Let us further assume that the treatment and comparison groups not only differ in height-weight, as assigned, but also in mother's IQ, which is perfectly possible in the absence of randomization. Last, let us momentarily assume for the sake of clarity, although there is no analytic need to do so, that mother's IQ is the *only* cause of cognitive development in the world other than a possible treatment effect, leaving behind height-weight, peer achievement, and all else. If we use the following equation,

$$(6\text{–}4') \qquad Y_i = a + b_A A_i + b_T T_i + e_i,$$

to estimate the parameters of Equation 6–4, using as data the study groups observed (which is the only population we care about from the standpoint of internal validity), and if we emerge with an apparent treatment effect, is it not possible, since the two groups do differ on mother's IQ, that the omitted variable X_2 may be responsible for this apparent effect? The answer is no.

To see why, assume that X_2 is correlated with A, but not perfectly, that is, many who are high (or low) on A are correspondingly high (or low) on X_2, but not with perfect consistency. We must now maintain a firm mental distinction between that part of mother's IQ that is correlated with height weight and that part that is independent of it. A part's being independent means that in most cases mother's IQ is fairly accurately predictable from the height-weight score of the child, but is still a little higher or lower than would be expected knowing height-weight alone.

1. To the extent that X_2 is correlated with A, *its causal impact on Y is reflected in the coefficient* b_A. In fact, since we are assuming for clarity that A is not a cause of Y, the entire magnitude of b_A is due to mother's IQ, and not to height weight at all! This confounding is known generally as specification error—error that results in incorrectly attributing an effect to an included variable because an omitted causal variable is correlated with it (see Johnston, 1972, pp. 168–169). It does not trouble us a bit here because we are not concerned with the true effects of A, but only of T. In fact, it works mightily in our favor because *some part of X_2—the part that is correlated with A—is now causally identified (even though omitted from the equation), controlled, and therefore unconfounded with T; some of the causal impact of mother's IQ is "soaked up," in a sense, by the coefficient on the control variable A.* That leaves only the remaining part of X_2 as a matter of concern, the part that is uncorrelated with A.

2. The part of X_2 that is uncorrelated with A still causes variation in Y. In fact, for every data point that is not exactly on the within-group regression line (of Y on A), its distance from the line must be entirely due to X_2 since that, we are assuming, is the *only* cause of Y scores in the world, other than a possible treatment effect. These distances of actual Y scores from the line then, that is, these residual effects of mother's IQ, are nothing but the disturbance terms, u_i and their estimates e_i in Equations 6–4 and 6–4′. As such, however, *they are also controlled and unconfounded with T. That is true because the disturbance is random with respect to A, and T is merely two subdivisions of A.*

Let us see why this is so. First, we note that the regression algorithm—the calculations procedure for arriving at the estimating coefficients a, b_A, b_T, and e—forces the error terms e to be uncorrelated with the independent variables in the equation, that is, e is random with respect to A and T. To take the next step, let us change the scenario a bit for clarity and assume now that mother's IQ never was related to the height-weight index in the first place; b_A reflects the true causal impact of A, but X_2 is still the only other outside cause of cognitive development. Since X_2 is unrelated to A and is omitted from the equation, its causal impact may be expressed in either or both of two remaining places: it may be in the error term e, which would be innocuous because e is randomly distributed with respect to T, and it might also be confounded with the treatment, that is, the treatment group might contain many of the high-IQ mothers and the comparison group the lower ones. In the last event, some of the causal impact of X_2 would be soaked up by b_T, giving a false treatment effect. It is precisely that danger that weakens quasi-experimental designs. Here, however, that is not a possibility, as the following paragraph will elaborate. Briefly, the reason is the rigid assignment procedure that ties the variable T to the variable A. Because mother's IQ is random with respect to A, it is also random with respect to T, with due allowance for ordinary statistical sampling error.

In fact, significance testing is applicable to the regression-discontinuity design for that very reason, and seeing why it is so will help to see the benign relation between an omitted cause (such as mother's IQ) and the treatment variable in this design. The function of the significance test here is the third one taken up in Chapter Five, the econometric-modeling function, but we are not bothered in this case by tenuous assumptions of a causal model. Mother's IQ as expressed in the error term *is* random with respect to A because of the algorithm (and we do not care if specification error means that some of it is already included in A or not, as explained in 1 above). Imagine that mother's IQ scores are a bunch of positive and negative numbers summing to zero that are written on chips. Express the randomness with respect to A by imagining that scores on A are a row of ordered canisters and that the chips are in fact randomly distributed into the canisters. The treatment group is the first half of the set of canisters and the comparison group is the second or higher half. Unless the number of chips is truly huge, it is unlikely that those in any one canister, or even in two together, are a faithfully representative subset of all of the chips even though they got there by a random process. We would not bet, in other words, that the chips in these few cans sum to zero. What is the probability, however, that the subset of chips in each half of the canisters is representative of the whole set, that is, that each has the same zero mean as the full set? If each does, it means that mother's IQ is not affecting the mean level of cognitive development observed in either group because, within each group, the IQ scores cancel each other out. Clearly, the probability of obtaining the population mean in any random subset is given by statistical sampling theory so that for a given total number of chips, the bigger the subset, the greater the probability. One canister would therefore be untrustworthy, but each of the two sets of half the canisters may very well represent so great a number of random chips as to be quite trustworthy. A significant result in this "experiment" means that the observed difference in cognitive development between the two treatment groups is highly unlikely to be due entirely to random distribution vagaries with respect to mother's IQ and must therefore be due in some measure to the only other possibility, namely, the treatment itself.

Clearly, the simplification devices used in the above exposition do not limit its generality. There is no need to assume either that A is completely noncausal or is completely unrelated to X_2. It may be partly causal and partly related. In that case, the coefficient b_A would indicate all of the effects of A, but would at the same time be augmented (or diminished, depending on algebraic signs) by some of the effects of X_2 as well. We don't really care what mixture is reflected by b_A. Nor is it necessary to assume that X_2 is the only other cause of Y; it merely stands for all other causes, some of which, or some parts of which, may be incorporated into b_A and the remainder into e.

In sum, the treatment effect depicted in Figure 6–1 is a real one. Any possible confounding variables—sources of possible selection bias—have been partially soaked up by b_A and, for the rest, are randomly distributed between the two treatment groups so that the extent of their impact on the difference is probably negligible and may be inferred, in any case, by means of an ordinary significance test.

THREATS TO VALIDITY

Being a comparison-group design, the regression-discontinuity design must meet the threat of selection bias to be considered strong and reliable. As we have seen in the previous section (where mother's IQ stood for all possible selection effects), it accomplishes that quite admirably. It is not as desirable as a randomized experiment, such as design 12, because it is less efficient, that is, it demands a somewhat larger study population to accomplish the same statistical sensitivity to a treatment effect as the R-comparative-change design (Goldberger 1972). Nevertheless, it is extremely powerful and is limited far more by the paucity of opportunities to assign by A than by the paucity of subjects to study in a given evaluation, or the expense of studying an adequate number of them. Like a true randomized experiment, contamination due to assignment, which is essentially selection bias, is not a problem here, but contamination due to the treatment or to the control of experimental conditions is, as always, a possible threat to internal validity. In this light, regression-discontinuity and experimental designs would seem similar in power. However, there are three additional threats that may be particularly severe in this design and that have received a great deal of attention.

Fuzzy Cutpoints

It has been emphasized repeatedly that the design assumes rigid assignment. By rigid assignment is meant that all subjects with the same A score are in the same group—E or C. An equivalent way of saying this is that all disturbance terms for a given A score are in the same group (each subject has a disturbance term, so that disturbances may be used as substitute language for subjects). The manifest way in which this would most commonly be violated is somehow having A scores near the cutpoint appear in both groups. This pathology is often called "fuzzy cutpoints" (e.g., Campbell 1984, pp. 29–37). It may occur in many ways (Cook and Campbell 1979, pp. 142–143); for example, knowing that those below a cutpoint will have remedial education, individual parents may prevail upon administrators to put their children into that group, in spite of the fact that their scores are a bit over the line.

One aspect of the resulting problem relates to the significance test. Imagine that some of the canisters near the cutpoint have been doubled, that is, two canisters are provided for each A score, one destined for the treatment group and the other for the comparison group. Some of the chips drawn for a given A score near the cutpoint now go into one of its two canisters and some into the other. If this suballocation were purely random, the problem would be minimized, but that would almost never be the case. Instead, arbitrary mechanisms such as feeling sorry for certain children might be the basis. Whenever that occurs, the two whole samples of disturbance terms for the study (E group and C group) are not random samples from the population of disturbance terms, and a sound justification for applying statistical theory is lost; the valuable significance test becomes irrelevant unless the transgres-

FIGURE 6–2a   No treatment effect

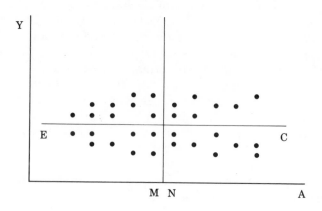

sions are few and minor. To preserve the randomness of the subsamples, it is essential that all of the disturbance terms for any given A score be in the same group (or be randomly assigned to E and C).

A second problem resulting from fuzzy cutpoints is that the overlap between the groups can do great violence to the visual and mathematical results. Consider that the assignment variable A is simply the initial of one's last name (this example emphasizes that A need not be related to Y; in fact, the procedure is tantamount to pure randomization when A is *not* related to Y so that assignment to treatments by the alphabet might well be random assignment, although one could not be sure of it). If there were no treatment effect, the plot of the posttest results on the assignment variable would be expected to look like Figure 6–2a. Now assume, however, that there were carelessness in K-P, in such a way that the lower Y scores (indicating a better outcome) in this area went into the comparison group and the higher scores (worse outcome) tended preponderantly to go into the treatment or E group. This imbalance would clearly pull the overlapping ends of the two within-group lines toward the offending data points, as in Figure 6–2b, so that instead of a continuous flat slope, the result would be a regression discontinuity—an intercept difference that the trained evaluator would be tempted to classify immediately as a harmful treatment effect. If the area of overlap is known to be reasonably small, the analysis might simply be performed without including it at all, that is, using the whole area of overlap as the cutpoint (Cook and Campbell 1979, p. 143). It is quite possible, however, that leaving a gap of this nature would also leave some ambiguity about the slopes of the regres-

**FIGURE 6–2b Fuzzy cutpoint with biased allocation—
pseudotreatment effect**

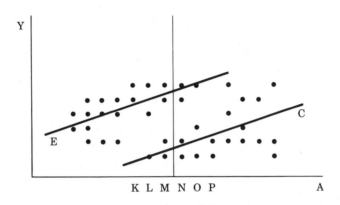

sion curves above and below the true cutpoint and thereby undermine confidence in the analysis.

Thus, analysis in the presence of fuzzy cutpoints may easily lead to a distortion of the effect of the treatment. As we saw, it is also handicapped by a loss of the applicability of the statistical test—a loss, that is, of one of the strongest attractions of this design. Strenuous efforts should therefore be made to ensure that the cutpoint be respected in any program to which regression-discontinuity analysis will be applied.

Random Measurement Error

In the midst of discussing three threats to validity that may be particularly severe, let us digress for a moment to consider one that might be feared as a threat but truly need not be, namely, random measurement error in the assignment variable. It is well known that random measurement error in the *outcome* variable, Y, does not bias the results, although it does make the design less efficient, so that a larger sample is needed for a given level of statistical significance (Reichardt 1979). In general, however, random measurement error in a predictor variable, such as a pretest, would indeed bias the results (see the presentation in Reichardt 1979, pp. 160–164). The issue will be discussed at greater length in the next chapter, but it should be noted here that random measurement error in A does not adversely affect the regression-discontinuity design. Here, the *measured* variable, not the true one (whatever that may be), is used for assignment to treatments. As long as the scale is scrupulously applied and the cutpoint rigidly adhered to, it is clear from the above exposition that the error term based on that measured variable will always be made random with respect to T (Reichardt 1979, pp. 202–203; Berk and Rauma 1983). Moreover, since all omitted causes of Y are made random with respect to T, it does not matter if other variables, such as mother's IQ, are included but measured with error. To the extent that an included variable, as measured and modeled, is a cause of Y, its impact is expressed in its own b coefficient and is unconfounded with T. To the extent that it is not a cause of Y, it does not concern us at all. To the extent that the measured variable *leaves out* a part of the true variable that causes Y, it is in exactly the same category as the omitted cause X_2 in the above description, that is, it is made random with respect to T by the combination of the assignment procedure and its random relation to A.

Nonrandom Measurement Error

A threat that has perhaps received less attention than it deserves is biased or *non*random measurement error in the assignment variable. It is similar in its effect to the fuzzy-cutpoint threat to validity, but it makes a connecting bridge as well to the final problem that will be treated in this chapter.

It was just noted that measurement error in A is not serious as long as assignment is based rigidly on the scores actually obtained, whether they measure an underlying characteristic accurately or not. This would seem to hold for any sort of measurement error, since scrupulous application and rigid cutpoints will always do their work of randomizing the error terms. On the other hand, it would seem that if a mischievous meddler were intentionally to fabricate some A scores so that people who would have done well on Y without the treatment (low scores) received comparison-group A scores, while some who would have done poorly (high scores) were scored to be assigned to the treatment group, a neutral program could surely be made to look harmful in spite of the fact that, on the scale used, a firm cutpoint was applied. Rigid adherence to a scale would seem to be powerless to protect the design against distorted measurement of this sort, whether intentional or not. How may this perspective be reconciled with the previous one, which showed that a rigid cutpoint on any scale randomized measurement error?

To answer, let us visualize an illustrative outcome that might result from intentional misclassification. In Figure 6–3, someone has tampered with the records of individuals whose last names begin with K–P, giving most of the probable high scorers (on the outcome Y) in this range false initials K–M and the probable low scorers N–P. As a result, assuming no treatment effect, the regression slopes have been pulled toward these biased data points in such a way as to resemble a harmful treatment effect, just as in the case of the fuzzy cutpoint. To clarify the issue under scrutiny, it is well to keep in mind what it means to say that e is random with respect to T in the regression-discontinuity design. One way of interpreting this is that *in the null case, the treatment-group regression curve will be a precise extrapolation of the comparison-group curve into the area beyond the cutpoint,* as in Figure 6–2a. If the treatment-group curve is in fact found in a different position, the cause of the discontinuity must be a treatment effect. In Figure 6–3, we have stipulated that there is no treatment effect—only a falsification of A scores. Therefore, given the italicized definition, above, there is no discontinuity. But there is! Just a glance at the figure makes this quite clear. Why in this case does there seem to be a discontinuity in the absence of a treatment effect? The problem is that we have been assuming that, in the null case, the functional form of the relation between A and Y is linear. By tampering with the A scores, however, we have no doubt made that null-case relation non-linear. This would be fairly obvious in the extreme example provided above since what was done in effect was to enforce assignment by a variable called true-initial-of-last-name-unless-mischievous-meddler-thinks-you-will-do-particularly-well-or-poorly. Such a variable could hardly be linearly related to anything! To depict with a smooth curve the true relation of Y to the assignment variable actually used would demand a cubic function, such as that rendered by the dashed line in Figure 6–3. Regarding that curve (if one only knew what it was), e is genuinely random with respect to T, there is no discontinuity, and no treatment effect is to be inferred. If, on the other hand, we assume a linear function, a treatment effect will be mistakenly inferred, provided that the intercept difference produced is large enough to be statistically significant. Intentional tampering is of course unusual. Unwitting nonrandom mistakes, however, are always possible, and when eligibility for a program depends on a qualifying score, there is likely to be a certain pressure toward falsification. These kinds of measurement errors can have the same effects as tampering.

A first conclusion from the above is that nonrandom measurement error in the assignment variable will distort the results when it makes the relation of Y to A nonlinear, or, more generally, when it makes incorrect the null-case functional form that is assumed. In applying the regression-discontinuity design, therefore, it is important to use an assignment variable and administrative procedures that are as unbiased as they possibly can be in their classification of individuals on A. Impartial measurement of a trait with a known functional relation to Y is critical; otherwise, one is in the extremely awkward position of

FIGURE 6–3   Misclassification. Pseudotreatment effect created by the assumption of linearity

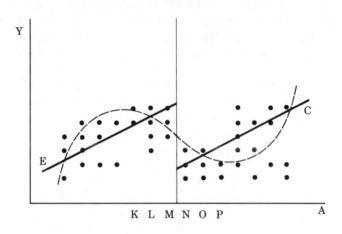

trying to outguess the bias by the application of new, and probably very strange, functional assumptions. It is best not to misclassify. There is not enough reported experience with the design to know how serious a problem nonrandom classification error will truly be. Fairness can to a great extent be controlled if the will is there; honest nonrandom mistakes by program personnel due to some clients' understating their incomes, for example, are difficult to discern and will vary with the nature of the assignment variable employed.

A second conclusion from the above is, of course, that the assumption regarding the form of the relation between A and Y in the regression-discontinuity design is critical. This problem seems serious enough to have received an enormous amount of attention (see Trochim 1984). In the following section, it is suggested that the problem is not serious enough to discourage judicious use of the design.

Curvilinearity

Clearly, if a linear relation between A and Y is assumed, as is so commonly the case in regression analyses, the validity of the results of the evaluation would seem severely threatened by the possibility of nonlinearities. In particular, as pointed out by Cook and Campbell (1979, pp. 138–139), one simple type of interaction (in which, for example, the treatment effect is greater the lower the A score of the individual) is

FIGURE 6–4 **Interactive treatment effect confounded with null-case curvilinear relation—Solid line = observed data; dashed line = linear assumption; dotted line = curvilinear assumption**

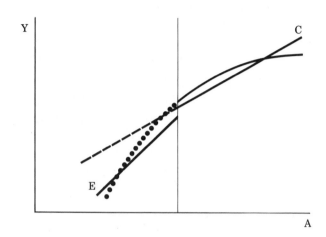

essentially impossible to distinguish from a curving, null-case relation. Figure 6–4 depicts both of these, the dashed-line assumption for the null case leading to an inference of a treatment effect and the dotted-line assumption leading to the opposite conclusion. In no way can the data from the impact analysis at hand communicate with confidence whether the steeper slope in the E-group is due to the treatment or, perhaps, to a null-case interaction (curvilinearity).

Nevertheless, nonrandom measurement error aside, the threat of incorrectly assuming the functional form of the focal regression may easily be exaggerated.

1. It is extremely common in program evaluation to have or to be able to have pretest data, that is, to have data relating current scores on the assignment variable to scores on the outcome dimension *before* the treatment is administered. We might, for example, have data on the relation of nutrition to *current* cognitive development, or income level to *current* school achievement. The functional form probably needed for the study can be obtained by fitting a curve to the pretest data and assuming that its form does not change when the outcome measure is taken a bit later in time, a fairly benign assumption in many cases.

2.   Most social programs by far are remedial, that is, they strive to make the lows higher, as with disadvantaged people and life's rewards, or the highs lower, as with high crime rates, physical incapacity, or pollution. One prominent illustrative program used in the regression-discontinuity literature has the aim of making the highs higher—giving merit scholarship aid to the best students (Campbell and Stanley 1966), but this is quite atypical. The far more typical case is depicted in Figure 6–1. There, a smooth curve that would make the actual treatment effect into a null-case outcome is so extremely convoluted as hardly ever to be found in practice (see Figure 6–3 for the general shape that would be implied). At least, one can say that in most actual cases such a complex curve (or a noncontinuous null-case outcome that simply followed the E and C lines in Figure 6–3 or 6–1) would be far-fetched enough to have negligible subjective probability. It is extremely difficult to imagine how ordinary real-world variables could possibly relate to one another in the fashion represented. This is one of the many instances in which presumption is likely to override a threat to internal validity. Thus, if a linear relation is assumed and a treatment effect is discovered on that basis in the ordinary remedial program, a nullifying underlying curve may often, probably in the great majority of cases, be so convoluted and causally far-fetched as to be ruled out as a serious factor in the policymaking process based on the results.

3.   Even in the less typical case, where the aim is to make the highs higher, a moderately strong true intercept effect demands a fairly unbelievable invalidating curve. A large intercept gap makes a cubic-type curve necessary to fit the data rather than the one-bend variety displayed in Figure 6–4. Consider Figure 6–5. If this were a time series, one might easily imagine some event other than the treatment that could cause such a jump in the natural course of things. In fact, the curve resembles the logistic or S curve of cumulative morbidity in an epidemic over time, or cumulative adoptions of innovations. In the regression-discontinuity case, however, the jump means that in the real world, Y rises gently across the lower regions of the A scale, but surges upward at a much greater rate for middling A scores and takes on a gently decreasing gain at the high end. It is admittedly more likely than the curve that involves a reverse in direction, as in the case of the previous paragraph (Figure 6–3 or 6–1), but it is unlikely enough that the problem should only be a caution and should not disproportionately discourage the regression-discontinuity design.

4.   The linear assumption is not mandated. Frequently, the circumstances of the design and the scales used to measure the variables will dictate the use of another simple curve as the assumed null-case outcome. Without a great deal of fanfare, for example, Berk and

FIGURE 6–5   Curvilinear null-case assumption needed to contradict a treatment effect when the highs are made higher

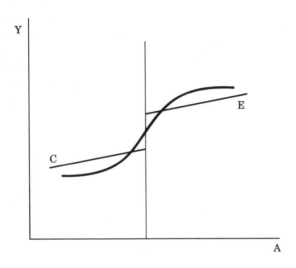

Rauma (1983) assume a logistic curve to manage the floor and ceiling effects of a dichotomous dependent variable.

5.   The evidence from the observed, within-group plots can be used to model the null-case curve. The difficulty with this approach, of course, is that the experimental-group plot is influenced in uncertain ways and to an uncertain degree by the treatment itself. Nevertheless, a great deal of study has been devoted to this problem in the context of the regression-discontinuity design and, for the technically oriented analyst or consultant, the results can be helpful (Trochim 1984).

6.   Last but certainly not least, if pretest data are not available, it should almost always be possible, usually at small additional expense, to obtain data on the relation of A to Y in some segment of the real world that is comparable, but in which the program has not been offered. No doubt, *comparable* cannot mean precisely similar, but if a linear or other simple function fits the data in a few additional settings, there is powerful reason to assume it in the evaluation at hand. This device in particular, as well as the first one listed, may help to distinguish between null-case curves and can pick up interaction effects, as in Figure 6–4. It is not a flawless alternative, but it will generally be a far better one than discarding the regression-discontinuity design in favor of ordinary quasi-experimental designs, whose power in principle is considerably less impressive.

SUMMARY

In sum, the primary limitation on the regression-discontinuity design should be its applicability, that is, the necessity of having enough control to assign subjects to treatments strictly according to their scores on a measured assignment variable. More experience with the design is needed, but there is good reason to expect that with the proper administrative and analytic procedures, when applicable, it is good.

Chapter Seven

The Comparative-Change Design

We return here to the consideration of designs in which selection is centralized but assignment is not randomized; that is, no strength can be drawn from the manner in which the assignment is carried out. Experimental and regression-discontinuity designs each draw protection against the threats of history, selection, and assignment contamination from a special calculated assignment process—randomization in experimental design and the randomization of residuals (selection by score on some quantitative variable, A) in regression discontinuity. In both cases, the special assignment process almost perfectly controls (makes predictable) the relationship between the treatment variable T and the outcome of interest Y in the absence of a treatment effect. In ordinary quasi-experimental design, however, there is no such specially calculated process; the assignment may as well be arbitrary insofar as so broad an ability to protect against threats to internal validity is concerned. Still, designs 3 and 4 may be improved upon. Without powerful assignment techniques, which demand so much control over who gets which treatment that they frequently cannot be used, there are still some methods by which the major threats may be substantially blunted.

In the present chapter we will consider one such method, the combined use of a pretest and a comparison group. In Chapter Nine, we will consider another, the interrupted time series, as well as its combination with the use of a comparison series. These methods comprise the fundamental technology of advanced quasi-experimental design. Before launching into this subject matter, however, it is well to note two facts that should always be kept in mind regarding these designs of intermediate power. (1) Although measurement and analysis procedures can make a study much more sensitive to treatment effects than it might otherwise be (see, especially, Judd and Kenny 1981, pp. 29–

32 and passim), protection against threats to internal validity will in general come almost entirely from selection and assignment processes and almost not at all from measurement and analysis. Thus, because they are so unsystematic in the assignment phase, all quasi-experimental designs are inherently weak. (2) In the final analysis, it is presumptive reasoning, assumptions, subjective and intersubjective probability that decide whether threats to internal validity are serious; they cannot be totally eliminated from consideration in any possible combination of design, measurement, and analysis. In this perspective, there are settings and circumstances in which quasi-experimental designs are adequate.

Design 5, the comparative-change design, has major importance in impact analysis because it represents a felicitous combination of practicality and power. For that reason, as many have noted, it is commonly employed (Cook and Campbell, 1979 p. 103). Unfortunately, there is somewhat less to recommend it from the standpoint of power than practicality, but it is a good start that can be improved on and is more likely to satisfy impact-analysis requirements than either design 3 or design 4. Best seen, in fact, as a combination of designs 3 and 4, it is diagrammed as follows:

$$(5) \qquad \frac{X_E \qquad T \qquad Y_E}{X_C \qquad \qquad Y_C}$$

Clearly, the before-after feature of design 3 is preserved, as well as the comparison-group feature of design 4. Each of these weaker designs has its own prominent threat to internal validity—history and selection, respectively—but each design also, it turns out, serves to blunt the threat to the other. The before measure blunts (but does not completely eliminate) the selection threat by enabling a control for differential starting points. The threat of history is neutralized by the comparison group; the comparison group is a recorder of the effects of history of all sorts so that any *difference* between the two groups is not due to their common history from pretest to posttest, but rather to the treatment or to some other threat. Unfortunately, the nonrandomized comparison group does *not* erase the threat of divergent history.

Let us leave aside in this consideration any divergent history or other contamination that may be due to the treatment itself or to the implementation of the program. The reason for doing so is not that these threats are irrelevant or negligible in connection with the comparative-change design (they are, on the contrary, potentially quite serious in some instances), but rather that they are universal dangers and thus do not serve to set this design apart from experimental or other designs. In truth, the comparative-change design is often less susceptible to the kind of contamination that results from unnatural variation within a field setting or communication among subjects because it is more amenable to geographically separated rather than intermingled groups. This, however, is a distinction of occasional practice and not a distinction in principle. Thus, the kind of divergent history about which to be concerned here is the kind that results from contamination in the unfolding of the assignment aspect of the design. The two groups may diverge (for reasons other than a treatment effect) because they somehow harbored the potential for such divergence even at the time of the pretest or before. As noted in Chapter Four, assignment contamination is, in its roots, essentially the same as the threat of selection-Q bias. It is accorded a separate category only to emphasize that some forms of selection-Q bias are essentially impossible to measure and control in the analysis; the later effects of these seeds can only realistically be neutralized by randomization or a similarly strong assignment procedure. Let us proceed then to analyze the threat of selection-Q bias in the comparative-change design.

SELECTION-Q BIAS AND COMPARATIVE CHANGE

Just as history is the threat to internal validity that is particularly relevant to design 3 (and, we will see, to the interrupted-time-series design) and selection is correspondingly paired with design 4, the personal nemesis of the comparative-change design is selection-Q bias. Considering it in a positive light, comparative change is a major step up from the weaker, comparative-posttest design in that it neutralizes selection-P bias. In a negative light, however, it differs from all stronger designs, such as experimental designs, in that it is vulnerable to selection-Q bias and assignment contamination (see Figure 4–1, reproduced on pp. vi–vii).

When the comparative-change design was formally introduced, it was suggested that this design neutralized the selection threat (Campbell and Stanley, 1966, p. 40). Although it was recognized that the treatment and comparison groups might differ in maturation and regression as the study unfolded, it was not emphasized that these are selection threats. For simple selection-Q bias, it is only necessary that the groups differ on some unmeasured variable that affects Y and has not yet affected X_1, or has not yet affected it as much as it will. Using an illustration from the previous chapter, for example, mother's IQ might be particularly important for later cognitive development when children are about four years old. Thus, group differences in that variable would not have affected the *pretest* on cognitive development as much as they will eventually affect the *posttest*. Such variables can be controlled, but to do so it is necessary to identify them—difficult, since they are potentially infinite in number—and measure them. Sometimes even that avenue is not open. As we noted in Chapter Four, the seeds of divergent events such as a heat wave or a crime wave can be essentially impossible to capture with measured variables. Similarly, divergent maturation and regression may result from causes that one cannot realistically expect to be able to capture beforehand. Therefore, the threat of selection definitely is not entirely neutralized by design 5. It is only selection differences on *measured variables* that may be neutralized in the analysis; if there are important differences in unmeasured or unmeasurable variables, the analyst can do little or nothing.

This is certainly not to say that inclusion of the pretest is a negligible gain. On the contrary, it is often extremely powerful because it is a funnel to the posttest through which most causes must pass. Of all of the possible causes of physical fitness, for example, or attitudes toward abortion, or crime rates or accident rates, a very large proportion will have taken their toll by time 1: the ordering of individuals or cities on such variables will not be substantially different at time 2. Many factors will no longer cause variation on the outcome dimension at all and many others will cause much less after time 1 than they did before. Thus, the pretest, when applicable, is a powerful screening device, reducing substantially the seriousness of the problem of infinite possible causes. This then is a second important function of the pretest in evaluation research, added to its role in increasing statistical sensitivity, as explained in Chapter Four. Nevertheless, it is surely not as good as randomization, and just how good it is—how much it has screened out and how much potential for selection-Q bias has been allowed to pass through—always remains unknown.

Since a pretest and other control variables provide a highly specific null-case prediction for the treatment group depending on where it starts out, and since this predicted value is located on a regression surface in convincing mathematical fashion, it is difficult to see how selection-Q bias works without placing it in the regression framework. Moreover, the regression framework conceptualizes the bias with a valuable clarity. Let us then turn to regression as we turn also to the forms that selection-Q bias may take in the context of the comparative-change design.

Intercept Bias, Matched Groups

Leave program evaluation behind for a moment and consider a simple study to record the progress of body weight over a certain period of time. Our model is the following:

(7–1) $$Y_i = \alpha + \beta_1 X_{1i} + u_i$$

(7–2) $$\bar{Y} = \alpha + \beta_1 \bar{X}_1,$$

as in Equations 5–1 and 5–1c. Collecting data on some group of interest and carrying out the regression calculations, we find that posttest weights observe the following pattern:

$$(7\text{–}3) \qquad Y_i = -1.5 + .95X_{1i} + u_i$$

$$(7\text{–}4) \qquad \bar{Y} = -1.5 + .95(200),$$

or

$$\bar{Y} = -1.5 + 190 = 188.5.$$

Thus, our group started out at an average weight of 200 pounds but ended up at only 188.5. Why did this happen? The possibilities, as expressed by the regression coefficients, are infinite. For example, looking at $\beta_1 = .95$, which means that on the average these people lost 5 percent of their body weight over the period, other things being equal, it might just be that a holiday or vacation period preceded the pretest so that people were unusually heavy then and regressed to the norm over time. Moving to the finding that $\alpha = -1.5$, it might just be that many respondents experienced heavy stress of the sort that tends to make one lose interest in food, such as viral infections or divorces, so that the average weight loss for the group from such sources was 1.5 pounds. It might also be that the scale on which people were weighed at time 2 was off by 1.5 pounds. Infinitely many scenarios could explain these results.

We might have carried out exactly the same study on a different group of people, or an additional group, and of course the results would not be expected to be the same. Let us suppose, for example, that in this second group the results were

$$(7\text{–}5) \qquad Y_i = 2 + .95X_{1i} + u_i$$

$$(7\text{–}6) \qquad \bar{Y} = 2 + (.95)(200) = 2 + 190 = 192.$$

In the second group, the initial weight also happened to average 200 pounds and the slope coefficient is again .95, but the intercept this time is 2 pounds instead of -1.5. These results are also explainable by infinitely many scenarios. Let us say that recovery from the same vacation period occasioned the 5 percent weight loss, but there was at the same time a uniform or randomly distributed weight *gain* of 2 pounds, perhaps attributable to the fact that many in the group gave up smoking during this period and gained weight in the process. The fortunes of the two groups may be diagrammed as the solid regression lines in Figure 7–1.

With this sort of possible real-world experience in mind then, let us return to impact analysis and design 5. Assume now that the lower line in Figure 7–1 represents the results of a weight reduction program

FIGURE 7–1 Weight change in two groups, where the average initial weights and the slopes are the same, but the two intercepts are different

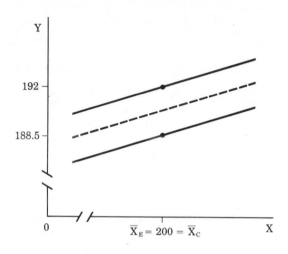

that is being evaluated, while the upper line represents the comparison group for the comparative-change design. Letting T be the treatment (the weight reduction program), as before, the analysis would be based on Equation 5–3, which is repeated here for convenience:

(7–7) $Y_i = \alpha + \beta_1 X_{1i} + \beta_T T_i + u_i.$

Before proceeding, it is well to note that in our present example the treatment and comparison averages are *matched* on the pretest (at 200 pounds). Since the slope β_1 functions to provide a null-case expectation for $\bar{Y}_E$ *when the two groups started out at different places* on the pretest (i.e., $\bar{X}_{1E} \neq \bar{X}_{1C}$), it is without function here in assessing the difference between actual and expected outcome in the group that received the program. Since the two groups started out at the same weight, the expected outcome for the treatment group in the absence of an effect of the program is simply the comparison group's (mean) outcome (see Equation 5–1c):

(7–8) $\hat{Y}_{0E} = \alpha + \beta_1 \bar{X}_{1E} = \alpha + \beta_1 \bar{X}_{1C} = \bar{Y}_C.$

Yet another way of saying the same thing is that there can be no selection-P effects in this example. Thus, the pervasive difficulty that is about to be demonstrated as inhering in the comparative-change design applies even when groups are matched on the pretest (and, in fact, on all other measured variables as well). Matching the treatment and comparison groups beforehand on certain variables does not achieve equality and, in fact, may easily make matters worse, as will be pointed out below (see Campbell and Erlebacher 1970).

The difficulty referred to enters in the following way when trying to discern based on this design whether there has indeed been a treatment effect. When the data are used to estimate Equation (7–7), β_T will equal -3.5, that is, there will be an apparent treatment effect of -3.5 pounds. That will clearly be true because the difference in intercepts $\alpha_E - \alpha_C$ will be $-1.5 - 2 = -3.5$. Having seen, however, that such a difference *may easily* arise, in the absence of any treatment whatever, from natural causes (such as viral infections, divorce, and quitting smoking) in both groups, we must be fundamentally uncertain whether to attribute it to such natural causes (selection-Q bias) or to the weight reduction program.

It will help in connecting this discussion to others in the book to view the difficulty slightly differently. Consider an outcome such as that depicted in Figure 7–1 with a new device, a hypothetical population norm, added to the analytical picture. An illustrative possibility is shown in Figure 7–1 as the dashed slope between the two solid lines we have discussed so far. We imagine that both the treatment and comparison groups belong to a larger population and, from the standpoint of design critique, we would like to be able to assume (we could not actually know) that they are both precisely typical of that population in the null case except for random error. In that fashion (*a*) we could reach a conclusion in the evaluation based on the solid foundational information that the only difference between the two groups is T, the program, and (*b*) if the population were a real one and were identified, we could generalize the results of the study to that body. In the constructed example of Figure 7–1, the two groups actually are typical of the population in the slope of posttest weight on pretest. As for intercept, however, the comparison group is surely nonrepresentative, and perhaps the treatment group as well. Such nonrepresentativeness could easily be due to the factors that were illustratively devised above (smoking, etc.). Of course, there need not be such unrepresentativeness; either one or both groups might fall exactly on the dashed population line in the absence of the treatment.

The point to be made in connection with design 5, however, is that since neither group was selected from the larger population at random, *one can never know* whether one group or the other is representative or not. The disturbances in the regression model are randomly distributed in the population, but they are not necessarily randomly distributed to the two groups under observation. (Nor is there a cut point on X_1 as in the regression-discontinuity design that would ensure the distribution of *all* disturbances for any given X_1 score to one and only one group; disturbances for the same X_1 score have generally been distributed to some subjects in one group and some in the other, but not, as far as we can know, at random.) Thus, a significance test, which would tell us just how lopsided a random process might have been, is irrelevant; what is needed is information on the distribution of disturbance terms in the *non*random process that was used in assigning the groups, but that, of course, is categorically unavailable. An outcome such as that depicted by the solid lines in Figure 7–1 then might result either from the treatment or from unrepresentativeness in one or both of the groups. That is the fundamental weakness of the comparative-change design—the potential for selection-Q bias—and there is no amount of post hoc statistical analysis of any sort that can cure it. The guarantee of representativeness may only be obtained *before* selection and assignment, not afterward. The only hope is to modify the design itself, a tactic to be considered in the next chapter and in Chapter Eleven.

Intercept Bias, Unmatched Groups

In design 12, the R-comparative-change design, selection-Q bias is of course not a problem. There, the dashed line in Figure 7–1 represents the combined group before randomization (or, in rare cases, the larger population from which both the experimental and control groups have been sampled at random). In fact, it would be precisely the observed control-group line, give or take a small amount for random sampling error, because the randomized control group is representative of the combined study population to start with and, we assume, has not been affected by the treatment or contaminated by faulty controls. The two resulting groups differ from one another in unmeasured variables only through the vagaries of the random procedure, so that null-case differences of various magnitudes are determinable by significance testing. Thus, one may project the expected or null-case intercept of the experimental group's line directly from the observed comparison group's line since the experimental group would also be precisely there, or very close to it, without the treatment. The expected null-case outcome $\hat{Y}_{0E}$ is then the point on the comparison-group regression line vertically above $\bar{X}_{1E}$. Given that the groups in this first illustration are perfectly matched in average pretest score as in Figure 7–1, this expected outcome is precisely $\bar{Y}_C$.

Note, however, that the two groups need not be perfectly matched. Through sampling vagaries, $\bar{X}_{1E}$ might differ slightly from $\bar{X}_{1C}$. This introduces no new procedures or problems; in that case, the point on the comparison-group regression line vertically above $\bar{X}_{1E}$ is still the expected null-case outcome, but it is now no longer identical with $\bar{Y}_C$. Because the two groups started out in different places on the X_1 axis, they are naturally expected to end in different places on the regression

FIGURE 7–2 Intercept bias due to selection-Q effects or random measurement error in unmatched groups

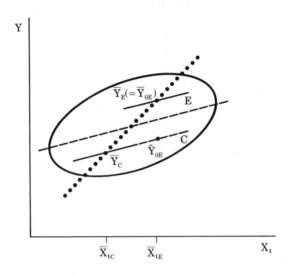

line of Y on X_1, with the magnitude of the difference in Y given by β_1 and the initial difference on X_1, that is, $(\hat{Y}_{0E} - \bar{Y}_C) = \beta_1(\bar{X}_{1E} - \bar{X}_{1C})$.

The complication of unmatched rather than matched groups introduces no new principles in the quasi-experimental context either but it does introduce an additional nuance. Figure 7–2 shows the hypothetical case in which the two groups start out in different places on X_1 and in which, we will continue to assume, there is no treatment effect. Rather, there are selection-Q effects in both groups that cause an intercept difference that *looks* like a treatment effect. If we assume (unwarrantedly) that there are no selection effects whatever, we can only assume further that $\bar{Y}_E$ in the null case (i.e., $\hat{Y}_{0E}$) would have fallen exactly on the comparison-group regression line—not at $\bar{Y}_C$ in this case, but vertically above $\bar{X}_{1E}$. If the assumption happens to be incorrect and selection effects are indeed present, it is clear that their unique contribution is *not* to make the mean null-case outcome for the treatment group differ from the outcome of the comparison group; that would have occurred anyway due to different starting positions. Rather, the more general rule is that they make it differ from the null-case outcome *expected* on the basis of β_1 and $\bar{X}_{1E}$.

Thus, the potential intercept bias (from selection-Q effects) in unmatched groups is bad, but no worse and no different in principle from the intercept bias in matched groups. In fact, the reverse may be true;

an intentional process of matching on one or two variables may easily
aggravate the selection bias it is generally designed to minimize (see
Campbell and Erlebacher 1970). If the treatment group consists of
somewhat unusual subjects, such as extreme scorers, so that it is difficult to find matching subjects, those found may well be unusual or
extreme for different and temporary reasons. The process in that fashion builds in selection-Q differences that are almost bound to have a
biasing impact. Divergent regression, for example, is highly likely to
occur and to produce quite misleading results. Campbell and Erlebacher (1970) present strong evidence for suspecting such effects in an
early evaluation of the Head Start program. If the treatment group is
extreme, or if matching subjects are in any way difficult to obtain, it is
far better not to try to match on one or two particular variables, thus
risking dangerous mismatches on others, but rather to select the comparison group from average, plentifully available individuals and rely
on statistical controls to adjust for differences in the would-be matching variables.

Finally, it is sometimes thought that if one can have near perfect
prediction of Y, which statisticians would often refer to as having a
high R^2, selection bias evaporates and the design becomes as good as
an experiment. It is only necessary to bring all of the predictors into
the analysis as adjusting variables or controls. After all, if one has
perfect prediction without the treatment all departures from the predicted values must be due to the treatment itself. The first response to
such a conjecture is that it will rarely happen in the evaluation of programs. Even the pretest, coupled with a few other good predictors, will
still generally leave the R^2 low enough to allow ample room for selection-Q bias to do its work. Second, it is important to add that such
reasoning is valid only for a high R^2 that pertains to the *combined*
treatment and comparison groups. But one never knows that R^2. The
treatment has been applied and has ruined forever one's chances of
knowing how well a set of variables excluding the treatment would
have correlated with Y. Once the treatment has been applied, one can
only calculate the *within-group* R^2s, which may easily be quite different from the population R^2. In fact, if there has been selection-Q bias,
that very bias would often raise within-group R^2; high R^2 would then
be the result of the very force (selection bias) whose nonexistence it is
supposed to demonstrate.

This may be seen by considering one kind of example of selection-
Q bias, as pictured in Figure 7–3. Assume that there is no treatment
effect whatever. Plainly, there is in this illustrative case low prediction
accuracy of Y from X_1 in the population to which one would like to
generalize, as indicated by the wide scatter of points denoted by the
large ellipse. The treatment and comparison groups are not widely separated because of the treatment but rather simply happen to have been

FIGURE 7–3   Selection-Q bias tends to yield a higher R^2 within groups than in the population as a whole

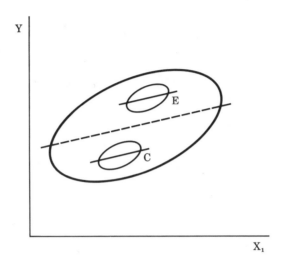

assigned from narrow ranges of individuals by selection-Q effects so that there is not only a separation but, within each group, Y is very highly predictable from X_1 (indicated by the narrow scatter of points around the within-group regression lines). These subjects are likely to be very similar to one another on some variable-set Q within groups, and different from one another across groups; that is why their Y scores show the similarities (within-group) and differences (between-group) they do. Therein lies the selection-Q bias. It is almost bound to work in this general fashion. Because of the intercept gap, one would of course be strongly tempted to infer a treatment effect when, in this illustration, there is none. Because of the high R^2 within groups, one would be further tempted to infer that the apparent treatment effect is real. But it is not. Instead, the very fact of selection-Q bias has itself yielded the high predictability of Y from X_1 within each group as a by-product of their distant separation within the constraints of the variance of the population. This example does not illustrate an arcane event. Almost all of modern quantitative social science shows us that a relation that is strong in one population (analogous to one of our two groups) may easily turn out to be weak in another (analogous to our whole population—the large ellipse), the difference being that some Q conditions are more *variable* in the second group than in the first (see Mohr 1982).

FIGURE 7–4   Evaluation results in which the slope of posttest on pretest is different for the two groups

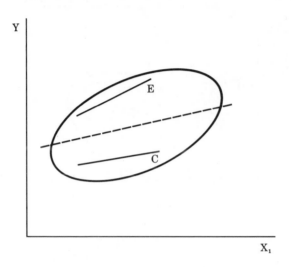

Bias in Slopes

Selection-Q bias may also extend to slopes; it is not confined to intercepts. Consider, as an analyst, being confronted with comparative-change evaluation results that resemble Figure 7–4 (of course, the hypothetical population regression line and the ellipse containing the scatter of its points are not observable). This sort of result can immobilize an impact analysis; that is, it does not provide a basis for going on to examine the possible intercept effect of the treatment. To do that, using Equation 7–7, it is necessary to estimate β_1. Since the two within-group slopes of Y on X_1 differ so sharply here, what should be used for β_1—the treatment-group slope, the comparison-group slope, or some compromise between the two? There is in principle no way to answer this question and, if the policy implications of the study rest on which alternative is chosen, as they easily might, the analysis must simply come to a frustrating halt.

The result depicted in Figure 7–4 presents no problem in the context of the counterpart experimental design, the R-comparative-change design. In that case, a more general equation than Equation (7–7) is used to estimate the treatment effect and other parameters, as follows:

(7–9) $Y_i = \alpha + \beta_1 X_{1i} + \beta_T T_i + \beta_2 X_{1i} T_i + u_i.$

FIGURE 7–5 Experimental design—the difference in slopes may appropriately be incorporated into the treatment effect using an interaction model

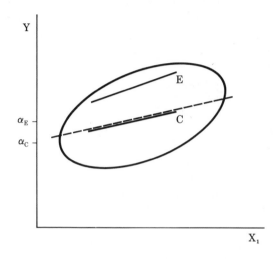

This equation incorporates one additional term, an *interaction* between the treatment and the pretest. Instead of β_T alone, the treatment effect is now given by the combined coefficients of T, namely, (β_T + $\beta_2 X_{1i}$). In other words, the treatment effect is not the same for every subject but has, rather, a common component plus an additional component that depends on the pretest score. An illustrative case is shown in Figure 7–5. The control-group regression line is the population line, plus or minus random sampling error. If not for the treatment, the regression line for the experimental group would be just the same. Since it is not, we infer a treatment effect such that, in the illustration shown, any experimental-group member may be presumed to have gained a certain positive amount, the intercept difference ($\alpha_E - \alpha_C$), plus an additional positive amount that depends on his pretest score— the higher the pretest score, the larger this additional impact. If the treatment were grants to small businesses to aid exports, for example, the results would tell us that exports tended to grow a certain amount no matter what they were to begin with but, on top of that, the higher they were to begin with the more they grew as a result of the grants. The key to the interpretation of the difference in within-group slopes is that, because of randomization, the two groups would have been the same in the absence of a treatment; *any* emerging difference, then, including a difference in slopes, is attributable to the treatment.

This interpretation is not available in the quasi-experimental version of the design. Since there has been no randomization, any presumption of null-case equality is problematic. The possibility of selection-Q effects must be allowed. These may well have caused all or part of the observed difference in slopes (as well as the intercept difference). Thus, it is impossible in principle to unconfound the effects of the treatment and the effects of selection on the slope of Y on X_1, and β_1 is indeterminate. If the difference in slopes is negligible as determined by a significance test—the fourth or strength-of-relationship function of significance testing given in Chapter Five—Equation 7–7 might be applied and would yield a weighted average of the two as the estimate of β_1. If the difference in slopes is *not* negligible, there really is no basis for continuing the analysis except a bracketing approach (e.g., Gramlich 1981); that is, an approach that allows for both possibilities and everything in between. If the analysis were continued anyway and Equation 7–9 were applied, thus estimating β_1 from the comparison group alone, one must bear in mind that the analyst is assuming away selection-Q bias in slopes—simply assuming, that is, that the difference in slopes is due to the treatment.

Furthermore, *even if both slopes are the same or negligibly different,* Equation 7–7 and further analysis may be inapplicable. One slope, after all, may incorporate a treatment effect and the other a selection effect of approximately the same size. Indeed, both slopes may incorporate the same selection effect and the inference will still be biased. It would seem that no harm would be done in this case because both groups are subject to the same hidden influence, but that will not be true unless their pretest means are matched (in which case the slope of Y on X_1 does not matter at all in predicting $\hat{Y}_{0E}$). Otherwise, the false comparison-group slope gives a false null-case expectation $\hat{Y}_{0E}$ no matter what the slope in the treatment group (see Figure 7–6). This difficulty, in fact, is exactly the source of bias when there is random measurement error in the pretest (Reichardt 1979, pp. 160–164). Ordinarily, the program evaluator looks for intercept effects and gives no attention at all to slopes; we have seen that even when the within-group slopes are identical this practice incorporates assumptions whose invalidity may seriously distort conclusions.

Such is the weakness of the comparative-change design and the role of selection-Q bias as its basic source. This is not to say that the design is useless—far from it. Its primary utility is for those instances in which (*a*) a comparison group is available that seems quite persuasively not to be different from the treatment group in important ways that cannot be measured; (*b*) it seems helpful, as it almost always will be, to capture a large segment of potential selection-Q bias by trapping

FIGURE 7–6 Treatment effect erroneously inferred when both slopes are identically false

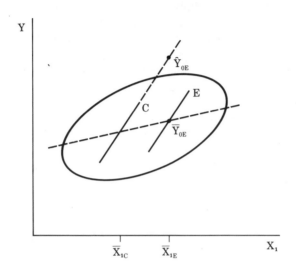

it in a pretest; (c) it seems helpful, as it almost always will, to make a possible effect stand out more by reducing error variance; and (d) a more powerful design is either not feasible or, for some reason, not desirable. The reader is reminded that the quantitative result of a significance test is not a valid basis for decisions about program effects when the comparative-change design has been employed. One uses exactly the same estimating equations as are used for the experimental version of the design, but one must make one's judgments based on the sheer magnitude of the coefficient b_T, not on its level of statistical significance. The direction and magnitude of the coefficient must then be weighed against one's conjectures and fears about the direction and magnitude of selection-Q bias.

Thus, making an inference from the comparative-change design with confidence must depend largely on what we have called presumptive reasoning, that is, on recognizing the potential of selection-Q bias for damaging one's conclusions but being able to reason that, in the particular evaluation considered, selection is not a serious threat. In the educational-performance-contracting experiment, for example, the treatment group was selected from the lowest performing schools in each district and the comparison group from the next lowest (Gramlich and Koshel 1975). Both groups, however, were very large and spread out across all regions of the country. Many would be willing to accept that there were no differences between the two groups beyond their initial test scores in reading and math (the measured pretests) sufficient to bias the results seriously. Others would feel enough of a nagging doubt to prefer a stronger design. Sometimes one can reason cogently that if there is any selection bias it is in the conservative direction so that if a program does show an effect, its true impact is, if anything, even greater than the statistical results appear to indicate. This would appear to have been the case, for example, in the performance-contracting experiment, where the comparison group was drawn from slightly higher-ranking schools than the treatment group.

Experimental design should always be given careful consideration and, in the educational-performance-contracting experiment, it might actually have been a possible alternative. We will turn in the next chapter, however, to one way of strengthening the comparative-change design that does not require such complete control over the selection process as is demanded by the randomization procedure.

RANDOM MEASUREMENT ERROR

It is necessary to consider briefly one additional threat to internal validity that has nothing to do with selection effects, namely, random measurement error in the pretest. It was noted in the previous chapter that the regression-discontinuity design provides good protection against random measurement error. The R-comparative-change design does so as well, for the following reason. The effect of random measurement error in the pretest is always to attenuate within-group slopes, that is, instead of observing a straight line connecting $\bar{Y}_C$ and $\bar{Y}_E$ in the null case (the dotted line in Figure 7–2), both the E- and C-group lines are rotated clockwise a bit on their centers, so that the analyst sees two separated shallower slopes, as in Figure 7–2. An intercept difference that is really the effect of random measurement error, then, would certainly tend to be read as a treatment effect. Except for ordinary sampling error, however, there is no expected bias from this source in design 12 because randomization makes the expected value $\hat{Y}_{0E}$ exactly equal to $\bar{Y}_C$ (see Reichardt 1979, p. 163); the two would not be separated from one another and connected by a straight line (or other curve). In that case, it does not matter if the within-group slopes are attenuated because, passing through the same midpoint, being equal, and being attenuated by the same amount, the two lines would appear one on top of the other no matter how steep or shallow they were. There would be no intercept gap in the null case. Randomization tends to equalize the pretest means and, therefore, the null-case posttest means. Statistical expectations aside, however, the farther apart the *actual* pretest means, the more serious the effects of any existing random measurement error, even in a true experiment. One can only say that the larger the experimental and control groups, the less chance for this possible bias to enter through the medium of unequal group mean pretest scores.

Since some difference in group mean pretest scores is likely in design 5, no matter how large the samples, random measurement error is likely to cause a bias. However, it will often be difficult to consider this a serious possibility because it is added to the fear of the selection-Q bias that already exists. Imagine that Figures 7–2 (using the dotted line to depict the imaginary, perfect-measurement case), 7–3, and 7–7 all depict instances of zero treatment effect; that is, an intercept gap has appeared, but for reasons other than an impact of the program (quitting smoking, divorces, measurement error, etc.). Selection-Q bias can cause a result resembling Figure 7–2 just as well as the other two; all look essentially the same to the analyst. From this perspective, random measurement error is an additional possibility that may either be magnifying or damping selection-Q effects. This is not a negligible concern, but it may well be a subordinate one unless the anlayst is operating with substantial confidence that selection-Q effects are absent.

It is well to bear in mind that random measurement error would generally produce a conservative bias. Consider the *direction* of such effects. The rule is that random measurement error always separates the two groups in the positive direction, that is, it makes the high group appear to end up higher than expected, or the low group lower. Therefore, if one of those is what the treatment is trying to do, random measurement error will tend to make the program look better than it actually is. If, as is more frequently the case, the treatment is trying to make the highs lower or the lows higher, random measurement error will make the program look worse than it actually is. Exactly how that would balance out with selection-Q effects depends, of course, on their direction.

Random measurement error should definitely not be ignored, but it is not a major issue in much of impact analysis for program evaluation. In many cases, a good correction factor can and should be applied (Campbell and Boruch 1975, pp. 223–241). More importantly, some designs are inherently resistant. Those that are not would rarely be vulnerable to random measurement error alone, but only in conjunction with other threats to internal validity that are generally harder to manage. The possible effects of all sources of invalidity should surely be carefully considered but, above all, concern for random measurement error should not distract. Successfully managing that problem, often with much attention and effort, should not lull the investigator into neglecting the problem of selection bias in quasi-experimental designs.

Chapter Eight

The Random-Comparison-Group Design

Although there are times when quasi-experimental designs will give results that, by the operation of external information and presumptive reasoning, are completely adequate, those designs in most cases are weaker than the evaluation situation requires. The weaknesses cannot be overcome by statistics; there is essentially no way in which data analysis tricks can neutralize the effects of history or selection in basic quasi-experimental designs such as designs 3, 4, and 5. If more confidence in the inference of direction and extent of treatment effect is needed, the best way to obtain it is by improving the design itself. We will see, for example, that the before-after design is improved by taking a large number of before and after measures spread out over time, instead of only one of each. This particular modification is so important and prevalent that it has always been treated as a separate design, the interrupted-time-series design. We will devote specific attention to that design in the next chapter, but note at this point that the basis of its improvement over the before-after design is not in any statistically or mathematically connected rigor. Rather, it lies in better support for the operation of presumptive reasoning. The time series shows the effects that history has had on the outcome of interest in the normal course of things; if a more pronounced change occurred just after the treatment, presumptive reasoning makes it unlikely that something unusual arose at just that particular time to cause the observed departure from the historically established pattern. Modifications that similarly affect the basis of presumptive reasoning appear in the literature on program evaluation (see Cook and Campbell 1979, pp. 103–136, 218–225). For example, one's faith might be considerably increased if one could introduce and withdraw the treatment several times in succession and observe what happens each time. Such modifications can be extremely valuable and their possibility should always be explored when the prospect of a standard quasi experiment leaves one feeling uneasy. Their drawback, however, is that one rarely has the control or the data required to implement them.

THE DESIGN IN CONCEPT

The best sort of change would be a change from quasi-experimental to true experimental design, but that again is often infeasible because of lack of control. In this chapter, the design reviewed is one that does provide a statistical basis for a more confident inference, as well as a stronger informational base for presumptive reasoning, and that also is applicable in a wide range of situations without more control over the world than is usually available.

Recall that in the last chapter we used the true population regression of Y on X_1 as a device to help visualize and conceptualize the idea of selection-Q bias in the comparative-change design. That regression provides a norm or anchor of correctness by which to identify a selection effect (in the parameters α or β_1) in either group observed in the study. Without the device of the population norm, a concern for selection-Q bias is a concern that the two groups studied might be different *from each other* in the null-case regression of posttest on pretest. It must necessarily be viewed in that way because in neither one of the two groups may the regression line be viewed as especially "correct." If different, the two groups are simply different; there is no wrong or right. A population norm, however, provides a standard of correctness. The selection-bias concern then becomes not whether the two groups differ from one another, but whether either group differs from the norm. With that change, each group may be viewed separately as a possible source of bias.

In the random-comparison-group design, the population norm functions similarly, but it is no longer merely a hypothetical device for clarity; it now becomes an integral part of the design itself. The basis of the design is to identify the population of concern and actually use it, or a random sample from it (whence the name of the design) as the comparison group. Thus the possibility of selection bias is confined to one group only, the treatment group; the comparison group parameters are correct because they comprise the population norm itself. The random-comparison-group design therefore stands somewhere between experimental and quasi experimental. It is still quasi experimental in that assignment is not random for the treatment group. That allows the possibility of null-case unrepresentativeness, or selection bias, in that group. It tends toward the experimental, however, in that assignment for the comparison group is at random from the population of concern—or is the whole population itself—except for the part of it that receives the treatment.

We will soon see that the device of using the population of concern for the comparison group paves the way for applying elements of classical statistics in the estimation of program effect. It should also be noted that it serves to minimax the bias, that is, it minimizes the maximum possible bias. If both groups can be unrepresentative of the population of concern, then they can be unrepresentative in opposite directions—one too high and the other too low—making for a very large bias (see Figure 7–1, for example). When only one group can be unrepresentative, however, the potential bias in any parameter is effectively cut in half.

THE POPULATION OF CONCERN

Randomization is often not possible because administrators and evaluators do not have complete freedom to select the group that is to receive the program. Political or ethical considerations may intervene, or the selection may already have been made before the evaluators were called in, or a whole jurisdiction must be included, and so forth. Even so, however, it is almost always the case that one does have complete freedom to select a group to compare with the one that receives the program. If the possibility of any comparison group at all exists, the choice is rarely mandated by moral, legal, or other outside authority; in general, nobody but the evaluator cares about comparison groups—at least until the time comes to use the finished evaluation in decision making. Therefore, there is generally no reason why the population of concern may not be designated as the comparison group and the whole population or a random sample from it observed as necessary for the study. The limitations, which would be mainly logistical, are generally not prohibitive.

The question becomes then which population to designate as the population of concern. The first and most obvious requirement is that *it be a population to which the treatment group belongs* so that the treatment group may be expected to be governed by its parameters in the null case. Infinitely many populations, however, satisfy that requirement. For example, if the treatment group is homeowners in Ann Arbor, Michigan, the population might be all residents of Ann Arbor, homeowners in Michigan, in the Midwest, in the United States, in cities having more than 100,000 residents, in college towns, in cities with large per-capita income, and so forth. Given the estimation procedures to be described for the random-comparison-group design, several populations might serve equally well, but the selection is considerably narrowed by two additional important requirements.

Having established that the population must include the treatment group, the second requirement is that *it be large relative to that group.* That is necessary because the comparison group will not be the population itself, but the population with a bite taken out of it (namely, the treatment group) to avoid the sort of contamination in which part of the comparison group receives the treatment. Thus, the treatment group should be a negligible segment of the population; its removal should, to the greatest extent possible, leave the population parameters unchanged.

Last, we will see that, for several considerations of internal validity, there must be at least a moderate number of population members (even though the particular ones may not be identified) whose Y scores duplicate the treatment-group counterfactuals. The best way to assure the desired coverage of the treatment group counterfactuals is to *make the population not only large but varied as well.* In that way, if the treatment group, by selection-Q effects, would in the null case have shown a particular error or distance from the predicted population value, the population will also be likely, within the variance of its random disturbance term, to contain additional elements with the same departures. In particular, it would not serve well to call the population something like Ann Arbor and Detroit and designate as the comparison group, homeowners in Detroit. There is too high a probability in such a construction that the two self-constituted groups would tend to vary only narrowly within themselves on certain characteristics, but differ fairly widely from one another.

If the treatment group happens to consist of volunteers for the program, as often occurs, it is critical in view of this requirement not to select as the comparison population a group that voluntarily declined to enroll (for example, states that did not pass a particular law in contrast to those that did). Rather, to make the population contain elements with the treatment group's potential, it should consist of similar volunteers for the program or, more likely, *of a group that never had the opportunity to volunteer or decline,* that is, one that simply was not offered the program or that somehow never considered it. Commonly, such a population would contain many members that would volunteer if given the chance, thus reflecting the treatment group counterfactuals to the extent that being the type to volunteer would have determined them.

ESTIMATING THE TREATMENT EFFECT

To simplify the discussion let us consider that only one control variable is employed—a pretest. Using regression techniques, it is essential in any comparison-group design to estimate the slope of posttest on pretest—the parameter we signify by β_1. To know where the treatment group would have ended up without the treatment, it is necessary in part to multiply its starting point $\bar{X}_{1E}$ by our estimate of this parameter. Perhaps the sharpest distinction between the random-comparison-group design and experimental and quasi-experimental designs is that it uses only one group—the comparison group—to estimate this parameter whereas the others pool the data and use both groups. Unless an interaction model is employed in design 12 (the R-comparative-change design; see Equation 7–9), randomization makes both groups equally good bases for estimating β_1; they are both correct. In design 5 (the comparative-change design), there is no more reason to suspect one group than the other of being a source of selection bias in this slope; as far as the analyst knows, they are equally correct or incorrect and might as well both be used. In the random-comparison-group design, however, the comparison group, being the criterion population, represents the correct slope, whereas the treatment group, both because it has received the treatment and because it is a nonrandom sample of that population, is an untrustworthy basis of estimation. We therefore leave it out.

It will be recalled from Equation 6–3 that a general estimator of treatment effect is,

(8–1)   Treatment Effect $= \bar{Y}_E - \hat{Y}_{0E}.$

This mode was not used literally before, however, because when the data on both groups are pooled, it is more efficient and correct to estimate β_T with a single operation, such as that represented by Equation 7–7, than to obtain the estimate $\hat{Y}_{0E}$ based on comparison-group parameter estimates and subtract it from $\bar{Y}_E$. When the data are not pooled, however, as in the random-comparison-group design, Equation 8–1 becomes a basis of calculation as well as a definition. In the balance of this section, we therefore consider methods of deriving an estimate of the null-case outcome for the treatment group, such as $\hat{Y}_{0E}.$ The discussion must be a bit more elaborate than one would desire because we must have a method of providing an allowance for the selection-Q bias that might remain in the treatment group, even though such bias has been eliminated from the comparison group.

A basic tool in deriving null-case estimates is the scatterplot for the regression of posttest on pretest in the comparison group. Since the comparison group is the population of concern, this scatterplot represents all the Y scores in the population when there has been no treatment. Organized as a regression, it also presents all the Y scores for each individual X_1 score, namely, the vertical row of points above any particular score on the X_1 axis. The scatterplot is represented by an ellipse, as in Figure 8–1a, which must be imagined as filled with a scatter of data points. Presumably, the null-case treatment-group data points are also included in the ellipse since the treatment group is part of this population, but we cannot be entirely sure of that because the treatment group was in actuality removed as a nonrandom sample. The more typical the treatment group is of the remaining population, the more its null-case data points will be represented by other subjects within the ellipse.

Assume that the actual treatment-group outcome is at the point Y_E in Figure 8–1a, or the same point $\hat{Y}_E$ in Figures 8–1b, c, and d. Since this actual outcome is well outside of the ellipse representing *null-case* outcomes in the population, we would like to infer that there has been a treatment effect. How large can we estimate the effect to be? The answer depends on how typical the treatment group really is. It started out at the point X_{1E} in Figure 8–1a or at the mean $\bar{X}_{1E}$ in the other three plots in Figure 8–1. If it is exactly average for subjects in the population with that starting point, it would have ended right on the regression line, at the null-case estimate labeled $\hat{Y}_{0E}$. The magnitude of the treatment effect would then be $\bar{Y}_E - \hat{Y}_{0E}$. Since the treatment group is a nonrandom sample, however, we may not have complete faith that it is exactly average so that we must impose a conservative hedge on our estimate.

To do so, we first pick a point to be called the outlier point. All subjects with Y scores further from the center than this point we will call outliers. This point will function quite analogously to a confidence level in classical inference. If we were to pick the 2.5 percent point as the outlier point, we would fix it such that 2.5 percent of the population with a given X_1 starting point had Y scores that were further distant from the regression line than our point (that location would be 1.96 error standard deviations from the population regression line, as represented by the comparison group [$1.96s_{uC}$], assuming that the error were normally distributed). Let us assume the 2.5 percent outlier point for convenience. It will mean that we risk a 2.5 percent chance of error in our inferences so that a different point might be chosen if a different level of risk were preferred.

Perhaps the major point at which the random-comparison-group design is weaker than experimental design is in the necessity to assume a certain percentage of the treatment group that would have ended beyond the outlier point in the null case. That is, it is necessary to assume the percentage that would, even without the treatment, have had such favorable Y scores that they would have been among the most advantaged 2.5 percent of the population anyway, some of them perhaps even falling outside the boundary of the observed population ellipse. If we were to assume that exactly 2.5 percent of the treatment group would have fallen beyond the population outlier point, just as in the population itself, that would be tantamount to assuming that the treatment group is a random sample. We cannot do that; we must be a bit more conservative. Thus, presumptive reasoning enters not only in the rejection of contamination as an explanation of the outcome, as in experimental design, but also in the assumption of a certain percentage of null-case outliers. That assumption, however, can

FIGURE 8–1   Interval estimates of program effect

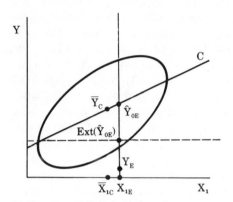

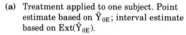

(a) Treatment applied to one subject. Point estimate based on $\hat{Y}_{0E}$; interval estimate based on $\mathrm{Ext}(\hat{Y}_{0E})$.

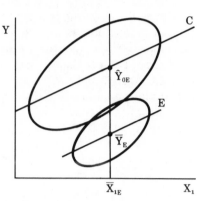

(b) Observed outcome; treatment applied to an experimental group.

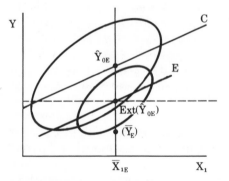

(c) Null case presumed for outcome in 8-1b when estimation is by Equation 8-3.

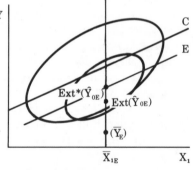

(d) Null case assumed for outcome in 8-1b when estimation is by Equation 8-4.

E:	Experimental group	
C:	Comparison group	
X_1	Pretest	
Y	Posttest	
$\hat{Y}_{0E}$:	Estimated null-case experimental-group outcome, with E treated as though it were a randomly <u>chosen</u> group having pretest score $\overline{X}_{1E}$.	

$\mathrm{Ext}(\hat{Y}_{0E})$:	Extreme $(\hat{Y}_{0E})$. Conservatively estimated null-case experimental-group outcome.
$\mathrm{Ext}^{*}(\hat{Y}_{0E})$:	Not quite so conservatively estimated null-case experimental-group outcome.

be quite a conservative one and can be guided substantially by empirical data.

If there were only a single subject in the treatment group, as depicted in Figure 8–1a, it would be quite legitimate to worry that the individual concerned might have been an extreme outlier in the null case—might have ended right on the border of the ellipse, perhaps, or even at Y_E itself. Clearly, little or no treatment effect could then be inferred. One subject, after all, might have ended anywhere. If there is a sizable treatment group, however, with variance in its Y scores, it becomes quite far-fetched to assume that essentially the whole group are null-case outliers—a large bump on the null-case population ellipse as in Figure 8–1b. What is needed is a conservative, but not needlessly crippling assumption. For the assumption that fully half of the treatment group would have been outliers, which is extremely conservative but would still frequently allow an inference of treatment effect, the null case would appear as in Figure 8–1c. For the assumption of only 10 percent outliers, which, given that the selection of a population has followed the guidelines suggested in the previous section, is still quite conservative but reasonably so, the null case would appear as in Figure 8–1d. With a normal distribution of error terms, and considering that the whole population has been measured for the comparison group, each of the three assumptions we have mentioned is connected with an estimate of treatment effect as follows (if a random sample is used rather than the whole population, another very small factor is needed in the estimates; see Mohr 1982a; Jackson and Mohr 1986; and Johnston 1972, pp. 153–154).

Taking the first of the three, if it is assumed that the treatment group is essentially a random sample of the measured population, then the following is a point estimate of the true treatment effect, β_T (actually, with this unlikely assumption, Equation 7–7 or 7–9 could be used, as though this were an experimental design; Equations 8–2 through 8–2b are nevertheless presented here as a necessary foundation for the models to follow):

(8–2)
$$b'_T = \bar{Y}_E - \hat{Y}_{0E,}$$

(8–2a)
$$\hat{Y}_{0E} = a + b_1\bar{X}_{1E,}$$

where a and b_1 are the estimates of α and β_1 derived from applying Equation 8–2b to the comparison group alone:

(8–2b)
$$Y_i = \alpha + \beta_1 X_{1i} + u_i.$$

These three equations instruct the analyst to: (1) regress Y on X_1 in the comparison group alone (Equation 8–2b); (2) apply the estimates a and b_1 so derived to the treatment group's starting point, $\bar{X}_{1E}$, to obtain an estimate of the counterfactual (Equation 8–2a); (3) subtract this estimate from the actual treatment-group outcome to obtain the estimate of the treatment effect (Equation 8–2).

Second, if it is assumed that 50 percent of the treatment group would have been outliers on the favorable side in the null case, then the following is the *interval* estimate of treatment effect implied:

$$(8\text{--}3) \qquad |b_T| \geq |\bar{Y}_E - \text{Ext}(\hat{Y}_{0E})|,$$

$$(8\text{--}3a) \qquad \text{Ext}(\hat{Y}_{0E}) = \hat{Y}_{0E} \pm 1.96s_{uC},$$

where $\text{Ext}(\hat{Y}_{0E})$ is read as Extreme $\hat{Y}_{0E}$, s_{uC} means error standard deviations in the comparison-group regression of Y on X_1, and $\pm$ must be *either* plus *or* minus as needed to place the outlier point at the top or bottom of the ellipse, whichever is the favorable side. The standard error of the comparison-group regression s_{uC} is our basis for setting the outlier point: assuming a normal distribution of errors, we move out 1.96 error standard deviations from the line to establish the point where 2.5 percent of the *population* remain yet further away. Equation 8–3a sets the null-case *treatment group* mean $\text{Ext}(\hat{Y}_{0E})$ at this point so that half the weight of the treatment-group disturbance terms is closer in, half further out. Figure 8–1c depicts the null case under this assumption and shows the elements of the right-hand side of Equation 8–3, which expresses the *minimum* size of the estimated treatment effect (minimum in that the true effect will be greater than the right-hand side of Equation 8–3 when the treatment group is actually more average or representative than is stipulated by the rather extreme assumption of 50 percent outliers).

Finally, if it is assumed that 10 percent of the treatment group would have been outliers in the null case, then the minimum magnitude of the treatment effect is larger than that given by Equation 8–3, but still smaller than that given by Equation 8–2, and the following is the interval estimate implied:

$$(8\text{--}4) \qquad |b_T{}^*| \geq |\bar{Y}_E - \text{Ext}^*(\hat{Y}_{0E})|,$$

$$(8\text{--}4a) \qquad \text{Ext}^*(\hat{Y}_{0E}) = \text{Ext}(\hat{Y}_{0E}) \pm 1.28s_{uE},$$

where s_{uE} means error standard deviations in the treatment group regression and $\pm$ must be either plus or minus as needed to bring $\text{Ext}^*(\hat{Y}_{0E})$ back in closer to the center of the ellipse than $\text{Ext}(\hat{Y}_{0E})$. Error standard deviations of the *treatment group* s_{uE} are used because the function of this term is to move the treatment-group ellipse toward the center, to the point where 10 percent of *its* errors stick out beyond the outlier point. Figure 8–1d depicts the null case under this assumption and enables the right-hand side of Equation 8–4 to be read as the minimum size of the treatment effect.

Looking at the representations in Figure 8–1, it is clear that the distance of the true outcome $\bar{Y}_E$ from the border of the ellipse is crucial for the ability to infer a treatment effect. If $\bar{Y}_E$ is far above or below the ellipse, even the extremely conservative assumption behind Equation 8–3 will enable a sizable treatment effect to be inferred with confidence. If $\bar{Y}_E$ is close to the border or inside the ellipse itself, even the less conservative assumption of 10 percent outliers would pick up only a small effect or none at all. Two factors control the distance concerned. The first is the true magnitude of the treatment effect. If it is very large, sending $\bar{Y}_E$ far beyond the level of posttest scores experienced in the population in the absence of the treatment, even the extremely conservative assumption will discover it. The other factor—perhaps not so obvious—is the vertical size of the population ellipse, that is, the magnitude of the error variance of the regression or, in other words, the accuracy with which Y is predicted from X_1. For a given fixed location of $\bar{Y}_E$ (as in Figure 8–1, for example), the critical distance would be comfortably large if the ellipse were very narrow in the vertical dimension, but it would become small to nonexistent for fatter and fatter ellipses. A small ellipse, that is a small error variance in the regression, is produced by having effective explanatory variables. One way to increase the R^2 (improve the explanation), is to add variables; any variables that can be measured and that will help the R^2 should on these grounds be included. The other way is to have *good* variables. The pretest, in this perspective, is critical. Predicting after from before may be of little interest in theoretical science, but it can be of great value in program evaluation because the prediction is likely to be extremely accurate, thus upgrading the power or sensitivity of certain designs. This is another manifestation of the same sensitivity function of the pretest we encountered in Chapter Four. Provided that the comparison group is trustworthy, as in experiments or in the random-comparison-group design, a good prediction from a pretest will have the effect of making the analysis sensitive to quite small treatment effects, even with fairly conservative assumptions. The other side of the coin is the following: Because one must make a conservative assumption to cover possible selection bias in the treatment group, the random-comparison-group design is not likely to be satisfactory unless a good prediction of Y scores in the comparison group is obtained from a pretest or other equally satisfactory variables.

Jackson and Mohr (1986) applied the random-comparison-group design to a housing subsidy program administered by the Department of Housing and Urban Development (HUD). The treatment group consisted of disadvantaged families in eight cities, picked on a nonrandom basis by the department. The comparison group was a random sample of similarly disadvantaged families taken from the Annual Housing Survey, a national housing census also conducted by HUD. Pretest scores on outcome measures such as rent, rent burden, housing quality, and crowding were quite strongly related to the posttests, in the range of $R^2 = .5$ to $.8$, so that a fairly sensitive analysis was possible. Many items of data indicated that the treatment group was tantamount to a random sample of the population but, as a necessary hedge, the conservative assumption of 10 percent outliers was applied. Noteworthy treatment effects were found on some of the outcomes of interest but not others. To illustrate the sort of inferential statement that one makes on the basis of the random-comparison-group design, the following conclusion from the housing subsidy evaluation may be cited:

> Assuming that as many as 10 percent of the treatment group might have been population outliers on the favorable side—i.e., beyond the $-.025$ level without the treatment—one may say with 97.5 percent confidence that one of the effects of the program was to lower average rent paid by $43.18 or more. (Jackson and Mohr 1986, p. 505)

It was possible to corroborate at least tentatively the accuracy of the findings and the conclusions based on them by putting together the results of a number of former studies, each smaller and less rigorous in design than the random-comparison-group study. No other applications of the random-comparison-group design have been reported to date, but experience with this first example was encouraging.

THREATS TO VALIDITY

Internal Validity

Since this is a comparison-group design, the most important threat to internal validity is selection bias. Selection-P effects are neutralized if there is a pretest, which there will almost always have to be if the design is to have sufficient sensitivity to make up for the conservative estimation technique. Selection-Q bias in the treatment group, and therefore contamination due to assignment, may remain; it is blunted and in many cases effectively neutralized by the use of interval estimates based on conservative assumptions regarding null-case outliers. This sort of estimation device is made possible by selecting the comparison group as a population of concern that includes the treatment group so that the scatterplot of the treatment-group regression may be included in the scatterplot for the comparison group. We will see in Chapter Ten that this property of the random-comparison-group design, that is, its particular sort of strength against selection-Q bias, provides a defense against one of the most formidable problems in program evaluation, namely, the problem of working with *volunteer* subjects.

History is not a threat in this case because the design is a comparison-group design. However, contamination due to the treatment and faulty controls does of course pose a threat to the random-comparison-group design, just as it does to experimental and other designs.

Random measurement error in the pretest is in principle a problem here just as it is in design 5, the comparative-change design. The fact of random measurement error means that something is left out, some piece of the true X_1 score, and if that piece is related to the treatment variable, this misspecification leads to a selection-Q bias. In the case of design 5, it was noted that such selection-Q bias may in fact matter little because the regression model is generally quite underspecified anyway so that there must already be the fear of essentially unmanageable selection bias from whole omitted variables. In the case of the random-comparison-group design, random measurement error may similarly cause selection effects, but unless the measurement error is very severe, the bias is accounted for by the conservative estimation techniques; these are, after all, designed to hedge against any selection bias remaining after application of the device of selecting the comparison group at random from the population of concern.

Interaction

Using the experimental R-comparative-change design, we saw in connection with Equation 7–9 that, if the two within-group slopes of Y on X_1 are different, an interaction model should be applied. In that case, the treatment effect is $(\beta_T + \beta_2 X_1)$, rather than β_T for all subjects regardless of X_1 score. Thus, differences in slope present no problem for experimental design. In design 5, the ordinary comparative-change design, when there is a difference in the within-group slopes it is unclear whether that difference results from interaction, selection-Q bias, or some of both. Interaction may thus present a major problem. Unfortunately, the random-comparison-group design is closer to design 5 in this respect than to design 12. The random comparison group minimaxes selection effects in slopes just as it does for intercepts, but any remaining difference between the observed within-group slopes is ambiguous in origin; it may be due to interaction, in which case the treatment effect is $(\beta_T + \beta_2 X_1)$, or to selection bias, in which case the true treatment effect equals β_T for all subjects regardless of X_1 score. Unlike design 5, however, the inference of mean intercept effect in the random-comparison-group design is firmly based; therefore, if there is a substantial difference in within-group slopes in the data, one is not faced with the dire prospect of giving up the analysis altogether. Rather, building on the foundation of a firm estimate of β_T, it is advisable to use the bracketing technique (Gramlich 1981): one presents *both* of these estimates of treatment effect, β_T and $(\beta_T + \beta_2 X_1)$, so that they become the boundaries between which the true effect for any individual subject is to be found.

External Validity

External validity is more solidly founded in the random-comparison-group design than in most others. First and foremost, one has a definite rather than a completely vague population to which, at a minimum, the results of the study are to be generalized. One would always be in this position when both the treatment and comparison groups are drawn from a single, larger population, but in no other case is that sort of selection built into the structure of the design itself. The quality of the generalization, of course, depends on following the rules, given earlier, for selecting the comparison population, so that the experimental group is made to be as representative as possible in the absence of random sampling. Second, one has a basis for generalizing that is similar to the basis one would have with a randomly chosen treatment group, but weaker in two respects: (*a*) the assumption of a certain percentage of null-case outliers, and (*b*) the solidity of the ground under an inference of interaction involving measured variables. The interaction concern is central to external validity; *interaction* is the statistical term for whether the treatment affects different subjects to different degrees. If the comparison group were a random sample from the whole population of concern and the treatment group were another random sample from the same population so that the design were a true experiment, one would appropriately generalize the precise treatment effect inferred in the study—point or interval estimate, with or without interaction with measured variables—to all the balance of the population. If the treatment interacted with a variable *not* measured, one's generalization would be wrong in the case of some individuals or groups: prediction from means is never correct for *all* individuals. Such a design is optimal, but rare. With a nonrandom treatment group and analysis based on the random-comparison-group design, the same benefits actually obtain except that (*a*) the treatment effect generalized is an interval estimate with a minimum, as in Equation 8–3 or 8–4, based on a given assumption about the percentage of null-case outliers, and (*b*) if apparently meaningful differences in within-group slopes are observed, the bracketing technique described in the previous section would be used as the basis of a tentative generalization of interaction effects. The tentativeness results from the uncertainty still remaining, and not covered by bracketing, that some interaction with measured variables just might happen to be hidden by offsetting selection effects. Interaction with unmeasured variables could, of course, lead to error just as in the completely random case, but the ground is much better here, given the intentional subgroup-to-group relationship, than when the observed subjects are special groups, such as freshman psychology students, people who answer an advertisement, or just subjects who are handy. Thus, the content of generalizations would be neither as precise nor as sound as under totally random selection, but then (1) it is so much stronger than the basis for the content of a generalization associated with designs 3, 4, and 5 as to be in a qualitatively different category; (2) the degree of precision with the random-comparison-group design may in many cases be quite satisfactory; (3) there is in this case a definite population to which to generalize, something that in practice is almost always lacking in the implementation of other basic designs, including not only designs 3, 4, and 5, but experimental designs as well; and (4) while the treatment group is not made to be representative by random sampling, it is devised to be as representative as possible by careful stipulation of the comparison population.

CONCLUSION

In conclusion, it may be observed that the random-comparison-group design has its relative weaknesses, particularly the need to hedge against a specific percentage of null-case outliers and the ambiguity that might still remain concerning interaction effects. Nevertheless, when experimental design is not feasible or for some reason not desirable, this design has a great deal to recommend it over the traditional strictly quasi-experimental approach; there is little reason to select just any convenient comparison group when a random comparison group is a feasible option, as it frequently will be.

One further type of improvement on quasi-experimental design remains to be discussed in Chapter Eleven.

Chapter Nine

Time-Series Designs

It was noted in the last chapter, that one way of improving on the before-after design would be to obtain additional observations over time both before and after the treatment to create a time series. Intuitively, faith in our presumption that the treatment rather than history is the cause of some observed change should be increased if we see the kinds of patterns in the outcome measure that history has tended to produce in the past and observe that the change after the treatment is a noticeable departure from those patterns. History in its various forms still remains a threat to internal validity, but it becomes more far-fetched, not so severe. That is why a time-series design in any of its various possible forms is classified as a quasi-experimental design, and not an elementary quasi-experimental design.

One might expect that an additional and very substantial improvement could be made by introducing a comparative time series, that is, a comparison group for which the same sort of time series data are available as are observed in the experimental group (or unit). That way, the threat of history would seem to be dispelled altogether. That is true enough in the technical sense, but one still is left with the possibility of divergent history, especially by assignment or selection-Q effects, and these are severe enough in the time-series context to make it questionable whether one gains much by introducing the additional data.

In this chapter, we will first consider the ordinary interrupted-time-series design before concluding with an exploration of the comparative-time-series design. Time-series analysis is a highly technical subject area on which much has been written both of great importance and great complexity. The treatment that follows will be oriented toward an appreciation of the primary ideas and issues for program evaluation rather than the sophisticated techniques of analysis that will often be required. It is therefore assumed that the reader who wishes to carry out such an analysis will have the aid both of a good computer package and either advanced technical skills or competent consultation.

THE INTERRUPTED-TIME-SERIES DESIGN

As is the case with the before-after design, the counterfactual here is derived from measurements on the treatment group or unit over an earlier period of time. In this case, there are a good many such observations before and also preferably after the point of treatment or, as it is more often called in this context, the intervention. Time-series analysis for program evaluation differs from standard time-series analysis by the existence and importance of this intervention point, which is reflected by the term *Interrupted* in the title of the design.

The impact of the intervention in the interrupted-time-series design is, as always, indicated by the difference between the observed result and the counterfactual. It would rarely be calculated in that way, but the meaning of the impact coefficient(s) is still the same. Obtaining the counterfactual presents no conceptual problem in this design, although it might be quite a complicated technical task. The counterfactual is a projection of the correctly modeled before series into the time periods occurring after the intervention point. If, for example, the time series were a straight, upwardly sloping line, the counterfactual would simply be an extension of the before line beyond the intervention point, as shown by the dashed line in Figure 9–1. The idea of result is, of course, even more straightforward and clear conceptually, being the Y outcomes actually observed after the intervention point. One possible example is also shown in Figure 9–1—a straight line starting a few points higher than would a simple extension and having a somewhat steeper slope than the before series.

It might be said that the individual data points in a cross-sectional design, such as design 5 or design 12, have little importance in themselves. Their primary conceptual function in an analysis is their contribution to aggregate summaries of themselves, such as their mean, a regression line, an error variance, and so forth. That is not the case in time series. There, each individual data point is a part of a process— part of a story, as it were, about what happens to Y as time marches on. Because of that, the impact of a program is not so clear a concept here as it has been in earlier chapters, even though neither the result nor the counterfactual may be at all ambiguous. The problem lies in choosing how much of the detailed story of the difference between the result and the counterfactual to include in a description of the impact. Let us approach both the idea of the description of a time series and

FIGURE 9–1   The counterfactual series; the result series

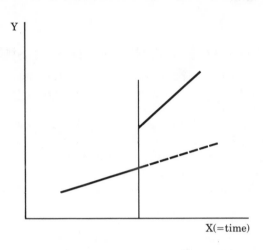

the description of an intervention effect by contrasting time series with simple before-and-after analysis.

One might reduce an available, interrupted time series to two points, one somewhat before the intervention and the other somewhat after, as in Figure 9–2a so that each series consisted in a single point and the inferred impact would be the difference between the two. If the before-after difference were appreciably greater than zero, for example, one would no doubt be tempted to infer that the intervention had had an effect. Having complete time series data available, however, and assuming for illustration that the data took the form of a continuous line, as in Figure 9–2b, it is clear that basing an intervention effect on the difference in two points would be naive: the series shows a trend upward over time, and the after point is precisely where knowledge of this trend would predict it should be without any effect of the intervention whatever. Clearly then in describing the intervention effect, one must take account of the magnitude and direction of the underlying trend of the series over time.

Another kind of error in reducing an interrupted time series to a difference between two points would occur if the series resembled Figure 9–2c. Time series are rarely perfectly straight lines. Usually, they are oscillating lines; they wander up and down to picture a general trend, but with a continuing pattern of departures from it. Departures from an understood pattern or trend are generally called error or noise.

FIGURE 9–2   Time-series analysis compared with analysis of two time points

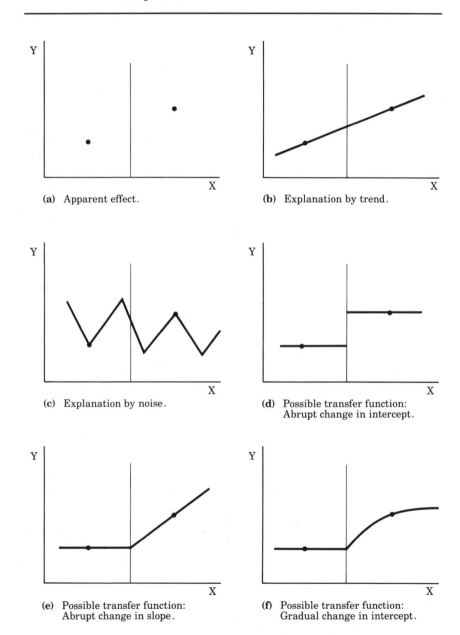

(a) Apparent effect.

(b) Explanation by trend.

(c) Explanation by noise.

(d) Possible transfer function: Abrupt change in intercept.

(e) Possible transfer function: Abrupt change in slope.

(f) Possible transfer function: Gradual change in intercept.

Completely random error is called white noise. Taking into account the established pattern of departures from a flat line in Figure 9–2c, it is again highly likely that the treatment had no effect; the difference between the two points would seem to result simply from taking observations at different locations in the regular pattern of noise. Another way of expressing the same idea is to say that the Y score for the point after the intervention is not surprisingly high because the noise pattern incorporates that level as a fairly common occurrence. Thus, one will also want to include the noise in a description of the series.

Even if one knew that the trend were flat and that the noise were small in amplitude, the two-point characterization of treatment effect could still be naive. Consider, for example, the differences in Figures 9–2d, e, and f. In the first case, there has been a simple, abrupt change in intercept. In the second, there has been an abrupt change in slope; the after point is quickly left far behind and therefore has little intrinsic meaning. In the third, the after point occurs part way through the process of a gradual change from one intercept or level of stationarity to another. The three are so different in their implications that one would want to describe each as fully as possible. When expressed mathematically in the context of the interrupted-time-series design, these various outcomes are a few examples of what are called transfer functions. The label is neutral in the important sense that its terminology makes it refer only to the empirical change in the time series after the intervention point. The cause of the change, whether the treament or history or both, is quite another issue that must be considered once the transfer function has been adequately characterized.

Thus, to determine the change in the time series it is necessary first to model both the time trend and the noise; then, to characterize the change, one must be prepared to use a varied array of descriptions both of slopes and intercepts. There are three methods in common use for taking account of trend and noise and for characterizing the change in the series. One is visual analysis—just "eyeballing" the graph of the raw data, arriving at a subjective conclusion about the existence, magnitude, and nature of the change, if any, and possibly supporting the conclusion by reading off a few numbers directly from the axes of the graph. This is a relatively good method. More will be said about how good once some of the quantitative issues in estimation have been considered. A second method is regression analysis, although we will see that the simplest type of parameter estimation, ordinary least squares, is not so likely to be appropriate for the interrupted-time-series design as it is for the designs covered previously. Lastly, there is ARIMA modeling, a less versatile and more esoteric technique than regression analysis, but one whose utility in this context is bringing it into increasingly common use.

Regression Analysis

The simplest form of regression model for analyzing interrupted-time-series data would have the standard assumptions of ordinary-least-squares regression and the following specific equation:

$$(9\text{--}1) \qquad Y_t = \alpha + \beta X_t + \beta_T T_t + u_t.$$

Here, we follow the standard practice of using the subscript t which indicates individual time periods rather than i as employed in cross-sectional analysis to indicate individual subjects. The variable T is, as usual, the treatment dummy, in this case scored 0 for all periods in the before series and 1 for all periods after the intervention point; β_T is then still the treatment effect, in this case the difference in intercept, or the vertical space between the lines representing the before and after series. The regression line involved is the plot of Y, the outcome of interest—the time series whose possible change due to the treatment we are investigating—on X, which represents time—scored, for example, as 1 for the first period (year, month, quarter, etc.) of the series, 2 for the second, and so on consecutively through the intervention point to the last period for which data are being used. The disturbance term u is assumed to be randomly distributed to the periods in the series.

In the representation of Equation 9–1, the trend is expressed by the coefficient β on the time variable, X. A coefficient of 2, for example, would mean simply that Y goes up two units each period. Using this simple model, we are therefore anticipating a linear trend over time, but a curvilinear trend could easily be accommodated by introducing terms in X^2 or other powers of X, as is frequently done in regression analysis to accommodate curvilinearity. With X in the equation as a control variable, β_T represents the treatment effect once the trend over time has been accounted for.

The transfer function for the treatment in this simple model is β_T; the effect of the treatment is expressed entirely as an abrupt change in intercept, or level of the series, as in Figure 9–2d. If it were desired to accommodate a possible change in slope, as well, that could be accomplished in straightforward fashion by adding an interaction term to the equation:

$$(9\text{--}2) \qquad Y_t = \alpha + \beta X_t + \beta_T T_t + \beta_2 X_t T_t + u_t.$$

This equation now accommodates the kinds of result depicted in Figures 9–1 and 9–2e. The interaction term $\beta_2 X_t T_t$ will be zero before the intervention (where $T = 0$) so that the mathematical characterization of the before series is left exactly as it was in Equation 9–1. The basic change in level may be read as the difference between the expected value of Y in the first period after the intervention point based on a simple projection of the before series, and the expected value of Y in the same period based on the estimation of Equation 9–2 from the data at hand (see, for example, Lewis-Beck 1979, p. 1143). Alternatively, and much more simply, the intervention point may be set at $X = 0$ (with negative values of X for the before series), by which device the intercept change may be read directly as β_T. Whereas the slope of Y on time in the interaction model is β alone before the intervention, it changes to $(\beta + \beta_2)$ afterwards. Thus, setting the intervention point at $X = 0$, the transfer function comprises an intercept change of β_T and a change in slope of β_2, and the treatment effect at any point X_t after the intervention is equal to $(\beta_T + \beta_2 X_t)$. In impact analyses, it is rare to find more complex transfer functions discussed for the regression approach than the one given by the interaction model of Equation 9–2.

In the present treatment of regression analysis for the interrupted-time-series design, the noise component has been left for last because it is the most troublesome. First, the noise—defined as the departures of the Y scores from their simple regression on time—can be reduced by introducing further explanatory variables: X_2, X_3, and so forth. Note that each must be in time-series form, covering essentially the same periods of time. It may well be that the departures of X_2 from its trend line do cause the departures in Y, so that a year in which disposable income is especially high, for example, may be a year in which consumer spending is also especially high. The noise in a series tracing traffic density on the interstate system might be substantially reduced by introducing variables representing income and gasoline prices. Some noise, however, and generally most noise, will inevitably remain. To have an accurate and statistically useful quantitative estimate of the effect of the intervention, it is essential to have an accurate model of the disturbance term in the regression equation—the remaining noise. A noise model always contains assumptions. In particular, if one assumes that the individual disturbance terms are independent of one another, one program-effect estimate will be obtained, but if one assumes them to be correlated, or dependent on one another in some fashion, a different estimate may well result. As all elementary treatments of time series analysis explain, disturbances in the time series context (as contrasted with much cross-sectional analysis) are highly likely to be correlated, that is, given any period t departures from the trend line in near-neighboring periods u_{t+1}, u_{t+2}, and so forth, or in seasonally repetitive periods, for example, u_{t+12} in a monthly series, are unlikely to be random with respect to u_t. Such models are said to contain autocorrelation. The ordinary-least-squares regression model, however, assumes independent, random disturbances—the absence of autocorrelation.

Elementary treatments also emphasize (*a*) that ordinary-least-squares estimators are unbiased in the presence of autocorrelation, but (*b*) that their variances tend to understate the true variances—the variances as they would be if the autocorrelation were taken correctly into account. It is appropriate to stop and consider what these terms mean in the evaluation context. First, to say that our estimator b_T is unbiased means that, even in the presence of autocorrelation, if the disturbances were dealt out to the time periods over and over for an infinite number of iterations, the mean of the infinite number of b_Ts we calculated would be the true parameter β_T. In other words, any b_T we obtain tends on the average to be correct. That is perhaps comforting, but bear in mind that it does not solve our primary problem, which is the threat of history: the coefficient may tend on the average to be correct, but it is uncertain whether it represents the effect of the intervention, some external event occurring at about the same time, some preexisting condition that begins to make itself felt at about the same time, or some mixture of these.

Next, turn to the issue of understated variance. One implication is that with a deflated variance, it will be much easier than it should be to get a statistically significant result. To place this apparent problem in perspective, we must again bear in mind that significance tests may be quite a minor matter; in the econometric-modeling function of significance testing, the model must be correctly specified; in the interrupted-time-series context, however, one must in general assume that there may be misspecification due to the omission of external events or other forms of history. That means that a significance test on the treatment coefficient is rather pointless. Thus, with an underestimated variance, the significance test might easily mislead us into considering the result statistically significant when in fact it is not, but since statistical significance tells us very little about the causal impact of the intervention anyway, it is of relatively small concern. What is truly needed is the confidence, which cannot legitimately come from statistics, that whatever change did occur was due to the treatment and not to something else.

The more serious side of the implications of an understated variance for classical statistical inference has to do with confidence intervals. We may be fooling ourselves on accuracy. If the variance of the estimate is in fact much larger than we think, then even though b_T is unbiased over infinitely many trials, our own particular b_T is untrustworthy because, on the average, it is far from the mark. Now, we may not know what the coefficient of supposed treatment effect *means* (in the causal sense), but it would at least be convenient to know what it *is*. Otherwise, it is hard to see that constructive thinking about analysis can even begin.

Just to begin, then, and bearing in mind that even precise estimation leaves the causality question unaddressed, it would be well to neutralize the effects of autocorrelation. In fact, it is relatively easy to tell whether autocorrelation is present or not (see, for example, the Durbin-Watson test presented in most texts and the more elaborate diagnostic techniques that are part of ARIMA modeling), but it is not at all an easy matter to get rid of it. Commonly, it is advocated that some form of generalized-least-squares estimation be employed in the presence of autocorrelation rather than ordinary least squares. To do so, however, requires developing a model of the dependencies among the disturbances terms, either based on good theory or previous knowledge, which are generally lacking, or based on the actual data at hand. Either way, however, it is possible, and indeed common, that autocorrelation cannot be adequately managed by regression techniques. The dependencies may not be easily modeled. If tests show that there is no autocorrelation in one's interrupted time series, it would seem reasonable to have available *both* a visual analysis and easily obtained, reliable, quantitative calculations of the coefficients—whatever their causal meaning may be (see, for example, Mazur-Hart and Berman 1979, or Lewis-Beck 1979, where most of the above elements of regression analysis for the interrupted-time-series design are exemplified in the absence of autocorrelation). If, however, as will frequently be the case, the autocorrelation persists, or takes an elaborate modeling effort to reduce, the benefit of the regression analysis comes into serious question. Is it better than visual analysis alone? Let us consider that issue in the following sections.

Visual Analysis

The true alternative to generalized-least-squares analysis or ARIMA modeling in the presence of autocorrelation is not ordinary regression. It is difficult to think why one would prefer quantification that is likely to be inaccurate to quantification that is more accurate, even if the former takes less time and trouble. The truly serious alternative is no statistically modeled quantification at all, but just the inspection of the graph of the series. By visual inspection, one usually (not always) obtains quite an immediate and strong impression of trend just by noting whether the series seems flat or moves generally up or down over time. In the same way, one has an impression of the noise component from looking at the amplitude of the oscillations. The transfer function is assessed by using a vertical line at the intervention point and looking separately at the before and after series. One notes whether the same trend has carried over from before to after and whether there seems to be a change in the overall level of the series that occurs at the intervention point or a bit later. If the change is small and even somewhat uncertain, one must mistrust it. If a moderately large change is evident, however, it is unlikely that a statistical adjustment for autocor-

FIGURE 9–3   Visual analysis of well-behaved series

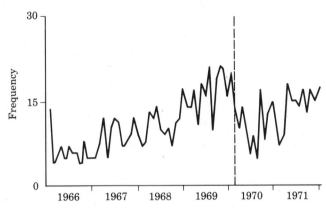

(a) The change in level is 8.59.

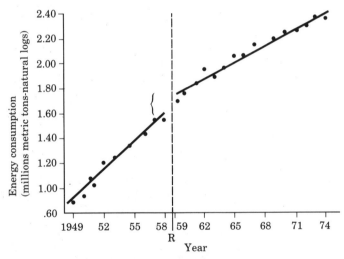

(b) The change in level is .089; in slope, −.032.

Source: (**a**) F. E. Zimring, "Firearms and Federal Law: The Gun Control Act of 1968," *Journal of Legal Studies,* 1975, p. 189.

Source: (**b**) Michael S. Lewis-Beck, "Some Economic Effects of Revolution," *American Journal of Sociology* (March 1979), p. 1142.

relation would erase it; one would then proceed to probe the issue of its cause—treatment or history.

Furthermore, if an interrupted time series does not contain a great deal of noise and does not present definite or possible changes of slope,

FIGURE 9–4   Series in which changes in level or slope or both are difficult to estimate by visual analysis

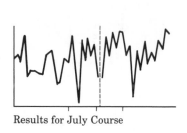

Results for July Course

(a)

Monthly average of hourly readings of O₃ (pphm) in downtown Los Angeles (1955-1972)*

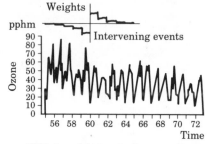

(b)   *With the weight function for estimating the effect of intervening events in 1960.

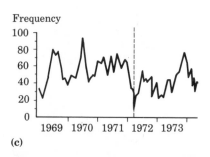

(c)

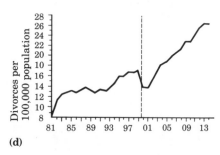

(d)

Sources: (**a**) Mary L. Smith, Roy Gabriel, James Schott, and William L. Padia, "Evaluation of the Effects of Outward Bound." In Gene V. Glass (ed.), *Evaluation Studies Review Annual* 1 (1976), p. 407. (**b**) George E. Box and George C. Tiao, "Intervention Analysis with Applications to Economic and Environmental Problems," *Journal of the American Statistical Association* 70, no. 349 (March 1975), p. 70. (**c**) Donald T. Campbell, "Focal Local Indicators for Social Program Evaluation," *Social Indicators Research*, 1976, p. 129. (**d**) G. V. Glass, G. C. Tiao, and T. O. McGuire, "Analysis of Data on the 1900 Revision of German Divorce Laws as a Time-Series Quasi-Experiment," *Law and Society Review*, 1971, p. 542.

it is a fairly simple matter to read the quantitative change in level, if any, from the axes of the graph (see, for example, Figure 9–3a). When the series is extremely well behaved, even a change of slope does not seriously undermine visual analysis, although the precise slope coefficients are not so easily estimated as the change in level (Figure 9–3b).

When the noise is marked, however, or changes in slope begin to complicate the transfer function, visual analysis begins to furrow the brow and visual quantification becomes hopelessly confused at worst or relegated to crude terms such as *quite small,* or *apparently greatly increased* at best (Figure 9–4). In practice, there are far too many cases in which visual inspection leaves the analyst in perplexity to give up the quest for a descriptive statistical quantification.

Nevertheless, visual analysis remains important. No matter what the coefficients of the transfer function, one's intuitive grasp of the series and the basis of one's insights into its implications are generally enhanced by a good look at the graph. Fortunately, one may almost always have both the numbers and the picture, and implementing an interrupted-time-series analysis in the absence of visual inspection may be putting oneself at an unnecessary disadvantage in understanding and interpreting the experiment.

ARIMA Modeling

The acronym stands for "Autoregressive, Integrated, Moving Average." The method as it applies to time series analysis in general was developed primarily in Box and Jenkins (1970), and the modifications necessary for adaptation to program evaluation were initiated at that time, with further development particularly in Box and Tiao (1975). Quite a full interpretation of the approach in terms of the needs and traditions of program evaluation was introduced by Glass et al. (1975). The goals of ARIMA modeling in the context of the interrupted-time-series design are the same as those of regression, namely, to establish the trend and get rid of or take account of the autocorrelation so that only white noise remains and a transfer function may be accurately estimated. One goes about it in a different way, however. Instead of introducing meaningful variables and relations into the equation to explain the pattern of the series insofar as possible, only past values of the series variable itself and of its disturbance term are employed as independent variables. This procedure eschews an *understanding* of the pattern in favor of a more reliable technique for reducing the residual to random movement. I am convinced that no brief treatment can equip a reader to undertake or even to critique an ARIMA analysis. Several weeks of training and practice are essential. Since this is not a technical manual and since ARIMA modeling, unlike regression, does not serve to illuminate the general concepts and principles of the broad spectrum of impact analyses for program evaluation, no effort will be made to develop here the fine points of the art.

As noted, the primary advantage of ARIMA modeling over regression modeling in context of the interrupted-time-series design is that it provides a nearly certain means of getting rid of autocorrelation. It will occur that a time series of one's outcome of interest can be reduced to white noise in regression analysis by the addition of control variables and/or the disturbance-modeling techniques appropriate to the generalized-least-squares procedure. In such cases, the choice of ARIMA or regression is mainly a matter of the analyst's preference. It should be noted that, if autocorrelation is present and is not easily and quickly eliminated, either technique represents a fair amount of trouble for what may sometimes be a relatively small gain over visual analysis. Having reliable numbers to accompany the visual inspection will generally make the effort worthwhile; what is needed is more widespread facility with the technology of interrupted-time-series analysis, so that the additional effort required becomes ever smaller.

THE COMPARATIVE-TIME-SERIES DESIGN

One approach to neutralizing the threat of history proceeds neither by presumptive reasoning nor by statistics, but by research design, that is, one adds a comparison group. In the present context, that translates into the addition of a comparison time series—a time series on the same outcome of interest, Y, but for a different unit from the one in which the intervention occurred or was introduced. One must conclude that it is better to consider a comparison series than not to have one available at all; nevertheless, the gain is not always large. There are two difficulties that tend to make the comparison-group approach less effective here than in the cross-sectional case (i.e., in cases such as the comparative-change or random-comparison-group designs). One difficulty concerns the techniques available for inferring the effect of the treatment based on the two groups or units; the other has to do with the seriousness of the remaining threats to validity. Let us examine the latter consideration first.

In principle, as we have reviewed several times, a comparison group neutralizes the effects of history; however, the threats of selection and divergent history arise to take its place. Primarily, the concern is that there may be selection-Q effects; one group may simply be different from the other in unmeasured characteristics that, whether directly or quite indirectly, affect the observed outcome. The term *indirectly* is meant primarily to reference the problem of divergent events, that is, the two might be different in some ways that make one but not the other prone to experience particular external events around the time of the intervention.

In the interrupted-time-series context, the selection-bias problem is compounded by the likelihood that the units observed will be single entities rather than groups. For example, one country might be compared with another, or one state with another, or one type of crime, one occupation, and so forth (examples of most of these may be found in Campbell 1977). The danger is that a single peculiarity may throw one or the other series off course around the time of the intervention, thus producing a biased impression of the intervention effect, whereas in a group of people or other subjects cross sectionally, a peculiarity connected with a single subject will be mitigated considerably by the experience of all the other subjects in the same group. In short, the subjects in time series analysis are time points, and because they are all descriptors of the same city, economy, occupational group, and so forth, there is a strong *dependence* among them; one event or preexisting characteristic can easily affect every subsequent score.

Even if the comparison series were derived from multiple units, such as one would have in comparing one state in the United States with all other states, the treatment group will rarely be more than a single unit. We saw in connection with the random-comparison-group design that a treatment *group* enables a less conservative inference than a single subject. In the same way here, but taking the other side of the coin, a peculiarity of the treatment unit might well have made it extreme within a population of its counterparts in the null case so that inference must be extremely conservative and the value of the comparison group becomes tenuous.

Let us now consider the first problem, that of the techniques available for bringing the comparison series into the estimation of treatment effect. In cross-sectional evaluations, using the R-comparative-change design or the regression-discontinuity design, for example, the data on the two groups are pooled in the calculations that yield the estimate of β_T (they are pooled automatically in the regression procedure). Even in the random-comparison-group design, the comparison-group slope estimates are employed to compute the treatment-group counterfactual. In comparative time-series analysis, pooling is highly problematic because one may be quite unwilling to assume that the processes producing the two time series are equivalent. The problem is not entirely dissimilar to that of design 5, where pooling may be illegitimate because one might be incorrect in assuming that the null-case slope of posttest on pretest is the same in both groups. Even there, however, because one tends to be concerned only with means, the problem is obviated if both groups start out at the same mean level on the pretest. In time-series analysis, however, every data point counts. Means over time periods are relatively useless. In the time-series context, "starting out at the same place" can only mean that the two series, aside from intervention effects, are generated by identical processes. Thus, time series may rarely be pooled with the thought that doubling the number of data points simply helps to determine the common parameters of the two series. Either the pooling cannot take place at all, or it must be done on some basis of less-than-complete similarity. Let us examine these two alternatives in turn.

Without question, some rough value may be derived from the comparison series by assuming that the possibly confounding effect of history is exactly the same in both series, even if their equations are different. Then, the data do not have to be pooled; the two series may be separately analyzed in their own terms, whether visually or statistically, and the raw changes in one after the intervention point may be compared with those in the other. That is, if we note that both the level and slope of the comparison series changed slightly after the period of intervention, we would expect the same external events to produce exactly the same changes in the experimental series, regardless of other differences between the two, and any difference in change would be attributed to the treatment (or to divergent history—a separate problem covered just above). Since history is just another form of intervention, that expectation is tantamount to expecting an intervention always to have the same effect—an unrealistic assumption in a great many cases. One would not, for example, expect a devaluation of the currency or a restriction of the money supply to have the same effect on inflation everywhere, regardless of the previous level or rate of increase in inflation. Nor would one expect the introduction of high-yield seed to produce the same increase in agricultural output in any country, regardless of the previous level of output and rate and direction of change. In effect, time series differ from one another for *reasons,* reasons that may interact with history to produce different effects in different series. If the two series are dissimilar, therefore, substantial caution must be exercised in inferring to one from the experience of the other, even assuming the same history in both. In short, a treatment and comparison series need not be pooled. They may be separately analyzed, even if different, but doing so involves the risky assumption that history produces the same effects on Y in both.

Methods for parameter estimation by the pooling of time series do exist, both in the regression framework (e.g., Kmenta 1971; Pindyck and Rubinfeld 1976) and ARIMA (Tiao and Box 1983), although their application to the interrupted-time-series design is not straightforward (see Berk et al. 1979; Glass et al. 1975; Lee 1986). In order for such methods to be more useful than the comparison of the two or more series after separate analysis, some sorts of connections between the series must be assumed to exist, either in their parameters or their disturbances. Lee (1986), for example, concludes that the logic and assumptions of pooled ARIMA modeling will usually suit the needs of program evaluation better than the logic and assumptions of pooled regression techniques. The reasoning regarding the existence and form of such connections and the modes of their introduction into the analysis become quite complex and are well beyond the intended scope of this book, but the gains from pooling over the comparison of separate series analyses may be substantial, so that, when it may be legitimately carried out, pooling is surely desirable. (For regression, an excellent introduction is available in Berk et al. 1979, and an illustrative

FIGURE 9–5   **Effect of introducing a law in the experimental state requiring repayment of welfare costs from the deceased recipient's estate on the old age assistance case loads—monthly data have all values expressed as a percentage of the case load eighteen months prior to the change of the law**

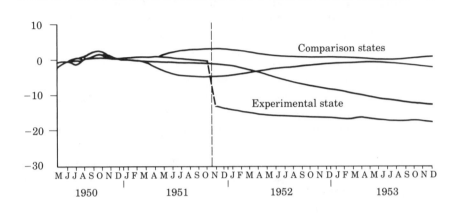

application of one approach in Moran 1985; for both regression and ARIMA, as well as a further application, see Lee 1986.)

Having now explored the ideas of the effects of history in a time series, the effects of the same history in two different time series, and the effects of divergent history in comparative time-series analysis, let us turn to a graphic overview of such problems by considering Figure 9–5. At first glance, it seems probable that the law introduced in the experimental state produced a substantial effect, and perhaps it did. At second glance, however, that inference is seen to depend heavily on which states are used for the comparison series. If only the two series that are uppermost by 1953 are used, the effect seems pronounced indeed. If all three are used, the effect still appears large because two out of the three comparison series are quite different from the experimental series. If only the third or lowest state were used, however, the inference would surely be in some doubt. It would appear then that the law brought about only a small effect in ultimate level, but hastened the pace of the fairly sizable change that would have occurred anyway. We see then how important the choice of comparison series can be; the trouble is that it is hard to tell from one's own data whether the comparison series is right or not. One's own data, after all, are all one has, and they show only similarities and differences, not right and wrong. Who knows, for example, what changes in inference might be induced by adding two or three *more* states to the analysis in Figure 9–5? At third glance, it is not even so easy to know what inference to make when all three states are used for comparison. Among the three—disregarding the experimental state—there appears to be an effect of divergent history. May not the experimental state merely be displaying a little more of the same sort of divergent history that occurred in comparison state 3? Taking a different perspective, if one had introduced the law into comparison state 3 and analyzed only that single series, one would have been prone to infer a slightly delayed but pronounced treatment effect, and if one had then compared this state with the first two, one would have become fairly certain of that inference. But one would have been wrong; the truth is that no such treatment was introduced in state 3 at all. Such are the possibilities, and confronting them in actual data such as these may with some justification introduce a fairly alarming degree of uncertainty into all interrupted-time-series analysis. In fact, Figure 9–5 is, from the perspective of the time-series analyst, rather a nightmare.

SUMMARY

In the end then, no matter how sophisticated the mode of analysis, informed presumptive reasoning about the likely possibilities must still play a role in both the interrupted- and comparative-time-series designs. The improvement over the before-after design is, in principle, huge: trends and noise are both taken into account and possessing an idea of the effects of *past* history constitutes a quantum leap in information on the possible effects of history at the intervention point. Nevertheless, sizable threats remain in principle; the time-series designs still have much in common with sister designs in the quasi-experimental category.

Chapter Ten

Ex-Post-Facto Evaluation Studies

The kind of study that is the focus of this chapter is rarely an intended design. It is, rather, what results when the experimenter has a lack of control over the design in a certain critical aspect, namely, the locus of selection. Unlike the one-shot case study, there is a built-in estimate of the counterfactual, so that the ex-post-facto design is a true impact-analysis design, but one must assign it to a category of lower power, in principle, than quasi-experimental design. As we will see, the ex-post-facto approach is extremely common, even though perhaps quite a bit softer than one would usually desire. It is important to have in mind, however, that every ex-post-facto evaluation study may be seen as having a quasi-experimental double, that is, there is always a design 4 or a design 5 underlying the ex-post-facto study, although it may at times not be clearly evident as such. It will generally be of substantial assistance to the critic or analyst to see the shadow quasi-experimental design and use it as a basis for thinking about threats to validity.

There are many differences between ex-post-facto studies and true quasi-experimental evaluations. A minor one is that, frequently, the subjects in ex-post-facto research will have any one in a large range of degrees or quantities of the treatment, rather than being scored only 0 or 1—receiving the treatment or not. Two of the more major differences are the following: the selection into treatments is decentralized rather than centralized, which is the defining characteristic of this design, and, as a consequence of that, spuriousness and time order become the focus of threats to internal validity rather than selection effects as understood in connection with the designs presented previously.

THE EX-POST-FACTO DESIGN IN CONCEPT

The term *ex post facto* is perhaps not the most apt label for this design, but it is not misleading and it has the merit of having roots in Campbell and Stanley's original treatise (1963). Many different labels have been used, such as correlational, historical, and passive observation, but there is no real need to review or critique them. The most important thing to be said is that none of these labels, including ex post facto, has captured the essence of the difference between the supposedly distinct design so labeled and quasi-experimental design; the boundary has in general been left fuzzy. Of course, one is free to include under ex post facto (or any similar title) whatever design characteristics one chooses; it is only necessary in creating a classification that the categories be rigorously and productively distinct. Let us attempt, then, to pull together the major characteristics that have been associated with the idea of ex post facto.

Ex post facto is frequently understood to mean retrospectively documented. Often, it is correctly perceived that the time order of the occurrence of pretest, treatment, and posttest may be in doubt in this type of design (Judd and Kenny 1981). On the other hand, even if observations are made retrospectively, after all of the significant events have taken place, it is still quite possible to have ample evidence of the times of occurrence of these elements. We will return to this issue in a later section, but it would appear that time-order problems are better seen as being only occasionally problematic in retrospectively documented research and therefore not a basis for putting such research into a separate category.

A more basic culprit frequently singled out is manipulation. The experimenter is able to manipulate (i.e., apply and withhold) the treatment in a quasi-experimental study, but arrives too late—after the fact—in the ex-post-facto case, which is the derivation of the label. This criterion is not wide of the mark, but it does not quite hit it, and it will be worth a brief exploration to see why. First, it is clear that the presence or absence of experimenter manipulation does not consistently set impact analyses apart from one another. The treatment in interrupted-time-series designs, for example, is rarely implemented by the experimenter; it is usually a legislative act, sometimes occuring far in the past, such as the early drinking-and-driving laws in Scandinavia (Ross 1976), or a social movement such as the Cuban revolution (Lewis-Beck 1979), or some other externally generated or fortuitous event. Yet the interrupted time series is universally accepted as a quasi-experimental design. Nor is there experimenter manipulation in the so-called natural experiments, as, for example, when one studies dental caries in the children of communities with and without naturally fluoridated water supplies. In these cases, the evaluator definitely comes on the scene after the fact. It has never been clear just what the design status of the natural experiment is, yet they are generally considered quite strong. We will see that they are classic quasi-experimental designs. On the other side, in some studies, such as when groups are based on volunteering for the program or declining to do so, the experimenter may personally administer the treatment to every single subject but, in its essence, the design is still ex post facto. Consider the *Gentlemen's Agreement* study (Glock 1955). A survey of white Christians is carried out in Baltimore, including a pretest on anti-Semitism. The movie *Gentlemen's Agreement* is later shown, let us say in one theater. Later still, those who were pretested are contacted for a posttest on anti-Semitism and also asked whether they saw the movie. Manipulation of the treatment is showing the movie and is not at all ex post facto, yet, even if the experimenter had personally run the projector, the design can by no stretch be considered quasi experimental. The *volunteering* gives it a strong ex-post-facto cast, just as in any other correlational population survey, regardless of the clear manipulation.

Second, why would the criterion of manipulation of the treatment prompt the creation of a separate design category? The most commonly explicit answer is that the inability to manipulate the treatment can lead to ambiguity about precisely who has received the treatment and who has not (e.g., Cook and Campbell 1979; Judd and Kenny 1981). That problem is immediately recognizable as a problem of possible contamination. It is not clear that this kind of threat to validity should occasion a separate design category, but it is clear that the ambiguity involved does not necessarily go along with a study's being conducted "after the fact." In any after-the-fact time series, for example, such as those mentioned in the previous paragraph, it is perfectly clear which periods were before and which after. The ex-post-facto character creates no ambiguity of this sort. In a great many after-the-fact cross-sectional studies too, documentation makes it quite adequately clear who received which treatment, as in quality-of-medical-care studies, for example, in which the variation in treatment received is established from the study of patient records (Payne and Lyons 1978).

Rather than manipulation of the treatment, it is manipulation of the *selection process* that directly and inclusively speaks to the distinction that is apparently sought. Centralized versus decentralized selection offers a basis of classification that distinguishes between the ex-post-facto design and all others in a sense that would appear to underlie nearly all of the writing on the subject to date. It subsumes as all-too-likely possibilities the time-order and contamination problems just noted, and the perspective in which it places them would seem quite in the spirit in which they have been discussed elsewhere. What is more critical and definitional, however, is the problem of spuriousness. When selection is decentralized, the possibility of spuriousness becomes a truly salient characteristic, one that is distinguishing and that appears to require a separate category of impact-analysis design.

An ex-post-facto design is one in which no central authority decides which subjects are to receive the treatment and which are not, nor what intensity of treatment each is to receive. Rather, that decision is made by different persons for different subjects. To experimenters, analysts, program administrators, and so forth, selection for treatment conditions is therefore ex post facto rather than manipulated. Others have made some of the critical selection decisions, and the experimenter and even the program people themselves pick up the implementation after this fact. For example, if a youth employment program is offered to all eligibles, but some take advantage of it and others do not, and if the first become the treatment group and the second the comparison group in an evaluation of the program, then the selection decision has been essentially totally decentralized and the design is ex post facto (Somers and Stromsdorfer 1980). It is well recognized that such a study has a serious problem, usually referred to as self-selection.

Similarly, if a new drug for peptic ulcers is released and some patients receive it on prescription by their private physicians while others do not, and if the two groups of patients are used as the treatment and comparison groups in an evaluation, the selection decison has been decentralized and the design is ex post facto, although in this case, selection has been decentralized to individual physicians rather than to self (Geweke and Weisbrod 1984). On the other hand, if an experimenter or the local medical society or the U.S. Public Health Service decides that all ulcer patients in hospital A will receive the drug and all in hospital B will not, or if patients are assigned by the experimenter or the director of internal medicine either to receive the drug or not as they are admitted into the hospital, then the design is experimental or quasi experimental. And similarly, if Congress passes a 55-mile-per-hour speed limit and highway death rates in the years preceding its effective date are later compared to those after, the decision as to which years will be in the before group and which the after has been centrally made and the design, as with almost all before-after or time-series designs, is quasi experimental (Clotfelter and Hahn 1980). Natural experiments are quasi experimental in that Mother Nature is a central authority; they have exactly the strengths and weaknesses of quasi-experimental design, including the potential for selection-P and selection-Q effects, but not the problem of self-selection.

In this book, as in most other treatments of this subject, evaluation designs are distinguished from one another by category primarily on the basis of the logical seriousness of threats to internal validity. Validity in this context refers to the causal inference of treatment effect. It

FIGURE 10–1 Z is a source of spuriousness

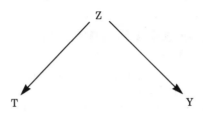

will help the discussion that follows if we review briefly what are generally considered the requirements for establishing that some variable (T) was at least a partial cause of another variable (Y) within a group of observations (see Selltiz et al. 1976, pp. 114–115). First, it is necessary to establish that T is related to Y in the group and setting observed, that is, as T varied from low to high, Y did not remain constant or vary randomly, but rather varied in some describable pattern—from low to high also, or from high to low, or parabolically, and so forth. Second, it is necessary to establish that Y was not causing T, which is usually done by establishing the time order in which the phenomena occurred: if Y preceded T in time, T could not have been the cause of Y. Last, it is necessary to rule out other causes of the observed relation between T and Y. Elsewhere (Mohr 1982, pp. 41–42, 46), I have proposed on logical grounds that other causes may be reduced to two factors: spuriousness and coincidence. *Spuriousness* is a well-accepted term in survey research that has a precise technical meaning. Z is a source of spuriousness for the relation between T and Y when its own variation causes *both* T and Y to vary in such a way as to be observationally related to each other, but not due to one causing the other. The standard, causal-arrow diagram for spuriousness is given in Figure 10–1. For example, quantity of robins and quantity of baseball are definitely related, not because robins cause baseball or vice versa, but rather because the variation in season (Z) causes concomitant variation in the two of them (Tashman and Lamborn 1979, pp. 159–160). Last, if T does not cause Y and Y does not cause T, and if no variable or set of variables Z causes them both to vary together, but yet they are observed to be related, then they must vary together by coincidence.

To this point in the book, our concern with internal validity has been overwhelmingly with coincidence as a possible alternative explanation for an observed relation between T and Y—treatment and outcome of interest. The sense in which that is so will be elaborated in a subsequent section. Before that may be accomplished, however, it is necessary to direct our attention to spuriousness.

SPURIOUSNESS AS A SOURCE OF SELECTION BIAS

There are two common types of ex-post-facto evaluation research. The first involves the necessity to reconstruct or perhaps to observe passively which subjects did and did not receive a treatment, or which more and which less, and perhaps to reconstruct also when that happened and what the outcomes or posttest scores were. Often, policies or social events or activities rather than discrete intentional programs are evaluated in this manner. The impact statistic that is computed is more likely than in previously discussed designs to be based on a multilevel treatment variable rather than a treatment dummy; for example, the level of police expenditures in different cities is examined for its possible effect on levels of crime (Cho 1980). It is this reconstruction type of study that has received most attention under headings such as ex post facto, correlational designs, and passive observation. Often, but not always, as noted above, the necessity to reconstruct implies uncertainty regarding the time ordering of the key events and ambiguity concerning treatment-group membership. *Every* illustrative example that I have ever seen, however, without exception, has involved decentralized selection. The following are some examples from Campbell and Stanley (1966, pp. 64–71). T is finishing high school and Y is success in later life (note that there are no time-order or treatment-group ambiguity problems here when the high school records are a basis of information); T is the education level of superintendents and Y is the quality of the school system; T is use of the turning signal by the car ahead and Y is its use by the car behind. Although there may be other problems in such cases, a universal problem is the need to worry about spuriousness because of decentralized selection (Campbell and Stanley 1966, pp. 64–71, see especially page 71).

The reconstructed type of study, however, is not the only one in which decentralized selection, and therefore spuriousness, becomes the basis of a potentially serious selection threat. The other type occurs when one offers a program and then administers it to those who volunteer for it, while composing a comparison group from nonvolunteers. There is little difference in implementation between this sort of study and a quasi-experimental evaluation, *except* in the source of selection and mode of assignment. Manipulation of the treatment, in particular, is the same in either case, as might well be the measurement of pretest and posttest and the computation of an impact statistic. There may be every bit as much of a sense of intentional *program* in this sort of ex-post-facto study as in a quasi experiment or experiment. Further, no reconstruction of the past is necessary. This type of evaluation has also been singled out for frequent special attention, usually under the rubric of volunteering, or self-selection. The volunteer-based evaluation study, however, is similar to the reconstruction-based study in the critical characteristic of decentralized selection so that the two may and in fact should be considered together in a classification of designs.

For either of these types of ex-post-facto study one may ask, Is the inference of treatment effect valid? Clearly, there is a severe problem of spuriousness or at least partial spuriousness introduced in both cases by the decentralized selection. If one compares the subsequent employment levels of those who did and did not volunteer for a job-retraining program, is it not possible that the first will come out way ahead, not so much because of the training, but because of the determination to work that made them volunteer in the first place? There is a strong possible selection effect here, in that the determination to work may be more prevalent or intense in one group than in the other, but note that it is a source of spuriousness as well. That is, it may cause T to be either 0 or 1, as well as causing Y to be either low or high. Similarly, consider jogging and heart disease. Is it not possible that those who jog tend to be more healthy in the first place, and therefore less prone to heart disease than those who choose not to jog? Again, the selection effect may be a source of spuriousness; general health condition affects the decision whether or not to jog as well as the later likelihood of developing heart disease.

The implied but unmeasured pretest is a common source of spuriousness (in both types of ex-post-facto design). For example, those who attend a lecture on the evils of nuclear power may already be against it; no wonder their attitudes are more negative on the posttest than the attitudes of those who did not attend! The gravity of the problem of spuriousness, however (although in this sense it is no different from the problem of coincidence), stems largely from the fact that its possible sources are unlimited. Not only the implied pretest but *virtually any variable* may determine, at least partially, both treatment group membership and outcome. The pretest *prior gas and electric bills* for example, may have little or no effect on who volunteers for energy audits in a residential energy conservation program, but education level and ownership of a single-family home may affect both participation and later energy-use habits (Berry 1983). Often, it is not the pretest but the desire to improve that is a cause both of volunteering or not and improving or not. Wanting to quit smoking, for example, may affect both signing up for a clinic and success in quitting. The problem would be the same whether we were evaluating one particular smoking clinic or were reconstructing whether people in a certain population went to smoking clinics or not. The point is that once the selection decision is decentralized, limitless characteristics of the individual subjects, whether anyone is conscious of them or not, may affect the assignment decisions reached, and many of these same characteristics may also affect the outcome of interest.

It is clear by now that the problem of volunteerism is almost synonymous with the idea of ex post facto. That is so because when the selection decision is decentralized, it is almost always, in point of empirical fact, decentralized to the potential subjects so that the decision regarding T is then essentially a decision by potential subjects of whether to volunteer. The three concepts of ex post facto, spuriousness, and volunteering are extremely closely linked. Thus, in the next section, we turn our attention to volunteering. Before doing so, it is perhaps well to mention once more that decentralization does not *necessarily* imply decision by the potential subjects. Teachers may assign certain students to the trial of some new teaching technology, for example, and reject others. Doctors may assign certain patients to receive a new drug and decide against prescribing it for others.

Volunteerism has long been recognized and lamented as a major problem for program evaluation. In the following section, however, it is shown not to be quite so great and intractable a problem as one might have thought. The analysis applies not only when decentralization is to the potential subjects themselves, but, in its main thrust and in almost all of its details, to the decentralized selection or "volunteering" of subjects by others, as well.

THE VOLUNTEER PROBLEM

At best, at least from the standpoint of good impact analysis, the programs, policies, and events to be evaluated should be applied to subjects without regard to their feelings in the matter (or, truly, without regard to *anyone's* feelings in the matter). In fact, however, the subjects of evaluation studies are frequently either people who placed themselves in a category of T or who were placed there by someone other than a central authority. Volunteering has long been considered a most serious problem for impact analysis, and it will continue to be so. However, it may be less serious than is sometimes thought for two reasons. To some extent the problem it causes is one of external and not internal validity, and there is a large class of cases in which the limitation on external validity that it causes is not a serious one. The second reason is that volunteering may frequently be confined to the treatment group, and there is a possibility that the right sort of comparison group can counteract the arising threat to internal validity.

It is first necessary to recognize that there are two types of volunteering effects, interactive and additive. They may easily occur simultaneously, and it may frequently be quite impossible to sort them out from one another, but it is nevertheless quite helpful to distinguish them analytically. In the individual case, one may then analyze how serious *each* might be if present, and what might be done about it. Often, by this means, one may place an evaluation totally beyond an attack that is grounded in the implications of volunteering.

The *interactive* effects of volunteering are those that occur to the extent that the subject never would have changed (from the counterfactual) without the treatment but, because of some quality, Z, the subject does change when and only when the treatment is received. The phenomenon of a possible interaction of this sort between the treatment and characteristics of the subjects has long been recognized (Campbell and Stanley 1966, pp. 19–20, 48–49). It may happen frequently, for example, that some subjects benefit from a program such as a smoking clinic because they are ready for it; others may well not benefit from the same program simply because they are not characterized by the Z that signifies the same state of readiness. Z, the readiness factor, is a source of spuriousness. It is clearly a cause of volunteering or not and is also a cause of outcome score if we interpret the term *cause* to include necessary conditions, even if not sufficient: for some, the clinic will not affect the Y score *except* in the presence of the readiness factor, and in that sense the latter is a cause.

It is critical to note regarding the possible interactive effect of volunteering that it is not at all a matter of internal validity. Thus, if one is dealing with an ex-post-facto evaluation, one knows that one does not have to worry about threats to internal validity from such interaction as one does from the second type of volunteering effect (to be discussed momentarily). It is clear that the interactive effect does no further damage to internal validity (remembering that other selection effects are always possible, as in a quasi-experimental design) when one recognizes that, in the absence of a true program impact, this sort of volunteering has no effect either on the result (R) or the counterfactual (C). To see this, note first that the status of the comparison group on the volunteer dimension has no impact on the counterfactual; that will come out the same regardless of whether the comparison group is composed either entirely or partly, (*a*) of subjects who are volunteers just as the treatment group, (*b*) of voluntary decliners, or (*c*) of subjects that never had the opportunity either to volunteer or decline. In all three cases, which exhaust the logical possibilities, there will be no improvement in the comparison group due to a readiness factor because no treatment has been administered, and, by definition, interactive volunteering or readiness alone is not enough to produce an effect. But neither does the status of the treatment group affect R, the result, apart from a true program impact. If the treatment group subjects are nonvolunteers, the program will not help them, and R will faithfully show that. If they are volunteers of the interactive sort they will be affected by the program and the impact will duly show up in the measurement of R. Thus, the comparison group never shows a confounding improvement and the treatment group measurement shows an effect only when the effect is truly there, so that internal validity is not at all threatened from this particular source. Assuming no *other* selection bias, the treatment effect discovered is real enough; only it would not be produced in all types of subjects.

What that means, clearly, is that the interactive effects of volunteering pose a threat to *external* validity; the true treatment effect discovered may be generalized only to volunteers and not to anyone or anything else. Or, considering that the treatment group is a group, the *mean* treatment effect discovered may be generalized only to a group with the same proportions of volunteers and nonvolunteers. We are dealing with external rather than internal validity then, but external validity is a most important and serious concern; one does not want to make the mistake of expecting the treatment to work on all subjects in some large universe when it will in fact work only on volunteers. Note that experimental designs are vulnerable to interactive volunteering effects as well as quasi-experimental designs and the ex-post-facto design; the results of an experiment would be generalizable only to groups with the same volunteer composition as the experimental and control groups used in the research. If the interactive effects of volunteering are unknown, therefore, as they always will be unless the treatment is tried on nonvolunteers, the generalizability of the results will be in serious question.

The saving grace, however, is that often the treatment is such that it would rarely if ever be applied to nonvolunteers. The smoking clinic, for example, may work only on volunteers, but that is probably no great restriction on generality because it is unlikely that we would ever be forcing people into such clinics anyway; the evaluation conclusion that the clinic works on volunteers is about as valuable as one could wish. A very large number of programs or treatments are of this variety. (Of course, the exact population to which one may generalize with validity is usually quite unknown, but that problem is fairly constant across almost all designs and has no different or special significance in connection with this one.) Note, however, that the reconstructed kind of ex-post-facto study may frequently produce an example on the other side. Caution must be exercised because such studies are sometimes undertaken precisely to generalize from volunteers to nonvolunteers, that is, a general law or policy is contemplated that will change certain behavior. For example, there may be interest in the impact of superintendents' education on the quality of the school system because one contemplates introducing a *requirement* that superintendents have some advanced degree, or there may be interest in the impact of police expenditures on crime because a grant program is contemplated as an *inducement.* One must be aware that these extensions may well not work because the communities might not be true, self-generated volunteers. The rule, however, remains: the interactive effects of volunteering are a potential problem only in regard to external validity and then only when there is a desire to extend the program from volunteers to nonvolunteers.

The *additive* effects of volunteering are quite different. In that case, there is some volunteering characteristic Z that produces an effect on the outcome all by itself. The previous attitude toward nuclear power would influence the posttest, for example, with or without the lecture, or the desire to quit smoking would in some people lead to a certain amount of success whether one attended the clinic or not. The treatment may produce an effect also, in which case the two effects would be added together to produce the total departure of Y from the counterfactual. The problem is to unconfound the treatment effects, if any, from the volunteering effects. This is an issue of internal validity. If the comparison group is, somehow, also composed of additive volunteers for the program, then there is no problem; the difference between them is due to the treatment. If it is composed of voluntary decliners, however, then the treatment group differs from it in two potentially influential ways—treatment and volunteering status—and attributing any difference in outcome between them to the treatment may be quite an erroneous leap.

If the design is purely ex post facto (that is, all levels of treatment, including no treatment, are voluntary on the part of all subjects), there is no sure method of unconfounding these two elements. The reader will find a great many sophisticated statistical techniques discussed in connection with this task in articles and books on program evaluation, but none is foolproof (e.g., Heckman 1976; Chronbach et al. 1977; Dunham and Mauss 1979; Blumstein and Cohen 1979; Cook and Campbell 1979, pp. 295–309; Somers and Stromsdorfer 1980; Hirst et al. 1983). They consist primarily in various ways of bringing explicitly measured Z-variables—characteristics of the subjects that might have caused them to arrive at their particular level of treatment or nontreatment—into the analysis as control variables. Such mechanisms are not at all to be disparaged as valueless. They may, in particular, improve the basis of presumptive reasoning by appearing to cover the major conceivable sources of spuriousness.

In general, however, applying control variables within the study group observed is not enough, even if they yield a high R^2 (controlling for T). If the control variables appear to provide a nearly complete explanation for Y, and b_T in that context appears to indicate a strong treatment effect, the result still may be spurious, that is, the apparent treatment effect still may be due to something other than the treatment. That is clearly true because, if the predictors leave variance for the treatment to explain, then they leave room for that "explanation" to be a false one. Consider, for example, that crime rate at time 1 is an excellent predictor of crime rate at time 2, but that changes in expenditures for police in the interim also are fairly strongly (negatively) related to time-2 crime rate, and therefore appear to constitute an effective sort of public policy. It still may be that, for example, unemployment changes in the interim have affected both expenditures and crime rates (the greater the increase in unemployment, the lower the expenditures and the higher the crime rate), causing them to be negatively related without any effect of one on the other at all. In general, even with control variables that yield a high R^2, awareness of some omitted factor of potential importance, or just the knowledge that there may easily be omitted factors of which one is *not* aware (the list of possibilities being infinite and unknown), will undermine confidence in internal validity, at least on the part of the sophisticated analyst or critic.

The only sure way to defeat the additive effects of volunteering is by research design. Two methods are commonly mentioned. One is to work only with subjects who have volunteered, dividing them into treatment and comparison groups (see, e.g., Berry 1983). This might often be done on a random basis, or it might have to be done on some nonrandom basis such as including earlier applicants in the program and excluding the later ones. The comparison subjects might be denied the program or, perhaps more commonly, delayed for a while in receiving it. Notice that this general sort of technique simply lifts the evaluation design out of the ex-post-facto category. The selection decision in such cases is not decentralized, but centralized; the individual subjects have made the decision to volunteer, but *all* of them have made the same decision (so that generalization to nonvolunteers is surely problematic), and it is the program administrator or the evaluator who selects the level of treatment to be received by each. Notice also that this method would generally not be available in the reconstructed sort of ex-post-facto design, as with the example of the effect of expenditures for police on levels of crime. In that sort of case, the assignment of T values has been made and there is nothing one can do about it. One cannot, for example, randomly assign high-expenditure communities to high or low expenditures; they have already assigned themselves. Nor can one make the high-expenditure communities wait to achieve their high-expenditure status; they have already achieved it.

The second method, not nearly so unambiguously successful, is to use posttreatment volunteers as the comparison group for the ordinary pretreatment volunteers. For example, those who volunteer for energy audits in 1981 are the treatment group and those who volunteer in 1982 are the comparison group, with the outcome variable for both being 1981 behavior, when the treatment group has already received the audits but the comparison group has not (Newcomb 1984). It will be profitable to consider this strategy with a bit more care than its general applicability might seem to merit because it helps to introduce the distinction between selection threats from spuriousness and coincidence.

It is a strategy that would also seem to be available occasionally in the reconstructed type of ex-post-facto design. One might use as the comparison group subjects that were in a low- or nontreatment category to start with, but later switched voluntarily and *gave themselves* the treatment, for example, low-expenditure communities that later became high-expenditure communities. Whether the treatment is administered by program personnel (energy audits) or is self-administered and must be reconstructed (police expenditures), a problem is presented because the outcome data for the comparison group must be obtained retrospectively rather than concurrently. Sometimes, as in the two examples cited, the problem is not severe because reasonably good documentation is available, such as heating bills or crime reports, and one needn't be completely dependent on human recall.

The important question that must arise, however, is whether the comparison group, which eventually did volunteer, was really a group of volunteers or nonvolunteers at the critical earlier time. If those subjects can legitimately be considered to have been volunteers, being late to volunteer because of some unimportant quirk, then selection is *centralized* (all are volunteers but some are put into the comparison group) and the design is quasi-experimental. There may well be important differences between the groups, as in any comparative-posttest or comparative-change design, but they are *coincidental;* they are not the result of differences in volunteer status because both groups were in the same category—volunteers. If, however, they may not convincingly be considered to have been volunteers at the earlier time, but rather nonvolunteers who subsequently changed in some important way, then selection was clearly *decentralized,* the design is ex post facto, and the danger of *spuriousness* enters in addition to coincidence (the very differences that made one group volunteer and the other not may also be responsible for differences in Y). Whether to consider the comparison group volunteers or nonvolunteers is a matter of some combination of information and presumption; the important item for the present discussion is that the decision on that issue determines the type of selection (centralized or decentralized) and the nature of the threats to validity (coincidence or spuriousness) and therefore the category of the design.

The two methods just presented for overcoming the additive effects of volunteering work, if they are successful, by lifting the design out of the ex-post-facto category and making it actually become an experimental or quasi-experimental design. They will only occasionally be

applicable because only occasionally does one have the control necessary to divide the volunteers into two groups and only occasionally will
the use of posttreatment volunteers be both a possible and a satisfactory expedient. A third method is available in some instances. The im-
pending ex-post-facto design can be transformed into a random-comparison-group design. The analytics of the latter are truly *made* for the
case in which there is concern that the treatment group may be atypical of the relevant population, as is precisely the concern with volunteers.

It is only necessary to select a population, as described in Chapter
Eight, and to use that or a random sample from it as the comparison
group instead of the group of voluntary decliners that would otherwise
be employed. The only special requirement for this use of the random-
comparison-group design, then, is that the population consist not of
decliners but of individuals who have never had the opportunity either
to volunteer or decline. In that case, the population presumably contains many individuals who are actually "volunteers" in their characteristics—individuals who are just like the treatment group—so that
the population scatterplot becomes a good basis for the treatment-
group counterfactual. Selection is then decentralized only in part since
the comparison group is determined by central decision. That, in fact,
was precisely the case in the housing subsidy evaluation summarized
in Chapter Eight (Jackson and Mohr 1986): those in the treatment
group were volunteers (the subsidies were of course not forced on eligible participants) and the comparison group, a national sample from
communities other than those in which the experiment was mounted,
never had the opportunity either to volunteer or decline. In some applications of the random-comparison-group design, the treatment
group will be centrally selected (e.g., a teaching technique is tried out
on a particular class), whereas in others it might be composed of volunteers. The difference between those two modes in the context and
framework of the random-comparison-group design is actually slight;
what matters is that factors that might otherwise make either sort of
treatment group "different" are well sprinkled throughout the population so that they have their effect on the variance in Y. This alternative
for overcoming additive effects would thus have good potential for application whenever the program, policy, or event does depend on volunteers, but in a geographically or otherwise restricted subdomain of
a larger population. Since a great many programs whose evaluation is
contemplated do depend on volunteers and are not national or universal in scope, the potential for application is appreciable.

What is not susceptible to amelioration by a shift to the random-
comparison-group framework is the sort of study in which T is some
behavior that is always voluntarily chosen at some level by all units in
the population of concern, such as expenditures for police or education

level of the superintendent of schools. That subcategory remains the weakest, in principle, of all true evaluation designs from the standpoint of threats to internal validity. The threat of selection bias from spuriousness is strong, and the possibilities for lifting the study into a higher design category are slim since even the random-comparison-group design is not available: all units in the population are either volunteers or decliners. Furthermore, as we will review briefly in the concluding section, the variables in such a study must usually be measured in retrospect so that special contamination and time order problems may undermine confidence as well.

Finally, it is now appropriate to consider a special case of voluntary attrition—an interactive effect in which the treatment causes attrition in nonvolunteers, that is, in subjects who would probably not have consented if given the choice originally. This may arise particularly in randomized experiments and may become a serious concern. An example is the case of a juvenile delinquency program in which many of the worst former offenders in the randomly assigned experimental group dropped out and would not show up for the counseling sessions (Berleman and Steinburn 1967). If valid posttest scores for the dropouts are somehow available there is no analytical problem, but often attrition means that no posttest is possible, as, for example, when the posttest is based on an attitudinal or informational questionnaire and the dropouts refuse to cooperate. It is necessary then to make assumptions about the missing posttest scores. To posit that the dropouts would show the mean Y score for the rest of the experimental group is incorrect: assuming that the dropouts are nonvolunteers and that the treatment is more likely to work on volunteers, the Y scores of the dropouts would have been worse than the mean of those who stayed on. A better assumption would be the mean score of the control group since the latter obviously did not benefit from the treatment and neither, presumably, would the dropouts. Even that, however, would not be correct if the dropouts were dissimilar in important ways. Particularly, some subjects in the control group may show *additive* effects of "volunteering" that would clearly not properly be assigned to dropouts, that is, some control-group subjects might just be ready to show improvement on their own. Last, perhaps the best assumption would be a projection of the Y scores of the dropouts based on their scores on the various X variables, thus taking at least measured dissimilarities into account. Even with this method, however, *unmeasured* additive effects of volunteering would contaminate the results. Thus, if the treatment has some likelihood of causing divergent attrition, and if one has not the luxury of being able to apply it to a known group of decliners, the best course may be to apply it only to volunteers! This would be especially desirable if generalization were needed only to future volunteers. One would either use an experimental design, randomly splitting the volunteers into two treatment groups, or one would apply the random-comparison-group design if such control were not feasible.

In sum, characteristics that would probably cause one to decline at the assignment stage if one had the opportunity can lead to selecting oneself out later on, causing a problem of nonreclaimable divergent attrition in some instances. Otherwise, although self-selection is all too common in evaluation studies and is, at worst, extremely damaging to confidence in results, the problem it presents is not severe (a) to the extent that interactive effects are the true concern, especially if the program will in general continue to be applied only to volunteers, and (b) to the extent that anticipated additive effects may be controlled by an appropriate shift away from an ex-post-facto design and toward an experimental, quasi-experimental, or random-comparison-group design.

COINCIDENCE AS A SOURCE OF SELECTION BIAS

The ex-post-facto design is distinguished from others by decentralized selection. That characteristic is chosen as a classifier primarily because it brings spuriousness into prominence; just as history has a special relation to single-group, over-time designs and selection to comparison-group designs, so does spuriousness—a particular source of selection bias—have a special relation to the ex-post-facto design.

It is not that spuriousness has no relevance for quasi-experimental designs, but rather that it can be considered fairly unusual in that context, somewhat strange, and therefore nondefining. To see this, recall that the precise meaning of a source of spuriousness is a variable that causes two others to be related by being a common cause of variance in both. The two other variables that concern us in impact analyses are those we have labeled T, the treatment condition, and Y, the outcome. In order for T and Y to be spuriously related, therefore, they must have a common cause. In quasi-experimental design, where there is centralized selection, the cause of T is the evaluator, or program administrator, or whoever is at that central decision point. Thus, for spuriousness to exist, Y must also be caused by that central authority. How could that occur? There is only one way of any prominence. If there is some characteristic of the subjects Z that is likely to influence their Y scores, and if the experimenter knows about this or is somehow aware of it, he or she could put subjects into treatment groups according to their scores on Z. Then Z would be causing Y and, indirectly through its effect on the experimenter, be causing T as well. In essence, the experimenter would be cheating—consciously or subconsciously, for good reasons or poor. Note that a natural experiment is superior in this respect because Mother Nature does not cheat. There is no question but that this occurs in program evaluation; no claim is made that the possibility should be ignored. As noted, however, it is so specialized a concern that one may make it an explicit exception for the purpose of classification of designs. With the exception of some sort of experimenter interference then, *spuriousness has no role in quasi-experimental design.*

We have certainly emphasized, on the other hand, that a certain characteristic of the subjects might differ across treatment groups in quasi-experimental design and might also cause Y scores. What are such differences if not sources of spuriousness? In fact, they are sources of selection effects by *coincidence,* which, indeed, is the only other possible explanation for a nondirectly causal relation between T and Y once spuriousness has been ruled out.

The appropriateness of the category may be seen by thinking first of randomized experiments. Consider our old example of nutrition and the cognitive development of children. T is nutrition supplements (the treatment group gets them and the comparison group does not) and Y is later cognitive development. Consider also mother's IQ as a possible source of selection bias. If participation were voluntary, surely mother's IQ could be a source of spuriousness: most high-IQ mothers might well both volunteer their children and independently contribute substantially to their later cognitive development through interaction in the home, whereas with low-IQ mothers both behaviors could easily be the reverse. The situation is quite different if the evaluation is a randomized experiment. Then, the two groups might well differ to some extent in mother's IQ, but that variable would not have been the cause of T; the relation is merely a *coincidental result* of the assignment method (randomization) used by the experimenter. The likelihood of various degrees of coincidental difference resulting from this mode of assignment is in fact determined by statistical sampling theory.

If we now consider a quasi-experimental design instead of a randomized experiment, the structure is similar. Assume that the nutrition supplements are given in the schools in city A, but not in city B. Barring cheating, mother's IQ does not cause city A to be chosen as the treatment group, but the schoolchildren in that city may be higher on mother's IQ anyway. Again, this is a coincidental result of the mode of assignment employed by the experimenter.

Coincidence should be random; in fact, it is essentially another way of saying *random.* If mother's IQ and other sources of selection effects are, because of centralized selection, distributed to treatment groups by coincidence, then, unlike the case of spuriousness, the likelihood of selection bias should be capable of determination by significance testing. Yet, the likelihood of various degrees of coincidental difference resulting from the quasi-experimental mode of centralized assignment is *not* capable of determination by testing. That is because

the mode of assignment of individual schoolchildren, even though centralized, is not by *independent* sampling. Each child is not an independent pick from a population; instead, the children are clumped into
cities. Because of that, they may well have strong similarities on variables such as mother's IQ within treatment groups and differences between groups. In principle, when a random assignment device is not
used, there is an unknown amount of dependence, or clumping, within
the study population, so that the statistically effective sample size—
the number of independent picks—is some *unknown* number, almost
invariably smaller than the physical number of subjects observed. In
our hypothetical nutrition case, the number of independent picks in
each group of children may be as low as one—city A and city B—because the variable "city of residence" may be a powerful cause of similarities and differences on mother's IQ. On the other hand, the effective sample size may not be quite so low; the scores of some subjects
may well be quite independent of one another in spite of the fact that
the subjects reside in the same city. There is essentially no way to tell.
Coincidental difference in mother's IQ is therefore indeed random, but
it may be a random difference between elements in a study population
of two. With only one independent subject to distribute to each group,
any apparent treatment effect is totally confounded with all preexisting differences, such as mother's IQ, so that neither mother's IQ nor
any other initial difference could possibly be ruled out as a cause of
observed differences in mean Y scores. In general, the lower the statistically effective sample size, the more chance for a lopsided distribution
of important characteristics, even if the distribution is random.

Thus, significance testing and confidence intervals as generally
practiced are not applicable to quasi-experimental design, as was
pointed out in Chapter Five, because the outcomes of these statistical
procedures are heavily determined by sample size. The larger the sample, the more statistically significant the result and the more precise
the interval estimate. In the absence of a random assignment mode,
even though differences between groups are coincidental, the number
of independent picks, and therefore the effective sample size, are unknown (and may be quite low). Significance levels and confidence intervals therefore cannot be determined even though the procedures are
technically applicable.

As a corollary of this reasoning, however, one senses why, in a
quasi-experimental design, there is justifiably greater faith in an inference of treatment effect when the difference in mean Y scores between the two groups is extremely large than when it is fairly small:
since not only the sample size but the size of the difference or relation
affects statistical significance (the stronger the relation, the more significant the result), such a large difference could well be statistically
signficant even if one assumed, as one must, that the effective sample

size were in fact quite small. Finally, as a second corollary, confidence in the results of a quasi experiment is likely to be greater, and justifiably so, the less "clumping" there were in the mode of assignment, and the more it resembled independent picks, even if not by a specific random device.

Having reviewed the above corollaries, let us pause to recognize an integral feature of quasi-experimental design. In a quasi experiment, by virtue of centralized selection and its relation to coincidence as the source of selection effects, the cause-and-effect logic of statistical significance applies. There is, however, a critical reservation regarding statistically effective sample size so that the quantitative results do not apply.

Note that whereas the before-after and interrupted-time-series designs are technically quasi experimental because of centralized selection, the mode of assignment—division by a moment of time—is such that they receive no benefit from the above feature. Clumping is so extreme and so arranged temporally that the statistically effective sample size is indeed one per group, before and after, and the designs are thereby left in a position of critical vulnerability. Other phenomena besides the treatment always occur at or near the intervention point. If one of these happens to cause a change in Y, that change will be confounded with the program's effect. The best that can be said, and it is no small advantage, is that such an occurrence is coincidental. Only presumptive reasoning applies, however, rather than statistical theory, in determining even roughly the probability of such a coincidence. If the design could be modified so that the intervention were serially applied and withdrawn several times, the statistically effective sample size would rise above one per group. Such a modification would make the design similar to quasi experiments involving comparison groups. The magnitude of the relationship, for example, would then become a very important item of information.

The corollaries hold for quasi-experimental design, barring experimenter interference, but they have no relevance for the ex-post-facto design. In a quasi experiment, selection effects are due to *coincidence*. Because coincidence is a random phenomenon, at least the idea of statistical inference is relevant, even if the quantitative results are not. In the ex-post-facto design, no matter how large the relationship between T and Y, and no matter how little clumping there would seem to be in a decentralized mode of selection, the voluntary nature of the assignment process is a foundation for *spuriousness*, the direct opposite of a random phenomenon and always a possible port of entry for truly serious selection bias. Combined with the other advantages that quasi experiments tend to have in practice, this technical distinction justifies a special place for that category in the classification of designs. It helps to clarify the importance of Campbell and Stanley's original treatise on quasi experiments (1963) as both a conceptual and practical contribution to the discipline of program evaluation.

CONTAMINATION AND TIME-ORDER PROBLEMS

In experimental and quasi-experimental design, characterized by centralized selection, one form that contamination may take is impurity of treatment condition. That is, even though it is decided centrally which subjects will be in the treatment and which in the comparison group, there may be some leakage of the treatment from one to the other, or comparison subjects may somehow sneak into the treatment category, or vice versa. In the sort of ex-post-facto design in which treatment condition is not only decided on a decentralized basis but must be measured by human recall or untrustworthy documentation, that sort of problem clearly has the potential for being much more severe. The conclusions of the research are likely to inspire little confidence if there is substantial uncertainty about which subjects received which level of treatment. This problem is not a necessary or universal one for the ex-post-facto design, but it crops up occasionally and, when it does, it can seriously undermine the results.

When it is necessary to reconstruct the past in order to measure T, Y, or X_1 (the pretest), errors in time ordering may also be a source of bias. It is conceivable that such a problem might arise in a quasi-experimental study as well, but the only instances of it that one finds in published evaluation reports occur when selection was decentralized.

One form the time-order problem may take is the possibility that Y actually preceded T. There are a great many ways in which this can occur. Rather than attempt to catalog them here, which would probably not be successful, it is simply well for the analyst to ask, in connection with all ex-post-facto studies, whether such a reversal could possibly have taken place. One example will be provided for the sake of clarity: T is scored 1 for states that inaugurated a mandatory program of motor vehicle safety inspection between 1950 and 1960 and 0 for states that had no such program by 1960. Y is the change in motor-vehicle accident mortality rate from 1950 to 1960 (Colton and Buxbaum 1977, pp. 137–138). The results show a drop in mortality rate from the beginning to the end of the period for both groups, but the drop was larger for the group of inspection states, so that there appears to be a beneficial treatment effect. It is possible, however, that the drop in many inspection states actually occurred before the inauguration of the inspection program, with a leveling off of the rate for the balance of the decade. Thus, Y actually occurred before T.

Another form of the time-order problem is the possibility that the treatment preceded the pretest. If that occurs, and if T actually influ-

FIGURE 10–2 X₁ is an intervening variable

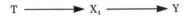

enced X_1, then the treatment has truly been effective. A hint of the true state of affairs would lie in a sizable correlation between T and both X_1 and Y. However, the causal model represented would be the "intervening variable" model (see Figure 10–2), and when the regression is run with the intervening variable X_1 as a control variable, the value of b_T will be near zero. One might mistake this result for a demonstration that X_1 is a source of spuriousness, taking the role of Z in Figure 10–1, in which the treatment truly is not effective. Both models, however, give the same result when controlling for X_1 (i.e., b_T tending toward zero), and distinguishing between them depends on knowing whether X_1 preceded T in time or followed it (see Blalock 1972, pp. 442–450).

This problem can occur just as the former one might—when one mistakes the times of occurrence of the critical variables. It may also occur for all practical purposes, however, when one fails to measure the treatment at the proper time, the time of its critical change. Let Y be crime rate at time 2 and X_1 be the crime rate at time 1. T is police expenditures for an intermediate year. Assume that T and Y are correlated. If X_1 is then brought into the picture, if the full regression is then run, and if b_T turns out to be near zero, X_1 will appear to be a source of spuriousness and the treatment may be taken as ineffective. (Possible explanation: A high previous crime rate is an indicator of an economically poor community, and vice versa. Poor communities have low subsequent police expenditures and high crime rates, and vice versa.) It is possible, however, that in many communities a critical change in expenditures actually occurred *before* X_1 and lowered the crime rate, thus explaining the correlation between T and Y: the public policy is in fact an effective one. One is simply mistaking the time at which the true "treatment" occurred; it occurred before X_1 rather than between X_1 and Y. The regression coefficient b_T in the full regression will then be zero because X_1 is an intervening variable, not a source of spuriousness.

That would not happen in a quasi-experimental design. There, one would select the communities to receive grants of some sort, which would be the critical change in expenditures, and the time order of the treatment would be properly established.

CONCLUSION

In sum, the true, defining, and universal threat to the ex-post-facto design is spuriousness. Nevertheless, decentralized selection also opens up ex-post-facto evaluation research to the possibility of serious problems of contamination and incorrect time ordering, and these threats must in general be considered by the analyst as well.

The moral of the tale is to *avoid* the ex-post-facto design. That is not easy to do, however, when attempting to assess the impact of a public policy choice that has been available in the past to the whole of the relevant population, such as expenditures for police or the education level of superintendents. An example often cited is the Coleman report on equality of educational opportunity—an attempt to discern just what factors are responsible for various levels of achievement in schools and on standardized tests (see Coleman 1976). It might possibly happen that the results of such studies are dramatic, unambiguous to all, and noncontroversial. It is far more likely, however, that the results will be doubted and disputed. Given the characteristics of such research and the implications of those characteristics as determined by evaluation technology, it is in fact likely that the results will engender endless inconclusive controversy both in policymaking circles and in the academic literature. Perhaps one can find a way to perform satisfactory small-scale experiments involving selected treatments, such as giving grants for police expenditures, or assigning superintendents to districts, or making selected changes in educational opportunity in a controlled population of school systems. If not, one must realize that not all programs, policies, and social choices may be soundly evaluated; if, when confronted with that kind of choice, one takes one's chances with a pure ex-post-facto design, one should embark on it with one's eyes open, that is, with the knowledge that the results are not likely to be persuasive.

Chapter Eleven

Subobjectives as Design

The subobjective design, or what I will call the *method of subobjectives,* operates through a particular and strong foundation for presumptive reasoning rather than by provision of a statistical basis for decision, but it is broadly applicable, and the reasoned analysis that it supports will in many cases be commonly shared and, in fact, well justified.

Cell a in Figure 3–1 represents the possibility that both the treatment-subobjective and the subobjective-outcome links are strong and that the treatment-outcome relationship is reasonably strong as well. These results, it was noted, do not necessarily prove that the program theory was correct, that is, that the treatment had a causal impact on the outcome. "However," we observed in Chapter Three, "the results certainly do not contradict the theory, and since what happened is exactly what was predicted, one's belief in the theory may be maintained and even strengthened." The quoted sentence suggests that inserting the subobjective into the analysis and obtaining these results does somehow increase internal validity, that these three relations are somehow better from the standpoint of inferring causality than knowing the treatment-outcome relationship alone. The suggestion was not elaborated in Chapter Three because that dealt only with the formative uses of subobjectives. Moreover, to obtain the proper perspective on the use of subobjectives as design, it was necessary first to have a conceptual base that included the ideas of internal validity, quasi experiments, coincidence, spuriousness, and the relations between program evaluation and classical statistical inference. Having developed that conceptual base, it is now possible to explore the sense in which one may indeed use subobjectives in the role of design, that is, a particular data format that enables inferences to be made regarding program effect. Put another way, we may now explore just how and why it is possible to strengthen internal validity by identifying subobjectives and collecting data that measure them.

The quoted sentence from Chapter Three emphasizes that, "what happened is exactly what was predicted." That is important. The use of subobjectives as design applies only to the case in which an apparent program effect has indeed been found, which means that there is a basic design already in place and one wishes to strengthen the inference from that design. The tentative proposal is that the evidence from the two (or more) subordinate links functions to increase confidence significantly in the causal nature of the relation that emerged from the basic design. It is not possible to use subobjectives to demonstrate that the treatment did *not* have an effect, which is some part of the thrust of all designs covered to this point. To show, for example, that the treatment did not lead to the subobjective or the subobjective to the outcome does not tend to prove that the treatment had no effect, but only that it had no effect through one particular channel. Thus, this aspect of design has a very specialized sort of use but, of course, an important one.

This chapter is a brief introduction to an area that is potentially large, multifaceted, intricate, and rewarding. It is hoped that much more will be done to develop knowledge regarding the various ways in which subobjectives can contribute to a demonstration of causality, as well as the true means by which this epistemological feat is accomplished, the kinds of basic designs and other conditions to build on that make the job easier or harder, the extent to which a pretest on the subobjective(s) strengthens confidence even further, and analysis schemes for the management of subobjective systems in the multiple-regression framework and others, particularly including path analysis and other forms of structural-equation modeling.

One way in which the idea may be applied has been elaborated by Scriven (1976), who calls it the *Modus Operandi* method of demonstrating causality (see also Mohr 1985). It is different from the method outlined below in that it is not attached to another design, one that uses a statistical approach, but rather stands alone. Y has occurred and the task is to demonstrate that T has caused Y. There are several other possible causes of Y: U, V, W, and so on. Each of these has a "characteristic path," that is, a mechanism or a known causal chain of events by which it would lead to Y if it were the true cause. The task of the analyst is to show that the characteristic path of T has indeed been actualized whereas the characteristic path of each of the other possible or plausible causes has not. This basis of determining causality is used frequently in many areas, such as detective work, cause-of-death determination or medical diagnosis, and troubleshooting in connection with machinery, as in auto repairs. If a car were overheating, for example, there are a great many possible causes. Each would have different implications for the status and motion of certain parts. By examining the proper ones, or perhaps just by taking the "case history," it is possible in some cases to pin the cause down precisely to one source or another.

THE LOGIC OF THE METHOD OF SUBOBJECTIVES

The method presented briefly here, one that is quite commonly applicable in program evaluation as currently practiced, operates by inserting measured subobjectives between T and Y, increasing confidence in the causality of the T-Y relation by decomposing it into two or more believable chained causal links. Confidence in causality regarding each link is accomplished by either or both of two mechanisms: magnitude of the relationship and causal proximity. The inserted subobjectives may of course be numerous. Furthermore, if several subobjectives are employed, they may be (1) additive within the equation for Y and not dependent on one another (e.g., learning both job-seeking skills and technical skills in a training program to affect employment), (2) interactive, and therefore multiplicative within the equation for Y and not dependent on one another (e.g., resources or knowledge on one hand and motivation on the other—the "behavioral" subobjectives of Chapter Three), and (3) chained, that is, dependent on one another, so that each appears as a subobjective in the equation for the one that follows. In the following presentation, we will assume that there is only one subobjective. Expansion to accommodate multiple subobjectives of these various types would involve a great deal of length, detail, and complexity. Such a discussion would be premature for a field so little developed, while at the same time not adding a great deal to an appreciation of the basic ideas.

There is a program logic as well as a validation logic to the method of subobjectives. The validation logic says that if the T-S and the S-Y links are both causal, then the T-Y relation is causal as well. The program logic says that if we know that S affects Y, then we need only implement some T that affects S to have an impact on the desired outcome.

The analysis scheme for the method of subobjectives rests on recursive structural equations (see, for example, Duncan 1975). Structural-equation models involve more than one dependent variable, and therefore more than one equation, with at least some dependencies among these variables themselves. In our case, both the subobjective S and the outcome Y function as dependent variables, but S is also an independent variable in the equation for Y. Recursiveness in structural-equation models is highly desirable in that it may enormously simplify the analytic task. In our terms, models would be recursive when dependent variables are not *mutually* dependent and not spuriously related by some omitted cause. The first requirement, not mutually dependent, is satisfied by our dealing with chains; the variables are ordered in time and generally measured in chronological sequence, for example, the training is given (T), the skills are measured at its conclusion (S), and the employment history is taken after several months (Y). In particular then, S may affect Y, but Y cannot affect S. There is no feedback loop. The spuriousness requirement may possibly not be met, but that, we will see, is an important focus of the analysis—it is not assumed away—and the possibility of spuriousness functions as a hedge or reservation on the conclusions.

The basic estimating equations for an analysis using the method of subobjectives are:

(11–1) $$S_i = a' + b_T'T_i + e_{Si}$$

(11–2) $$Y_i = a + b_SS_i + b_TT_i + e_{Yi}.$$

The first equation shows the T-S link, with b_T' being the estimate of the impact of the treatment on the subobjective. In the second equation, b_S shows the impact of the subobjective on the outcome—the magnitude of the S-Y link. The coefficient b_T shows the *additional* impact of the treatment on the outcome, over and above its impact through the subobjective. If its magnitude is appreciable, it means that the treatment is operating through another channel in addition to our measured S. (Note that we use the concept appreciable rather than significant. Subobjectives might well be used in true experiments for formative purposes, in which case statistical significance and interval estimates would be appropriate, but they will not add anything to the true experiment as a design. In the present context, the basic design within which subobjectives are included is understood to be a quasi experiment or, when applicable, a random-comparison-group design. Statistical significance may thus be used as an indicator of magnitude—the fourth function of testing given in Chapter Five—but it is mainly raw magnitude itself and not probability theory on which we must depend for our judgment of impact, which is why the term *appreciable* is appropriate.)

If either b_T' or b_S is unimpressive, the attempt to bolster confidence in validity has failed and is finished: in that case, one must be willing to entertain two sorts of possibilities, namely, that the treatment may have operated through another path, that is, through unmeasured and perhaps undreamed-of subobjectives, and, unfortunately, that history or selection effects rather than the treatment may be responsible for the observed T-Y relation. Let us assume then that both of the component relations *are* impressive. That is the single case that is germane to the present discussion. Let us also assume that S is essentially the only subobjective that actually operates, that is, that the analyst has measured and included in the system of equations all of the important channels through which T affects Y, assumed here for simplicity to be only one. Then $b_T = 0$. It will also be true then that, if the component links are causal, the summative correlation coefficient will be equal to the product of the two component ones: $r_{TY} = (r_{TS})(r_{SY})$, a relation that will be helpful in our analysis because it has implications for the magnitude of the component links.

Before looking more closely, however, it is necessary to consider the possible role of spuriousness. That is not a concern with respect to the relation between T and S; S is an ordinary outcome of a treatment in the setting of a quasi experiment and in that sense might just as well be labeled Y as S. Except for experimenter interference, only coincidence causes history and selection effects in the relation between T and S. That is desirable; to establish causality, it is far better to be dealing with a quasi experiment than with a strong possibility of spuriousness. With a quasi experiment, the corollaries from Chapter Ten become relevant. In particular, the size of the relation may become a matter of true interest in establishing its causal nature.

The S-Y link, however, is another matter. S, the proposed cause of Y, is not a treatment in the setting of a quasi experiment. The possibility therefore exists that the S-Y link should be considered an ex-post-facto link, and therefore one that might be at least partially spurious.

For example, there may be some natural variance in S in the comparison group or the before condition, indicating that there would probably be some variance even without the program in the treatment group as well. Considering both groups lumped together then, selection into S scores is not centralized. To the (generally unknown) extent that there would be natural variation in S, it is possible that the same natural forces might also to some extent be responsible for Y, making the S-Y relation spurious or partially spurious. Of course, it is not necessary that the relation in question be spurious. S may still be a true cause of Y. Since some amount of spuriousness is possible, however, it is clear that some dependable source of confidence that the S-Y link is causal rather than spurious would be welcome. Such sources are not in principle available within the ordinary ex-post-facto evaluation; we will see momentarily, however, that they do commonly arise when the relation involves a subobjective.

How about the extent to which the achievement of a given score on S is *not* just a natural occurrence but is induced by the program? This raises a most interesting connection between the two subordinate links: in truth, *the S-Y link is quasi experimental to the extent that T causes S*. The experimenter or other centralized source determines scores on T, so that if these in turn cause scores on S, the central source is thereby causing S as well, albeit indirectly. It is the same sort of manipulation as the direct assignment to treatment groups—a manipulation of status from the outside that breaks the possibility of spuriousness. Thus, for the S-Y link to be quasi experimental to some extent the T-S link must to that extent be causal. Since the T-S link is itself the result of a quasi experiment, presumptive reasoning and the corollaries from Chapter Ten become important.

Having found that the operation of the subobjective to increase one's confidence in the validity of the original causal inference depends on confidence in the causal nature of the two component links, it is necessary to examine the two bases on which such a foundation of confidence in the components must usually rest.

First is the magnitude or strength of the relationship. If it is strong, a quasi-experimental relation may still be evidence of causality, even under the assumption of a rather small statistically effective sample size due to the presence of some unknown amount of dependence in the selection of individual subjects. How strong is strong? The following rule contains many ifs, but will nevertheless be a useful guide. If b_T is zero in Equation 11–2 (i.e., if T operates only through the channel we call S and not partly through another subobjective), and if the component links are at least strong enough so that $(r_{TS})(r_{SY}) = r_{TY}$, then the case for causality is a good one. By the analysis of Chapter Ten, spuriousness in the first link, and therefore in the second one, thereby becomes dubious, and the leading remaining alternatives to causality become experimenter interference (conscious or subconscious), and sheer coincidence.

The other basis of confidence is causal proximity—a causal distance that is quite close. The causal distance is defined as the combined (multiplicative) likelihood (*a*) that event K will follow from event J if nothing intervenes, and (*b*) that nothing will intervene. The assessment of likelihood may be quite subjective, but it will often be based on information such as data from previous studies, or technical data from the laboratory, or widespread general experience. For example, the causal distance between seat belt use and accident fatality rate is quite close; one knows from tests on dummies and other data that K will follow from J, all else being equal. Of course, average driving speeds might increase, or there might be some other sort of intervening or offsetting factor. These contingencies are not impossible, but are fairly unlikely.

The point to be made in connection with subobjectives is that the causal distance for the links involving them is much smaller or closer than that for the usual relation between treatment and outcome. If one passes a seat belt law and the use of seat belts increases, one has little difficulty in attributing the last to the first. This does not mean that there is no need to collect data on the use of seat belts. One would not be bowled over with surprise if use were hardly to increase at all. That would mean that some circumstance intervened, as for example the fact that the police did not enforce the new law. Given that use did increase, however, the law will certainly be implicated as a cause. One will feel the need for the measures, therefore, but be willing to make the obvious causal connection if the measures come out as expected. Similarly, if seat belt use goes up and the fatality rate is found to go down, the causal connection will again be made. One would probably not be willing to allow seat belt use alone to be the outcome of interest on the assumption that a lower fatality rate is essentially certain to follow; average driving speeds might actually go up, for example, or the most risk-prone drivers might be just the ones who do not use their belts (Lee 1987), and so forth. Nevertheless, once "close" data like these *show the expected relation,* the reasoning that predicted it is vindicated.

When there are important subobjectives, whether measured or not, the causal distance is much greater between treatment and outcome than between either of these and the subobjective. Graphically, the difference is self-evident on the outcome line, where treatment and outcome are further apart than either one is from the intermediate subobjective. Empirically, the causal mechanism itself is not so immediate and direct in the T-Y relation and there are also more stages at which something may go wrong in the sense of interfering with the desired result. Thus, even if the fatality rate decreases after the seat belt law is passed, it will probably not be easy to muster abundant faith that one is the cause of the other—to rule out history as a threat to validity. To make such faith a reality, the documented occurrence of seat belt use, the subobjective that would carry the causal force from one to the other, is crucial—a midstream stanchion that enables one to build the full-length causal bridge.

APPLICATIONS OF THE METHOD

Before concluding, let us consider a few examples for orientation. (1) A law requiring motorcycle helmets to be worn is passed and the severity of injuries from motorcycle accidents decreases (Muller 1979). Confidence in the causal attribution is firmly nailed down by documenting that the use of helmets increased greatly after the law was passed and that severity of injury has a strong negative relation to helmet use. (2) A work-release program is initiated at some sites (prisoners are released during the day for six months before expiration of sentence to work for private employers in nearby communities) and criminal recidivism is less for the treatment group. Selection bias is a nagging doubt until it is shown that work release is strongly related to postprison employment and the employment variable is even more strongly related to recidivism. (3) A quasi-experimental, comparison-group program to provide nutrition to disadvantaged children shows an apparent effect on cognitive development. The results are welcomed but accepted with reservations until it is shown that the health of a portion of the brain does not deteriorate for the treatment group, whereas it does for the comparison group, and that the health of that portion of the brain is related to cognitive development. Then, most lingering doubts truly disappear.

It was noted in Chapter Four that two mechanisms—a strong relationship and causal proximity—may serve to yield adequate confidence in the overall T-Y relation in some instances even with an elementary quasi-experimental design, whereas divergent attrition or the possibility of contamination might undermine confidence at times even in an experimental design. In the quasi-experimental case, these two mechanisms will work to make confidence high when the causal distance between T and Y is so close that a subobjective could hardly be squeezed in, that is, when T and Y are related essentially as T and S might be in another program. In the present chapter, we have seen that when the design is quasi experimental but the causal distance seems a bit too great or the relation a bit too weak to yield high confidence in the inference of program impact, splicing with subobjectives can have the effect of activating these two mechanisms, enabling them to be brought to bear on an evaluation to which they otherwise would not become germane.

The evidence from the method of subobjectives is additive; the stronger the quasi experiment per se, the more likely it is that the evidence from subobjectives will tip the scales in favor of a confident causal inference. A comparative-change design is better than a comparative-posttest or before-after design. The random-comparison-group design, which might sometimes not be quite strong enough in itself because of the necessity to assume a percentage of outliers, would almost certainly suffice if subobjectives were added to the picture.

Not only is internal validity strengthened by subobjectives, so is external validity. Whenever one understands the causal mechanism by which a treatment affects an outcome, one is in a much better position to make it happen again. A goal of all evaluation should be to understand how treatments work so that they may be made to work when needed.

There is far more demand than supply for formative evaluations in the world, and subobjectives are their critical ingredient. One hardly needs further reason to devote greater attention to this part of the outcome line in program evaluation in the future. If one did seek other arguments, however, they are to be found in the possible contribution of the method of subobjectives to confidence both in internal validity and in generalizability.

Chapter Twelve

Multiple Outcomes

To this point, we have primarily referred to programs as though they had only one outcome of interest. In the technical sense of the word *program* this is a perfectly valid perspective; a program is *defined* by a single outcome line. In the administrative sense of the word *program,* however, the single outcome is a naive oversimplification. Most programs in both the public and the private sectors can have a large number of outcomes in the form of concerns both of program personnel and of interested outsiders. Furthermore, some impacts are concerns of no one; they are not intended. They are not even dreamed of in connection with the program or agency until new times or new events suddenly make them salient and the connection is made, yet they have been impacts of the program all along. Let us retain the sense of the word program as defined by one outcome line because it provides a fundamental unit with which to build. We must also recognize the multiple-outcome administrative program, however, and develop mechanisms for handling it in the context of impact analysis. The reason is that policymakers and other citizens often find it natural to wonder whether some administrative unit is effective, all in all—whether it is worth our continuing support as currently operating or requires drastic change.

There are five problems or functions connected with this issue of the effectiveness of a multiple-outcome administrative program. They are the problems of: finding, limiting, assessing impact, common-scaling, and weighting. Let us consider the meaning of these problems one by one.

1. *Finding.* Any given program might have a large number of impacts. How does one figure out which outcome dimensions might be affected?

2. *Limiting.* It might be that the number of potential impacts found is huge. If so, evaluating with respect to all of them is unrealistic. How does one decide which to pursue and which to ignore?

3. *Assessing impact.* How does one determine or estimate what has been the impact of the program on each outcome?

4. *Common-scaling.* If there are many outcomes and one wants an answer to the effectiveness question for the administrative unit as a whole, it would seem that the estimates of impact for the various outcomes would have to be combined in some way. But they are probably in different measurement units—percent of individuals helped, number of points' improvement on some attitude scale, number of hours saved, and so forth. How does one manage to put all of these things together so that the effectiveness of the whole may be appraised?

5. *Weighting.* Even if the various impact scores can be combined, it would be rare if they were all of equal importance. How does one decide how to weight the importance of each relative to the others?

Our concern is with the manner in which impact analysis deals with these issues. It is hardly possible to consider the subject, however, without comparing impact analysis with other evaluation techniques that confront the same set of issues. The two others that will briefly be examined for this purpose are benefit-cost analysis and multiattribute-utility-technology (MAUT).

There is one important distinction that can be made immediately between the impact-analysis perspective and these other two techniques. Some evaluation work is retrospective, where interest is in the extent to which a program actually carried out has been effective, and some is prospective, where interest is in the impact a program would have if it were carried out in the future. Benefit-cost analysis and MAUT may be employed as either retrospective or prospective evaluation techniques. Impact analysis, however, is purely a retrospective technology in its use of research design (see Hawthorne 1988). It is clear from previous chapters that all research designs covered compare the *results of having conducted the program* with something else, such as a control group or before data. The orientation is therefore necessarily retrospective. For that reason, this being a book about impact analysis, we will attend only to the retrospective function in this comparison of the handling of multiple outcomes in the three techniques. It is well to add, however, that there is considerable overlap in the concerns of prospective and retrospective evaluation, as different as they may be in some respects. Sherrill (1984), for example, suggests benefit-cost analysis to make projections into the future from data on the past generated by impact analysis. Much in the technology of impact analysis, including the principle of the outcome line and the treatment of multiple outcomes that follows in this chapter, is therefore valuable for the conduct of prospective evaluative studies of all kinds; it is primarily design that stamps impact analysis as retrospective and has little relevance for prospective studies.

BENEFIT-COST ANALYSIS

In the literature on this approach, very little attention is paid to the problems of *finding* and *limiting*. Analysts tend to include certain benefits and costs in their research because others have done so in the past. Thus, each sort of program develops its own conventions so that predictable sets of benefits and costs are treated depending on whether the program is a dam, a transportation system, a training program, a government regulation, and so forth. There also tends to be a certain amount of borrowing of ideas from one sort of program to another. Whatever the sources, it is clear from the literature that it is the analyst's responsibility to look beyond the obvious gains and losses to factors that are more indirectly or distantly implicated, but are nevertheless important. Gramlich (1981) mentions factors such as pollution, health, safety, waste of time, secondary market impacts, nonmonetary satisfaction from education, and impacts on marital and family ties (Gramlich 1981, pp. 4, 83, 160, 223).

At the same time, on the limiting side, analysts are cautioned to be sensitive to the possibility of duplication, or double-counting: including the same benefit more than once in different guises, particularly in the process of listing the benefits that accrue to different groups.

However, it is rare for the analyst to question whether he or she has included all of the relevant outcomes, and even more rare, it appears, to seek to determine how one would know whether the list employed is a complete and correct one or not. No systematic finding or limiting procedures are offered, although limiting because of difficulty of data accessibility and negligible expected impact are informally noted from time to time. In some measure, the functions of finding and limiting are performed by the connection of the concept of payment with the concept of utility, that is, the amount a person or group is willing to pay for any good, service, or condition is taken to represent all of the benefits derived—without identifying each one by name. The validity of such a blanket indicator is often uncertain. Further, it is clear to all that there are almost always parties who do not pay and whose benefits or costs are therefore not included unless special note is taken of their stake and special measurements are made, as in the case, for example, of enjoyment of a good environment or the gratification of the families of medical patients. It is common to encounter among students of benefit-cost analysis the feeling that much may be left out but that little can realistically be done about it. It is, in sum, a weakness of benefit-cost analysis that the technology includes no systematic procedures for finding or limiting; how serious this weakness is remains undetermined.

The function of *assessing impact* is central to benefit-cost analysis.

It is performed in highly complex ways and demands a great deal of expertise and creativity. It is done in so very many different ways, however, that it becomes extremely difficult to characterize the method or provide a definitive outline. As a rough approximation, one might note that there are two basic approaches. The first and by far the predominant one involves (a) the acquisition of at least some minimally essential amount of real-world data on prices and quantities—enough to provide at least a few anchoring points from which to work (including not only information about goods, but also such factors as wages and interest rates); and (b) economic theory as a basis of extrapolating and imputing from there. The theories themselves cannot, of course, be reviewed here, but some of the numerous concepts and devices from economic theory that are commonly employed in benefit-cost analysis to extrapolate or infer from basic data points are demand and supply curves, marginal cost curves, production possibility curves, indifference curves, consumers' and producer's surplus, cost-accounting techniques, discounting techniques for all of the effects of time, and the analytic geometry of two-dimensional graphs (see, for example, Gramlich 1981). The heart and soul of benefit-cost analysis lies in the creative application of economic theory to pertinent, retrievable, existing data for the purpose of assessing impact by inferring what would happen under a variety of conditions.

The second of the two impact assessment techniques is a blending of the first with exactly the designs described in detail in prior chapters of this book (see, e.g., Gramlich 1981, pp. 158–179). However, experimental and quasi-experimental research designs have no impact-assessment role in prospective studies (see Hawthorne 1988). Therefore, benefit-cost analyses using this second sort of estimation of impact are necessarily retrospective.

For the most part, the functions of *common-scaling* and *weighting* are handled quite simply in benefit-cost analysis. Any common scale could in principle be employed, but the one that is used nearly 100 percent of the time in practice is dollars (or some other monetary unit). In such cases, the effort is made to express all impacts in dollars. Not only does this obviously provide a common scale, but it also weights the various impacts for relative importance because $10 is considered always to represent twice the utility of $5 no matter what kind of benefit or cost each may represent. This common-scaling and weighting system is perhaps the most conspicuous characteristic of benefit-cost technology, although not the most important or central one. In fact, it is recognized that not all impacts can be successfully monetized. Analysts are urged to go as far as possible in that direction and, rather than ignore the nonmonetized impacts, simply to present them on the side, as it were, in their original scales (Gramlich 1981, p. 15).

There is another sort of weighting that may become important in benefit-cost analysis—the weighting of groups (even individuals) for importance in connection with the impacts of a particular policy. For example, the poor or unemployed may be weighted more heavily than the middle class. This kind of weighting is done subjectively by the analyst, often in consultation with others who have a concern regarding the policy. In this sort of case, the evaluator is urged in the professional literature to apply techniques such as "bracketing" or "sensitivity analysis" that provide decision makers with a *series* of results instead of only one, each depending on the employment of a different set of weights.

MULTIATTRIBUTE-UTILITY TECHNOLOGY

This is a term that has been used to designate a subset of scholarship in the large area of applied decision-making analysis. Many approaches to multiattribute decision making are available. The MAUT approach in particular is treated here because it is representative for our purpose and because it has been brought explicitly to bear upon the task of program evaluation (Edwards and Guttentag 1975; Edwards and Newman 1982). As noted above, it is akin to benefit-cost analysis because it permits and indeed specializes in prospective evaluation—deciding which alternative is better before any of them has been carried out. It is akin to benefit-cost analysis also in that it typically involves consideration of a large number of outcomes and permits their aggregation into one summary estimate of impact.

Whereas benefit-cost analysis has little to say about *finding,* however, this function is featured prominently in the MAUT technology. MAUT is generally considered as a tool for organizational decision making (the decision being concerned with what to do once the results of an evaluation are in hand). It is an assumption within the approach that the decision should be made on the basis of the goals of those members of the organization who have a stake in the decision because of their official responsibility or their probability of being affected by the results. Therefore, the question of a list of impacts is not an abstract one but rather one that is bounded by the concerns of certain individuals. In MAUT, these individuals are called stakeholders. There are no firm criteria for whom to consider a stakeholder, so that some ambiguity about the final list of outcomes is thereby introduced. It is presumed that for practical purposes the determination of relevant stakeholders can be made in satisfactory fashion by the evaluators along with responsible executives in the organization concerned. It also appears to be assumed that the stakeholders know what the relevant impacts are or should be so that whatever list they compose may be considered complete. MAUT does not entertain the possibility of an incorrect evaluative conclusion that is due to the omission of impacts by stakeholders. It is assumed, however, that discussion and the interchange of ideas will help the stakeholders to arrive at a full list. Thus, MAUT gets fairly high marks as an evaluation methodology insofar as the function of finding is concerned.

There are also guidelines, though quite weak and nonexplicit ones, for *limiting* the list once the full version has been elicited. These are primarily concerned with the elimination of duplication and overlap, as well as the noninclusion of potential impacts that are relatively unimportant. Long lists of impacts are resource consuming and they also tend to result in undervaluing the important impacts by dilution.

To analysts accustomed to impact analysis or benefit-cost analysis, the performance of the *impact assessment* function within MAUT will appear peculiar. No particular provision is made for the application of systematic methods such as economic theory or experimental or quasi-experimental design. It is rather presumed that the analysis will arrive at good estimates of the impact of each alternative on all outcomes by the most reasonable possible means. In a great many cases, the method envisioned is the subjective judgment of responsible organizational personnel. For some impacts, subjective judgment is as good an assessment technique as any. In fact, it is often known for certain just what the impact will be, as with the impact of a new office location on the travel time of personnel. In a great many other cases, however, subjective judgment or other rapid techniques would be considered by many a poor substitute for economic theory or rigorous research design; it is treating casually precisely what benefit-cost analysis and impact analysis are most pointedly designed to accomplish. The impact assessment step, then, is not a strong point of MAUT itself, although nothing about the approach inherently prevents taking as many pains with this function as may be desired.

The MAUT technology has quite a bit more to say about *common-scaling*. Since the primary purpose of the approach is to enable decisions to be made among several alternatives when a large number of outcomes or implications are at issue, it is considered important that impacts on the various outcomes be capable of aggregation in some fashion. While the literature does not specify why dollars are not the suggested common standard, it is fairly evident that at least two reasons apply: (1) MAUT is not a cost-driven approach; costs in the sense of resource inputs are frequently not considered at all or are considered separately after much of the other work has been done (Edwards and Newman 1982). There is therefore no pressure to put other impacts into dollars stemming from dollars' already being the scale of one central impact. (2) It would usually be far too much trouble to produce sound dollar-conversion schemes for the dozens of situation-specific outcomes generally considered in any one application of the technique. Therefore, a different sort of approach is adopted. For each outcome, maximum and minimum plausible or tolerable scores are provided by the stakeholders. These anchoring endpoints then become the common elements in all scales—all begin at the same place as one another and end at the same place as well. Thus, a raw score on any scale can always be converted to the common scale by putting it in percent of the distance from the beginning anchor point toward the ending one. A common-scale score, in other words, would read something like "28 percent of the way from the minimum plausible (or tolerable) to the maximum." Clearly, results of the evaluation will depend on where the anchor points for the various scales are set. Although there can be no system that guarantees their being set at the right place, so that results will often seem fragile or ambiguous to some, sensitivity analyses can be performed to examine the effects on the evaluation as a whole of moving any given anchor point a certain distance in one direction or another. But this process can take a lot of time and trouble. Common-scaling in MAUT, therefore, will no doubt seem fairly sound to some, overly subjective to others.

The scheme for common-scaling summarized above does not automatically perform the *weighting* function simultaneously, as does dollars. Five dollars spent on one item generally have the same importance as five dollars spent on any other, but 28 percent of the distance on one outcome may clearly not have the same value as the same distance on another. The remedy in MAUT is simply to get the stakeholders to assign importance weights subjectively to all of the outcomes so that outcome A is worth twice outcome B, which is worth 1.4 times outcome C, and so forth. The process is actually less time consuming and less arbitrary than it might seem, but it does introduce another strong element of subjectivity and, in addition, the problem of obtaining different relative weightings from different stakeholders. The solution to this last concern is to provide average weights, or average weights that are themselves weighted by the position or importance of the respective stakeholders, and/or different evaluation results for each stakeholder. The last solution is not outlandish; decisions often must be made collectively and it may well be better to let each party know where the issue stands in his or her own values rather than in some average set of values. Weighting then, like common-scaling, may be considered satisfactory by some people at some times and unsatisfactory by other people or at other times.

Summary

To summarize the above, benefit-cost analysis (1) has relatively little to say about the functions of finding and limiting, (2) depends for estimation primarily on the use of economic theory to extrapolate from relevant available data points, and (3) accomplishes weighting and common-scaling by putting outcome measurements in dollars. MAUT uses the interests of stakeholders to perform the functions of finding and limiting, has relatively casual content on estimation, weights by the values of stakeholders, and achieves common-scaling by converting actual measurements to percentage scores based on location between minimum and maximum plausible.

IMPACT ANALYSIS

Except for its obvious relation to the third of the five functions, assessing impacts, impact-analysis technology has been rather silent about these issues; in fact, there tends to be little formal recognition that programs have more than one outcome—or at most a few. Therefore, a recommended technology will be provided in the balance of the present chapter. For the finding function, we will suggest a modified version of the stakeholder approach. For limiting, rather drastic measures will be suggested based partly on the categories in the outcome line and partly on the relative value of including a particular outcome in the research. The function of impact assessment is based on traditional experimental and quasi-experimental research design, as elaborated in the previous chapters. Weighting is proposed to be accomplished on a personal private basis by each participant in decision making about the program, and it is recommended that common-scaling not be attempted in any way.

Finding

To assist in the discussion of *finding,* it will be helpful to recognize three different categories of outcome: objectives, constraints, and side effects.

Objectives are intended or desired outcomes of the program attributed to any interested party. That is, they include the program goals attributed to the unit's management or any other collection of its members, to the legislative or other funding authorities, and to anyone else who might in some way be a stakeholder, whether explicitly articulated by these parties or not.

Constraints are outcomes to be avoided by the program, again from the perspective of any interested party. The need to avoid pollution, for example, is a constraint of many manufacturing programs. Concern for the integrity of the merit system was apparently a constraint on the Civil Service Commission in its implementation of the Federal Affirmative Action Program during the early days (Rosenbloom 1980). From the perspective of any one stakeholder or group, *a constraint is subordinate or secondary to an objective* in that the program would never be advocated for the sake of the constraints. Rather, the program is conceptualized as having been created or desired for the sake of the objectives, but once it is clear that the activities will be undertaken, the constraints arise as limits to what those activities may be and how they may be implemented.

Side effects are outcomes that are neither sought nor avoided by a *particular* interested party (cf. unintended outcomes in Sherill 1984). The stakeholder may be ignorant of the side effect or may simply be indifferent toward it. If an unknown side effect suddenly comes to light, however, it may well become an objective or, more commonly, a constraint. It is this potential that causes evaluators to be anxious about side effects—the possibility that if the program were known actually to be having a certain impact, important stakeholders might consider that fact grounds for modifying the program substantially or even eliminating it. White flight from central cities to the suburbs has been a possible side effect of school desegregation programs that would be a constraint to some stakeholders if it could be convincingly documented. Similarly, if birth control education were actually to cause an increase in sexual activity among teenagers, as many claim, that side effect would no doubt become a program constraint for many stakeholders. Sometimes, constraints and side effects are more important to an evaluation than objectives. The objectives of a negative income tax, for example, would probably have to do with the living standards of the poor, administrative cost savings, and the economy of the country. Evaluations of this policy, however, have had most to do with a constraint—its possible negative effect on work incentives.

When a program has multiple outcomes, they may be perfectly consistent with one another, but they may also conflict in some way. A program that trains underemployed senior citizens to be home health aides and finds them employment in connection with chronically ill patients who otherwise could not afford that service is accomplishing two consistent objectives: the employment objective and the health objective (Lyons and Steele 1977). On the other hand, a park service may have two objectives that inherently or almost inevitably conflict: preservation of wilderness areas intact and provision of recreation opportunities for citizens. Sometimes, objectives conflict by competing for scarce resources. A housing subsidy program may have the objectives of reducing crowding and increasing housing quality, but to the extent that it pays for one it is generally prevented from paying for the other; more space and better space compete for resources (Jackson 1982; Jackson and Mohr 1986). Constraints commonly conflict with objectives. The cost constraint, for example, conflicts in principle with almost all objectives, although it is sometimes not an important concern (see Hawthorne 1988—it is in fact not considered important in most impact analyses). Similarly, the merit-system constraint was considered to conflict substantially with minority employment objectives in the early days of the Federal Affirmative Action Program (Rosenbloom 1980). Conflict among outcomes is one of the primary reasons for the weighting and common-scaling functions in a multiple-outcome evaluation; if a program has some costs and some benefits, there may understandably be interest in learning how it works out on balance, or in the aggregate.

Seeing objectives, constraints, and side effects in this way, it becomes evident that the function of finding is impossible to accomplish systematically because the outcomes of any program are infinite (Tribe 1972; Mohr 1983). It is impossible to know all of the side effects because, by definition, many side effects are unknown. As noted above, they are of concern nevertheless because they might easily become important constraints or objectives if and when they become known. Years ago, few dreamed of environmental pollution as an evaluation criterion, but it would rarely be overlooked today. Nord (1983) recently mentioned consumer sovereignty, the scope of the role of government in the economy, the vitality and independence of workers, the democratic nature of political institutions, stress and health in society, and the quality of family life as possible outcomes of many programs. Few would dream of these side effects as evaluation criteria today, but who can say that tomorrow they will not occupy the same sort of position as pollution? The possible side effects of a program are indeed infinite. Objectives and constraints are also infinite because it is impossible to know who all of the stakeholders are. The impact-analysis perspective has not attended to this issue of identifying all stakeholders because it has focused primarily on what needs to be done to maximize impact in connection with any one given outcome. Benefit-cost analysis and MAUT have tended to overlook or neglect it. Unfortunately, the infinite numbers mean that the problem cannot in principle be solved.

To make any headway on it at all, it is well to recognize two kinds of program evaluation: partisan and professional.

The *professional* case is one in which the evaluation is designed to serve the public interest—to be nonpartisan—no matter who is paying for it. The responsibility for inclusion and exclusion is that of the evaluator. The inclusion of outcomes must be determined by professional standards (nonpartisan ethics) and the technical methods at the disposal of the evaluation practitioner (to date, as noted above, the technical methods available for goal finding have been few, but some technical underpinnings are available for the limiting function, which is also critical in arriving at the final list of outcomes). Since there must be concern for all interests, it is recommended that an early part of every "professional" impact analysis consist in an effort to write down all of the *plausible* stakeholders and outcomes that the evaluation team, program personnel, and other experts can manage to think of as pertaining to that program. Evaluators must themselves reflect and also consult strategically to determine who the significant affected publics might be, and then reflect and consult again to determine the objectives, constraints, and side effects with which those publics will be concerned (Sherrill 1984; in some cases, good suggestions will be available from existing, theoretically oriented social science research—see Chen and Rossi 1980).

A *partisan* evaluation is one that is carried out for particular sponsors—who constitute an interest group concerning decision making about the program—and is designed to serve the interests of those sponsors. This is not to say that a partisan evaluation may not be professional in the sense of being planned and executed with the benefit of excellent training and competence, but rather that it is not the ethics of the profession that constitute the primary authority for determining content. Further, I mean in no way to imply that partisan evaluations have license to be unethical. Realistically, partisan evaluations will occur with substantial frequency. When they do, professional ethics and public responsibility still apply and the evaluator stands in much the same relation to client and public as does the responsible accountant. With these caveats understood, the outcomes to be considered in a partisan evaluation are those whose inclusion is likely to be of benefit to the sponsors. That makes the "finding" job a bit easier. It is obviously essential to work with the sponsors to elicit all of the objectives and constraints in which they believe they have an interest. This should often include the objectives and constraints of primary concern to the sponsors' opponents or other important parties to the eventual decision-making process, since such information may well be of benefit to the sponsors in mapping their strategy. It should also include any side effects regarding which the sponsors might benefit by having information, again because it enables the sponsors either to add to the weight of evidence on their side or to know, at least, what kinds of points are likely to be made on the other side. If, for example, one were interested in giving a fair trial to a voucher system for public education, one might well be concerned to investigate the claims of opponents that, "vouchers could foster segregation by race and class, undermine the Constitutional separation of church and state, encourage hucksterism in the schools, increase the tax burden for public support of schooling, undermine existing systems of professional tenure for teachers and administrators, and destroy the shared democratic values fostered by the traditional system of public schools" (Weiler 1976, p. 281).

The two major distinguishing characteristics of the partisan case concerning the finding function, then, are (1) that the evaluators are essentially advisers to a finite set of parties, perhaps just one group, so that the ultimate responsibility for what to include truly rests with the sponsors rather than the evaluators; and (2) only the concerns of a finite set of participants need be entered so that the infinity confronted is a very much smaller one than in the professional case.

These guidelines for the finding function are meager; they are, nevertheless, firmer than those that have previously been available and are in fact perhaps as systematic as they can be for the task.

Limiting

We turn now to a consideration of the function of *limiting* in the impact-analysis approach. The finding procedure might well yield a large list of outcomes that are candidates for inclusion in the research. Should all of them be accepted? One clear response is that only those entities that are true outcomes need be considered as such, and those must be considered in their proper role. In other words, the concept of the outcome line should be applied to the list. In the typical case, stakeholders will offer a great many outcomes that are in fact activities. These can be recognized as such, included in the research if the outcomes to which they pertain are included, and treated according to the guidelines for activities in Chapter Three. Furthermore, when one speaks of a multiple-outcome program, one does not refer to any and all impacts, but to multiple *outcomes of interest*. Even a single outcome line contains many outcomes; additional technology beyond that of Chapters One through Three is needed only because or when multiple outcome *lines* are indicated. The long list of impacts thus needs to be separated into distinct outcome lines, each with its own independent outcome of interest. To a great extent, the entries on the original list will then be seen to fall into groups, the number of groups being considerably smaller than the original number of impacts on the list. Each group will contain subobjectives, one outcome of interest, and further impacts that are consequent on that. Once activities, subobjectives, and consequent impacts (i.e., inherently valued outcomes beyond the outcome of interest) are assigned their proper places on the relevant outcome lines, so that the essential list now contains only the core member of each group—the true outcomes of interest in the project—much confusion is likely to be dispelled and the evaluator will confront a far more manageable task of selection, or limiting.

Although it may be shortened by applying outcome-line concepts, the list may still appear too long. Assume that it now contains only valid outcomes of interest of the program or administrative unit concerned. The evaluator faces a dilemma: a balanced and complete presentation of the effects of the program demands that all of these legitimate outcomes be included, but time and expense dictate that some be ignored or the evaluation will be impossible to conduct in a timely fashion, if at all.

At this point, it is important to recognize that completeness is neither an intelligent nor even a valid standard. We have emphasized the infinity problem. It means that, try as one might, one cannot include all potential impacts, nor even all of the important ones. In the 1950s, for example, public concern over air pollution led to the installation of tall smokestacks. What are the outcomes of interest in connection with tall smokestacks? One of them, extremely important, could hardly have been included at the time: acid rain. Tall smokestacks are now known to be a primary contributor to acid rain! Recognizing the inevitability of incompleteness but accepting the necessity to act with the benefit of as much information as possible, it becomes clear that an instrumental strategy is indicated. Consider the evaluation itself to be a program: usefulness then becomes its objective, adequate quality and quantity of information its subobjectives, and time and expense its primary constraints. Therefore, considering the objective and subobjectives, the list should not be reduced further by eliminating elements from it totally, thus banishing the very idea of certain information and perhaps reducing utility. On the other hand, in trying to keep within the constraints, it is not true that everything on the list has an equal claim to research resources. Some valid outcomes of interest of the original program cannot be researched, some need not be, and some should not be, under the circumstances. Let us elaborate briefly on these three bases for withholding research resources:

Some outcomes *cannot* realistically be researched, for example, because they would take more money than is available, because the results would not be available in time for the necessary policy making, or because the measurement technology is out of reach. One of the justifications offered for police diversion programs is that juveniles should not suffer the stigma of being labeled criminals as a result of court convictions (Klein et al. 1977). This outcome probably cannot be adequately researched. It would be essentially impossible to document and quantify the effects of such labeling—even in the short run and especially in the long run, which is more pertinent. Some outcomes *need* not be researched because the results are obvious, or assumed, or automatically achieved. For example, one aim of substituting the mediation of citizen disputes for court trials is greater privacy (Conner and Surette 1980): documenting such an outcome takes no special research. Some outcomes *should* not be researched, because they have too little impact on decision making about the program. In fact, outcomes may be loosely divided into major and minor as follows.

In finally reducing to manageable size the list of outcomes of interest to be researched, classifying them as major and minor can be extremely important. It is enough to obtain impact data on major outcomes because the minor ones are highly unlikely to change any action decision regarding the program. A major benefit (positively valued outcome) is one for which some level of attainment is potentially either necessary or sufficient to justify the program. A major cost (resource input or negatively valued outcome) is one for which some level of impact is potentially sufficient to make termination of the program or drastic curtailment desirable. If the outcome is minor—defined simply as anything that is not major—subjective estimates may well be as useful in the decision process as a full-scale analysis of impact would be. If classification as major or minor is uncertain, or if there is disagreement among stakeholders, the outcome must be left as major.

Finally, there may still be too many major outcomes left on the list to make a rigorous impact analysis of all of them feasible given the time and money available for the study. In MAUT, this will rarely be a problem because the techniques for assessment of impact are relatively inexpensive. The problem can arise in benefit-cost analysis, but even there the analysis costs tend to be mainly the time and energy of one or two researchers and these can be stretched to accommodate an additional benefit or cost of substantial importance. In the impact-analysis approach, however, assessment generally means applying an experimental or quasi-experimental design in the field, often involving questionnaires or extended observations, many subjects, expensive treatments, travel, and so forth. If there are multiple major outcomes of interest, each of them must have the same sort of impact analysis as if there were only one. Sometimes there are economies—the same subjects and observation periods serving more than one outcome, but frequently the doubling or trebling of outcomes means nearly doubling or trebling the resources consumed by the research. If it is possible to do the full job, that is the course to take, but if that is hardly practical, it is well to remember that all outcomes *need not* be rigorously researched to justify an evaluation. It is certainly true that decisions about programs are made time and again without the benefit of any systematic evaluation whatever. Further, not having information based on rigorous research does not mean excluding an outcome from consideration in the policy process; it simply means having a different and presumably lower quality of information about it. It was cautioned above that *no outcomes of interest should be eliminated totally from consideration.* All of those that cannot, need not, or should not be researched must then still be there; it is an important function of the evaluator to bring them to the attention of all concerned parties. One tries to research those that are most critical and those that can readily and inexpensively be studied; the rest, as with MAUT, must be managed with more subjective or at least less rigorous techniques.

Thus, while there is no algorithm that permits unambiguous limiting in the impact-analysis perspective, the above guidelines will go far toward reducing a large and confusing collection of potential outcomes to manageable proportions for the evaluation of programs of moderate scope.

Assessing Impacts

As its name suggests, impact analysis is almost entirely oriented toward implementing the third of the five functions, *assessing impacts*. The task is carried out, as has been noted, by means of certain research designs, with the implication that only past impacts are assessed. Since the subject was covered at length in the preceding chapters, it need not be addressed here.

Common-Scaling and Weighting

The final two functions, *common-scaling* and *weighting,* are ignored in the literature on impact analysis. One might try to put as many outcomes as one possibly could in dollars, as in benefit-cost analysis, or convert them to percent-of-plausible-distance scales and weight them subjectively, as in MAUT. There are so many pitfalls to both of these techniques, however, that they are not recommended for the general case (there may certainly be instances in which their application or partial application would be highly desirable). Too often, the benefits and costs dealt with in impact analyses are not possible to convert to dollars *with confidence*—outcomes such as attitude change, satisfaction, achievement in elementary school, mental health, cognitive development, awareness of political issues, divorce, environmental esthetics, extinction of animal and plant species, and so forth, to say nothing of human life and well-being. It is not that these conversions are impossible, just that their accuracy is so uncertain and that outcomes such as these occupy so extremely important a position in impact analysis that the necessity to use dollars would greatly undermine the utility of the whole approach.

MAUT is full of subjectivity. For decisions made by one person alone or when there is an unquestioned final authority, the disadvantages of subjectivity in common-scaling and weighting are not serious. When decisions are collective, however, as they so often are in the arenas of public administration and public policy, where impact analysis has been most frequently applied, the multiplicity of perspectives on plausibility and of preferred relative weights make aggregation into one outcome score rather pointless. Such averages of values can rarely be satisfying. One could derive a single outcome score for each interested party to the policy debate. That might help each individual concerned arrive at a preferred stance or bargaining position. But in the debate itself, whether in Congress, in bilateral bargaining, or in a staff meeting, these positions have to be justified. That cannot be done by reference to one's own, subjectively sculpted overall score. Others will not accept the weights and measures of the claimant. They have their own priorities and their own subjectively sculpted scores. Aside from rhetorical artistry, a stance on a policy can only be defended by reference to the actual results on salient individual outcomes expressed in original measurement scales.

All of this leads in the direction of leaving the results of impact analyses in the terms in which they were originally measured—attitude scales, lives lost, time saved, test scores in school, and so forth—eschewing the attempt to provide aggregate scores or relative weights of any sort. The common-scaling problem is not as important for decision making as one might think. Although it is logically impossible—beyond any shadow of a doubt—to make a rational choice among incommensurables, *human beings do it all the time.* We are past masters of the technique, whatever it is. If a person has to choose between so much health and so much time, for example, the choice is fairly readily made, *even though the same person might feel that conversion scales cannot be provided with confidence.*

Last, this procedure leaves participants in a decision process to make up their own minds individually about the action indicated and to arrive at a collective resolution by bargaining and politics instead of rational persuasion or demonstration. Decisions about public programs, however, and about many programs or projects in the private sector are generally taken in a political arena. Political processes are perfectly appropriate for many such decisions and in fact would be difficult to replace by any common-scaling and weighting schemes that are known. As long as the details of the application of such schemes are not perfectly consensual, they *cannot* shift the terms of the debate from the political to the rational. What is important is the availability of sound, convincing impact assessments on the right outcomes and subobjectives; the political and policy processes can handle the rest.

POSTSCRIPT: UTILIZATION

It has been claimed and demonstrated that program evaluations are not used as extensively as one would desire and expect (Leviton and Hughes 1981). Many reasons have been offered for this and suggestions have been made for improving the utility of evaluation research. Without quarreling with the data and speculation that have been reported on this subject, let us present a view of utilization in the particular perspective of this book. We have emphasized that impact analysis is not a long series of independent points and lessons, but rather an integrated structure, a logical whole. Let us then posit that the primary requisite for carrying out evaluations that will be used appropriately is high quality where quality refers to the whole scope of the integrated evaluation task.

In these terms, the present and previous chapters indicate that four aspects stand out:

1. *Comprehensiveness in the presentation of outcomes.* It is wrong to evaluate a program on one or two outcomes only, without any acknowledgment that certain others have relevance as well. The evaluator serves the policy process well by noting formally the range of considerations that may well be at stake in connection with the program under analysis.

2. *Correct choice of the outcomes that are to be submitted to actual research.* There are two kinds of issues here. One involves choice among outcome *lines.* As detailed in this chapter, many considerations enter into such a choice, including some that directly concern the probability that the results will be used. Can the variables be measured well enough for people to believe the data's message? Can the results be obtained in timely fashion, considering the needs of the decision-making process? Are the results really in doubt? Are they likely to be important or major? The second issue under this heading involves correct choice of the outcome of interest once a given outcome line has been indicated or selected. Here, the methods of Chapter Two, in particular, become important.

3. *Quality of selection and execution of research designs.* The evaluation must be carried out well in its more technical aspects. If it is possible to pick holes in the methods employed, those who are disinclined a priori to agree with the implications of the findings are highly likely to discover those flaws and to capitalize on them, even if the individuals concerned are not quantitatively sophisticated. Having an axe to grind makes one smart in pertinent areas.

4. *The evaluation should in most cases be formative.* People are rarely satisfied to know only that there is a certain impact, or lack of impact; they want to know why the effects are as they are and, above all, how it might be possible to make improvements. If the evaluation ignores this need, even the worthwhile information it contains will probably not be absorbed.

Program evaluations cannot be expected to determine the outcomes of policy processes. These generally involve politics, bargaining, and trade-offs with other policies, as well as personal considerations that even properly comprehensive goal-finding cannot and probably should not hope to include. The function of an evaluation is only to provide good information. However, that is a supremely important function. It is true that data will not always carry as much weight as pure rationality would dictate. What is important to recognize is that a sound evaluation with implications in favor of a certain policy alternative will provide powerful ammunition to the friends of that alternative and severe problems for its foes. That is why sound evaluation is important, where sound evaluation means recognizing the full scope of the task and doing the whole job well.

References

Baldus, D. C. 1973. "Welfare as a Loan: An Empirical Study of the Recovery of Public Assistance Payments in the United States." *Stanford Law Review* 25, pp. 123–250.

Berk, Richard A., Donnie M. Hoffman, Judith E. Maki, David Rauma, and Herbert Wong. August 1979. "Estimation Procedures for Pooled Cross-Sectional and Time Series Data." *Evaluation Quarterly* 3 (no. 3), pp. 385–410.

Berk, Richard A., and David Rauma. March 1983. "Capitalizing on Nonrandom Assignment to Treatments: A Regression-Discontinuity Evaluation of a Crime-Control Program." *Journal of the American Statistical Association* 78 (no. 381), Applications Section, pp. 21–27.

Berleman, William C., and Thomas W. Steinburn. 1967. "The Execution and Evaluation of a Delinquency Prevention Program." *Social Problems* 1 (no. 4), pp. 413–423.

Berry, Linda. December 1983. "Residential Conservation Program Impacts: Methods of Reducing Self-Selection Bias." *Evaluation Review* 7 (no. 6), pp. 753–776.

Blalock, Hubert M., Jr. 1972. *Social Statistics*. 2nd ed. New York: McGraw-Hill. First published in 1960.

Blumstein, Alfred, and Jacqueline Cohen. November 1979. "Control of Selection Effects in the Evaluation of Social Problems." *Evaluation Quarterly* 3 (no. 4), pp. 583–608.

Box, George E., and Gwilym M. Jenkins. 1970. *Time Series Analysis: Forecasting and Control*. San Francisco: Holden-Day.

Box, George E., and George C. Tiao. March 1975. "Intervention Analysis with Applications to Economic and Environmental Problems." *Journal of the American Statistical Association* 70 (no. 349), Theory and Methods Section, pp. 70–79.

Campbell, Donald T. 1977. "Focal Local Indicators for Social Program Evaluation." In Marcia Guttentag (ed.), *Evaluation Studies Review Annual,* Vol. 2. Beverly Hills: Sage, pp. 125–145.

―――――. 1984. "Foreword." In William M. Trochim, *Research Design for Program Evaluation: The Regression-Discontinuity Approach*. Beverly Hills: Sage Publications, pp. 15–43.

Campbell, Donald T., and Robert F. Boruch. 1975. "Making the Case for Randomized Assignment to Treatments by Considering the Alternatives: Six Ways in Which Quasi-Experimental Evaluations in Compensatory Education Tend to Underestimate Effects." In Carl A. Bennett and Arthur A. Lumsdaine (eds.), *Evaluation and Experiment: Some Critical Issues in Assessing Social Programs*. New York: Academic Press, pp. 195–296.

Campbell, Donald T., and Keith N. Clayton. 1961. "Avoiding Regression Effects in Panel Studies of Communication Impact." *Studies in Public Communication*, No. 3. Chicago: University of Chicago, Department of Sociology, pp. 99–118.

Campbell, Donald T., and Albert Erlebacher. 1970. "How Regression Artifacts in Quasi-Experimental Evaluations Can Mistakenly Make Compensatory Education Look Harmful." In J. Hellmuth (ed.), *Compensatory Education: A National Debate,* Vol. 3, *Disadvantaged Child.* New York: Brunner/Mazel, pp. 185–210.

Campbell, Donald T., and Donald W. Fiske. 1959. "Convergent and Discriminant Validation by the Multitrait-Multimethod Matrix." *Psychological Bulletin* 56, pp. 81–105.

Campbell, Donald T., and Julian C. Stanley. 1966. *Experimental and Quasi-Experimental Designs for Research.* Chicago: Rand McNally. Originally published as "Experimental and Quasi-Experimental Designs for Research on Teaching." In N. L. Gage (ed.), *Handbook of Research on Teaching.* Chicago: Rand McNally, 1963.

Chen, Huey-Tsyh, and Peter H. Rossi. September 1980. "The Multi-Goal, Theory-Driven Approach to Evaluation: A Model Linking Basic and Applied Social Science." *Social Forces* 59 (no. 1), pp. 106–122.

Cho, Yong Hyo. 1980. "A Multiple Regression Model for the Measurement of the Public Policy Impact on Big City Crime." In David Nachmias (ed.), *The Practice of Policy Evaluation.* New York: St. Martin's Press, pp. 264–288.

Clotfelter, Charles T., and John C. Hahn. 1980. "Assessing the National 55 m.p.h. Speed Limit." In D. Nachmias (ed.), *The Practice of Policy Evaluation.* New York: St. Martin's Press, pp. 396–411.

Coleman, James S. 1976. "Recent Trends in School Integration." In Gene V. Glass (ed.), *Evaluation Studies Review Annual,* Vol. 1, Beverly Hills: Sage, pp. 305–323.

Colton, Theodore, and Robert C. Buxbaum. 1977. "Motor Vehicle Inspection and Motor Vehicle Accident Mortality." In William B. Fairley and Frederick Mosteller (eds.), *Statistics and Public Policy.* Reading, Mass.: Addison-Wesley, pp. 131–142.

Conner, Ross F., and Ray Surette. December 1980. "Processing Citizens' Disputes outside the Courts." *Evaluation Review* 4 (no. 6), pp. 739–768.

Cook, Thomas D., and Donald T. Campbell. 1979. *Quasi-Experimentation: Design & Analysis Issues for Field Settings.* Chicago: Rand McNally.

Cronbach, Lee J., David R. Rogosa, Robert E. Floden, and Gary G. Price. 1977. "Analysis of Covariance in Nonrandomized Experiments: Parameters Affecting Bias." Occasional Paper. Stanford, Calif.: Stanford Evaluation Consortium, School of Education, Stanford University.

Deniston, O. Lynn. January–February 1969. "Migrant Camp Conditions Improved by Inspection." *Journal of Environmental Health* 31 (no. 4), pp. 338–346.

Deniston, O. Lynn. 1972a. "Program Planning for Disease Control Programs." Communicable Disease Center, Health Services and Mental Health Administration, Public Health Service, Department of Health, Education and Welfare.

_____. 1972b. "Evaluation of Disease Control Programs." Communicable Disease Center, Health Services and Mental Health Administration, Public Health Service, Department of Health, Education and Welfare.

Deniston, O. L., and I. M. Rosenstock. February 1973. "The Validity of Nonexperimental Designs for Evaluating Health Services." *Health Services Reports* 88 (no. 2), pp. 153–164.

Deniston, O. L., I. M. Rosenstock, and V. A. Getting. April 1968. "Evaluation of Program Effectiveness." *Public Health Reports* 83 (no. 4), pp. 323–335.

Duncan, Otis D. 1975. *Introduction to Structural Equation Models*. New York: Academic Press.

Dunham, Roger G., and Armand L. Mauss. August 1979. "Evaluation of Treatment Programs: A Statistical Resolution of Selection Bias Using the Case of Problem Drinkers." *Evaluation Quarterly* 3 (no. 3), pp. 411–426.

Edwards, Ward, and Marcia Guttentag. 1975. "Experiments and Evaluations: A Reexamination." In Carl A. Bennett and Arthur A. Lumsdaine (eds.), *Evaluation and Experiment: Some Critical Issues in Assessing Social Programs*. New York: Academic Press, pp. 409–464.

Edwards, Ward, and J. Robert Newman. 1982. *Multiattribute Evaluation*. Beverly Hills: Sage Publications.

Farquhar, John W., Nathan Maccoby, Peter D. Wood, Janet K. Alexander, Henry Breitrose, Byron W. Brown, Jr., William L. Haskell, Alfred L. McAlister, Anthony J. Meyer, Joyce D. Nash, and Michael P. Stern. 1978. "Community Education for Cardiovascular Health." In Thomas D. Cook and Associates (eds.), *Evaluation Studies Review Annual*, Vol. 3. Beverly Hills: Sage Publications, pp. 296–299.

Freeman, Howard E., Robert E. Klein, John W. Townsend, and Aaron Lechtig. 1981. "Nutrition and Cognitive Development among Rural Guatemalan Children." In Howard E. Freeman and Marion A. Solomon (eds.), *Evaluation Studies Review Annual*, Vol. 6, Beverly Hills: Sage Publications, pp. 339–359.

Geweke, John, and Burton A. Weisbrod. February 1984. "How Does Technological Change Affect Health Care Expenditures? The Case of a New Drug." *Evaluation Review* 8 (no. 1), pp. 75–92.

Gilbert, John P., Richard J. Light, and Frederick Mosteller. 1975. "Assessing Social Innovations: An Empirical Base for Policy." In Carl A. Bennett and Arthur A. Lumsdaine (eds.), *Evaluation and Experiment: Some Critical*

Issues in Assessing Social Programs. New York: Academic Press, pp. 39–194.

Glass, Gene V., George C. Tiao, and T. O. McGuire. May 1971. "Analysis of Data on the 1900 Revision of German Divorce Laws as a Time-Series Experiment." *Law and Society Review* 5 (no. 4), pp. 539–562.

Glass, Gene V., V. L. Willson, and J. M. Gottman. 1975. *Design and Analysis of Time-Series Experiments*. Boulder: Colorado Associated University Press.

Glock, Charles Y. 1955. " Some Applications of the Panel Method to the Study of Change." In Paul F. Lazarsfeld and Morris Rosenberg (eds.), *The Language of Social Research: A Reader in the Methodology of Social Research*. Glencoe, Ill.: The Free Press of Glencoe, pp. 242–249.

Goldberger, Arthur S. 1972. "Selection Bias in Evaluating Treatment Effects: Some Formal Illustrations." University of Wisconsin, Institute for Research on Poverty, Discussion Paper No. 123–72.

Goldman, Jerry. November 1979. "Resolution of Appellate Litigation: A Controlled Experiment." *Evaluation Quarterly* 3 (no. 4), pp. 557–582.

Gramlich, Edward M. 1981. *Benefit-Cost Analysis of Government Programs*. Englewood Cliffs, N.J.: Prentice-Hall.

Gramlich, Edward M., and Patricia P. Koshel. Summer 1975. "Is Real-World Experimentation Possible? The Case of Educational Performance Contracting." *Policy Analysis* 1 (no. 3), pp. 511–530.

Haefner, Don P. 1965. "Arousing Fear in Dental Health Education." *Journal of Public Health Dentistry* 25, pp. 140–146.

Hammond, K. R., and F. Kern. 1959. *Teaching Comprehensive Medical Care*. Cambridge, Mass.: Harvard University Press.

Hardy, Thomas. *A Laodicean*. 1905. New York: Harper & Row.

Hawthorne, Elizabeth M. 1988, in press. *Evaluating Employee Training Programs: A Research-Based Guide for Human Resources Managers*. Westport, Conn.: Quorum Books.

Heckman, James. 1976. "The Common Structure of Statistical Models of Truncation: Sample Estimation for Such Models." *Annals of Economic and Social Measurement* 5, pp. 475–492.

Hirst, Eric, John Trimble, Richard Goeltz, and N. Scott Cardell. December 1983. "Use of Synthetic Data in Dealing with Self-Selection: Improving Conservation Program Energy Savings Estimates." *Evaluation Review* 7 (no. 6), pp. 807–830.

Hook, J. in preparation. "Operation Whistlestop: An Interrupted Time-Series Analysis of a Community Crime Prevention Program." Evanston, Ill.: Department of Psychology, Northwestern University.

Hoole, Francis W. 1978. *Evaluation Research and Development Activities*. Beverly Hills: Sage Publications.

Hyman, Herbert H., and Charles R. Wright. 1971. "Evaluating Social Action Programs." In Francis G. Caro (ed), *Readings in Evaluation Research*. New York: Russell Sage Foundation, pp. 185–220.

Jackson, Bryan O. 1982. "The Linkage between Implementation Processes and Policy Outcomes: An Analysis of HUD's Administrative Agency Experiment." Doctoral Dissertation, The University of Michigan, Ann Arbor, Michigan.

Jackson, Bryan O., and Lawrence B. Mohr. August 1986. "Rent Subsidies: An Impact Evaluation and an Application of the Random-Comparison-Group Design." *Evaluation Review* 10 (no. 4), pp. 483–517.

Jason, Leonard A., Kathleen McCoy, David Blanco, and Edwin S. Zolik. 1981. "Decreasing Dog Litter: Behavioral Consultation to Help a Community Group." In Howard E. Freeman and Marion A. Solomon (eds.), *Evaluation Studies Review Annual*, Vol. 6. Beverly Hills: Sage Publications, pp. 660–674.

Johnston, J. 1972. *Econometric Methods,* 2nd ed. New York: McGraw Hill.

Judd, Charles M., and David A. Kenny. October 1981. "Process Analysis: Estimating Mediation in Treatment Evaluations." *Evaluation Review* 5 (no. 5), pp. 602–619.

Judd, Charles M., and David A. Kenny. 1981. *Estimating the Effects of Social Interventions.* Cambridge: Cambridge University Press.

Kelling, George L., Tony Pate, Duane Dieckman, and Charles E. Brown. 1976. "The Kansas City Preventive Patrol Experiment: A Summary Report." In Gene V. Glass (ed.), *Evaluation Studies Review Annual*, Vol. 1, Beverly Hills: Sage Publications, pp. 605–657.

Kelman, H. R. April 1962. "An Experiment in the Rehabilitation of Nursing Home Patients." *Public Health Reports* 77 (no. 4), pp. 356–366.

Kerlinger, Fred N. 1967. *Foundations of Behavioral Research.* New York: Holt, Rinehart & Winston.

Kershaw, David N. 1980. "A Negative-Income-Tax Experiment." In David Nachmias (ed.), *The Practice of Policy Evaluation.* New York: St. Martin's Press, pp. 27–40.

Klein, Malcolm W., Kathie S. Teilmann, Joseph A. Styles, Suzanne B. Lincoln, and Susan Labin-Rosensweig. 1977. "The Explosion in Police Diversion Programs: Evaluating the Structural Dimensions of a Social Fad." In Marcia Guttentag (ed.), *Evaluation Studies Review Annual*, Vol. 2, Beverly Hills: Sage Publications, pp. 549–568.

Kmenta, Jan. 1971. *Elements of Econometrics.* New York: Macmillan.

Larkey, Patrick D. 1979. "Process Models of Governmental Resource Allocation and Program Evaluation." In Lee Sechrest, Stephen G. West, Melinda A. Phillips, Robin Redner, and William Yeaton (eds.), *Evaluation Studies Review Annual*, Vol. 4. Beverly Hills: Sage Publications, pp. 284–317.

Lee, Yoon-Shik. 1986. "The Child Restraint Requirement Law: An Impact Analysis and an Exploration of Program Evaluation Using Multiple Time Series." Doctoral dissertation, The University of Michigan, Ann Arbor, Michigan.

Leviton, Laura C., and Edward F. Hughes. August 1981. "Research on the Utilization of Evaluations: A Review and Synthesis." *Evaluation Review* 5 (no. 4), pp. 525–548.

Lewis-Beck, Michael S. March 1979. "The Economic Effects of Revolution: Models, Measurement, and the Cuban Evidence." *American Journal of Sociology* 84 (no. 5), pp. 1127–1149.

Lyons, Morgan, and G. Alec Steele. November 1977. "Evaluation of a Home Health Aid Training Program for the Elderly." *Evaluation Quarterly* 1 (no. 4), pp. 609–620.

Mazur-Hart, Stanley F., and John J. Berman. 1979. "Changing from Fault to No-Fault Divorce: An Interrupted Time Series Analysis." In Lee Sechrest, Stephen G. West, Melinda A. Phillips, Robin Redner, and William Yeaton (eds.), *Evaluation Studies Review Annual*, Vol. 4. Beverly Hills: Sage Publications, pp. 586–599.

McCleary, Richard, Andrew C. Gordon, David McDowall, and Michael D. Maltz. 1979. "How a Regression Artifact Can Make *Any* Delinquency Intervention Program Look Effective." In Lee Sechrest, Stephen G. West, Melinda A. Phillips, Robin Redner, and William Yeaton (eds.), *Evaluation Studies Review Annual*, Vol. 4. Beverly Hills: Sage Publications, pp. 626–652.

Mohr, Lawrence B. 1982. *Explaining Organizational Behavior: The Limits and Possibilities of Theory and Research*. San Francisco: Jossey-Bass Publishers.

————. August 1982a. "On Rescuing the Nonequivalent-Control-Group Design: The Random-Comparison-Group Approach." *Sociological Methods and Research* 11 (no. 1), pp. 53–80.

————. 1985. "The Reliability of the Case Study as a Source of Information." In Lee S. Sproull and Patrick D. Larkey (eds.), *Advances in Information Processing in Organizations*, Vol. 2; Robert F. Coulam and Richard A. Smith (eds.), *Research on Public Organizations*. Greenwich, Conn.: JAI Press, pp. 65–94.

Moran, Garrett E. February 1985. "Regulatory Strategies for Workplace Injury Reduction." *Evaluation Quarterly* 9 (no. 1), pp. 21–34.

Muller, Andreas. 1979. "Evaluation of the Costs and Benefits of Motorcycle Helmet Laws." In Howard E. Freeman and Marion A. Solomon (eds.), *Evaluation Studies Review Annual*, Vol. 6. Beverly Hills: Sage Publications, pp. 80–114.

Murray, Charles A., and Louis A.Cox, Jr. 1979. "The Suppression Effect and the Institutionalization of Children." In Lee Sechrest, Stephen G. West, Melinda A. Phillips, Robin Redner, and William Yeaton (eds.), *Evaluation Studies Review Annual*, Vol. 4. Beverly Hills: Sage Publications, pp. 653–663.

Newcomb, Tim M. June 1984. "Conservation Program Evaluations: The Control of Self-Selection Bias." *Evaluation Review* 8 (no. 3), pp. 425–440.

Nord, Walter R. 1983. "A Political and Economic Perspective on Organizational Effectiveness." In Kim S. Cameron and David A. Whetten (eds.), *Organizational Effectiveness: A Comparison of Multiple Models*. New York: Academic Press, pp. 95–133.

Patton, Michael Q. 1979. "Evaluation of Program Implementation." In Lee

Sechrest, Stephen G. West, Melinda A. Phillips, Robin Redner, and William Yeaton (eds.), *Evaluation Studies Review Annual,* Vol. 4. Beverly Hills: Sage Publications, pp. 318–346.

Payne, Beverly C., and Thomas Lyons. 1978. *Evaluation and Improvement in Ambulatory Medical Care.* Final Report Grant No. R01 H5 01583-02. Washington, D.C.: National Center for Health Services Research.

Pindyck, Robert S., and Daniel L. Rubinfeld. 1976. *Econometric Models and Economic Forecasts.* New York: McGraw-Hill.

Reichardt, Charles S. 1979. "The Statistical Analysis of Data from Nonequivalent Group Designs." In Thomas D. Cook and Donald T. Campbell (eds.), *Quasi-Experimentation: Design and Analysis Issues for Field Settings.* Chicago: Rand McNally, pp. 147–205.

Rist, Ray C. August 1970. "Student Social Class and Teacher Expectations: The Self-Fulfilling Prophecy in Ghetto Education." *Harvard Education Review* 40 (no. 3), pp. 411–451.

Rosenbloom, David H. 1980. "The Federal Affirmative Action Policy." In David Nachmias (ed.), *The Practice of Policy Evaluation.* New York: St. Martin's Press, pp. 169–187.

Rosenstock, Irwin M. July 1966. "Why People Use Health Services." *Milbank Memorial Fund Quarterly* 44 (no. 3, part 2), pp. 94–127.

Ross, H. Laurence. 1976. "The Scandinavian Myth: The Effectiveness of Drinking-and-Driving Legislation in Sweden and Norway." In Gene V. Glass (ed.), *Evaluation Studies Review Annual,* Vol. 1, Beverly Hills: Sage Publications, pp. 578–604.

Scriven, Michael. 1972. "The Methodology of Evaluation." In Carol H. Weiss (ed.), *Evaluating Action Programs: Readings in Social Action and Education.* Boston: Allyn & Bacon, pp. 123–136.

————. 1976. "Maximizing the Power of Causal Investigations: The Modus Operandi Method." In Gene V. Glass (ed.), *Evaluation Studies Review Annual,* Vol. 1. Beverly Hills: Sage Publications, pp. 101–118.

Selltiz, Claire, Lawrence S. Wrightsman, and Stuart W. Cook. 1976. *Research Methods in Social Relations.* 3rd ed. New York: Holt, Rinehart, & Winston.

Sherrill, Sam. August 1984. "Toward a Coherent View of Evaluation." *Evaluation Review* 8 (no. 4), pp. 443–466.

Skipper, J. S., Jr., and R. C. Leonard. 1968. "Children, Stress, and Hospitalization: A Field Experiment." *Journal of Health and Social Behavior* 9, pp. 275–287.

Smith, Mary L., Roy Gabriel, James Schott, and William L. Padia. 1976. "Evaluation of the Effects of Outward Bound." In Gene V. Glass (ed.), *Evaluation Studies Review Annual,* Vol. 1. Beverly Hills: Sage Publications. pp. 400–421. Reprinted from Boulder, Colorado: Bureau of Educational Field Services, Laboratory of Educational Research, School of Education, University of Colorado, 1975.

Smith, William G. 1976. "Evaluation of the Clinical Services of a Regional Mental Health Center." In Gene V. Glass (ed.), *Evaluation Studies Review Annual,* Vol. 1. Beverly Hills: Sage Publications, pp. 343–355.

Somers, Gerald G., and Ernest W. Stromsdorfer. 1980. "A Cost-Effectiveness Analysis of In-School and Summer Neighborhood Youth Corps: A Nationwide Evaluation." In David Nachmias (ed.), *The Practice of Policy Evaluation*. New York: St. Martin's Press, pp. 67–79.

Tashman, L. J., and K. R. Lamborn. 1979. *The Ways and Means of Statistics*. New York: Harcourt Brace Jovanovich.

Tiao, George C., and George E. Box. 1983. "An Introduction to Applied Multiple Time Series Analysis." Working Paper No. 101. De Kalb, Ill.: Scientific Computing Associates.

Tribe, Laurence H. Fall 1972. "Policy Science: Analysis or Ideology?" *Philosophy and Public Affairs* 2 (no. 1), pp. 66–110.

Trochim, William M. 1984. *Research Design for Program Evaluation: The Regression-Discontinuity Approach*. Beverly Hills: Sage Publications.

Volpe, Anne, and Robert Kastenbaum. January 1967. "Beer and TLC." *American Journal of Nursing* 67 (no. 1), pp. 100–103.

Waldo, Gordon P., and Theodore G. Chiricos. 1977. "Work Release and Recidivism: An Empirical Evaluation of Social Policy." In Marcia Guttentag (ed.), *Evaluation Studies Review Annual*, Vol. 2. Beverly Hills: Sage Publications, pp. 623–644.

Warner, Kenneth E. November 1984. "The Effects of Publicity and Policy on Smoking and Health." *Business and Health* 2 (no. 1), pp. 7–13.

Webber, Melvin M. 1980. "The BART Experience—What Have We Learned?" In David Nachmias (ed), *The Practice of Policy Evaluation*, New York: St. Martin's Press, pp. 412–439.

Weiler, Daniel. 1976. "A Public School Voucher Demonstration: The First Year of Alum Rock. Summary and Conclusions." In Gene V. Glass (ed.), *Evaluation Studies Review Annual*, Vol. 1. Beverly Hills: Sage Publications, pp. 279–304.

Zimring, Franklin E. 1975. "Firearms and Federal Law: The Gun Control Act of 1968." In Gene V. Glass (ed.), *Evaluation Studies Review Annual*, Vol. 1, Beverly Hills: Sage Publications, pp. 511–577. Reprinted from *Journal of Legal Studies* 4 (no. 1), 1975, pp. 133–198.

Index

Index

A

Achievement measurement, 54
Activities, 1–2, 10
  definition, 14
  implementation analysis, 31–32
  multichannel treatment, 42
Additive effects of volunteering, 170,
  173–77
  overcoming effects by research de-
    sign, 174–76
Adequacy ratio, 2, 5–8, 87
After-the-fact time series, 165
A priori characteristics of subject, 63–
  64
ARIMA modeling, 154, 157–58
  advantages over regression modeling,
    157–58
  goals, 157
  methods of parameter estimation,
    160
  program evaluation, 160
Assessment; see Impact assessment
Assignment
  contamination, 62–64
  divergent, 62–63
  experimental design, 45, 97
  procedures, 98
  random measurement error, 107–8
  rigid, 101, 105, 108
Attitude measurement, 54
Attitude scaling, 5
Attrition, 52, 56–57, 177–78
Annual Housing Survey, 141
Autocorrelation, 154, 157
Autoregressive, Integrated, Moving Average; see ARIMA modeling

B

Basic bivariate regression equation,
  81–83
  modeling a treatment, 82

Basic experimental design; see Experimental design
Bay Area Rapid Transit System
  (BART) evaluation, 52–53
Before-after design, 49, 54–55, 132
  centralized selection, 181
  contamination, 64
  threats to validity, 57, 69
  time-series compared, 148
Behavior as outcome, 33–34
Behavior prerequisites, 33–34
Beneficial impact of program, 11–12
Benefit-cost analysis, 1, 195–97
  assessing impact function, 195–96
  common-scaling, 196
  data acquisition, 196
  economic theory as basis of extrapo-
    lation, 196
  finding, 195
  limiting, 195, 206
  weighting, 196–97
Berk, Richard A., 99, 108, 112, 160
Berleman, William C., 65, 69, 177
Berman, John J., 154
Berry, Linda, 169, 174
Biased measurement error; see Nonran-
  dom measurement error
Bias in slopes, 126–30
Bivariate linear regression equation,
  81–82
Bivariate regression for program evalu-
  ation, 83
Blalock, Hubert M., Jr., 93
Blumstein, Alfred, 173
Boruch, Robert F., 71, 131
Box, George E., 156–57, 160
Bracketing, 197
Buxbaum, Robert C., 182

C

C (counterfactual), 3
Campbell, Donald T., 44, 49, 52, 54, 62, 65, 68, 69, 71, 72, 76, 96, 97, 99, 105, 106, 110, 112, 116, 117, 121, 124, 131, 132, 156, 158, 164, 165, 171, 173, 175, 181
Causal chain, 12, 29, 70, 186
Causal distance, 190–91
Causal impact, 112
Causal inference function, 47, 91–96
Causality, 12
 Modus Operandi method, 186–87
 use of subobjectives to demonstrate, 186–91
Causal proximity, 190, 192
Causal relations, 28, 29
Centralized selection, 45, 49, 97, 165
 randomized and nonrandomized, 97
CETA program evaluation, 41
Chance, 95
Change over time, 53
Characteristic path of events, 186
Chen, Huey Tsyh, 203
Chiricos, Theodore G., 69
Cho, Yong Hyo, 168
Chronbach, Lee G., 173
Classic experimental design, 46
Clayton, Keith N., 72
Cohen, Jacqueline, 173
Clotfelter, Charles T., 166
Clumping, 180–81
Coincidence, 178–82, 189
 random, 179
Coleman, James S., 184
Coleman report, 184
Colton, Theodore, 182
Common-scaling, 194, 207–8
 benefit-cost analysis, 196
 MAUT, 198–99
 multiple -outcome evaluation, 202
Comparative-change design, 81
 compared to comparison-discontinuity design, 81
 internal validity threats, 115–31
 random measurement error, 130–31
 selection-Q bias, 117–30
Comparative methods of program organization, 41
 outcome lines, 43
Comparative posttest design, 58, 60
Comparative time series, 146
Comparative-time series design, 158–62
 effect of history, 159–60
 estimation of treatment effects, 159
Comparison group, 53, 55, 58, 115–16, 158

Comparison group—*Cont.*
 matched, 118–22
 unmatched, 122–26
 volunteering, 174
Comparison group design, 64
 estimating treatment effect, 135–36
 regression-discontinuity design, 101
 threat to, 65–66
Conclusion validity, 44 n, 46
Confidence intervals, 153
Conner, Ross F., 205
Construct validity, 44 n
Contamination, 49, 52, 66
 assignment, 62–64
 comparative-change design, 116–17
 ex-post-facto design, 165, 182
 incomplete or improper experimental controls, 64–65
 threat to validity, 59, 62–65
 within treatment delivery element, 64
Control group, 45
 increase of sensitivity, 47
 threats to internal validity, 55, 57
Control-group mean, 2
Controls
 contamination, 64–65
 incomplete or improper, 64–65
Control variables, 48
 pretest, 84
 regression equation, 83–87
 volunteering effects, 173
Cook, Thomas D., 65, 68, 69, 105, 106, 110, 116, 132, 165, 173
Correlational design, 168
Correlation between two sample variables, 90
Counterfactual (C), 3, 6, 47–48, 53, 62, 82
 estimating, 4
 outcome line, 21
 problem, 11
 quasi-experimental design, 52
 regression analysis, 62, 87
 time-series design, 147–48
Coverage level of measure, 2, 7–8
Cowbird control program, 36–39
Cox, Louis A., Jr., 56
Curvilinearity, 110–14
 null case assumption, 112–13

D

Data analysis, 80
 application to program design, 10
Decentralized selection, 97, 165
Decision-making analysis, 197
Deniston, O. L., 2, 4, 6, 10, 26, 33, 40, 56
Design
 characteristics of, 50–51

Design—*Cont.*
  comparative-change design; *see* Com-
    parative-change design
  comparative time-series design; *see*
    Comparative time-series design
  experimental design; *see* Experimen-
    tal design
  ex-post-facto design; *see* Ex-post-
    facto design
  framework for impact analysis, 48–
    49
  implementation, 62
  inadequacy, 48
  interrupted time-series design; *see*
    Interrupted time-series design
  nonexperimental, 44
  quality of, 64
    external and internal validity, 44–
      45
  quasi-experimental design; *see*
    Quasi-experimental design
  random-comparison group design; *see*
    Random-comparison group
    design
  randomized experiment, 44
  regression-discontinuity design; *see*
    Regression-discontinuity design
  subobjectives as design; *see* Subobjec-
    tives as design
  time-series design; *see* Time-series
    design
Detrimental impact of program, 11–12
Difference of means, 3, 83
Difference of proportions, 3
Discovery subobjective, 12, 13, 32–33
  example, 34
Disturbance terms, 105–6
Divergent assignment, 62–63
Divergent attrition, 59, 62–63, 65
Divergent events, 53–54, 59, 63, 65
Divergent history, 57, 62–63, 116–17
Divergent maturation, 55, 59, 62
Divergent regression, 124
Double-blind experiment, 64
Dummy variable, 82
Duncan, Otis D., 187
Dunham, Roger G., 173
Durbin-Watson test, 154

E

Econometric modeling function, 92–93,
  95, 103
Economic theory as applied to benefit-
  cost analysis, 196
Edwards, Ward, 197–98
Effectiveness ratio, 2, 4, 8
Effect statistic, 95
Elementary quasi-experimental design,
  50
Erlebacher, Albert, 71, 76, 121, 124

Error
  nonrandom measurement, 108–10
  random measurement, 107–8, 130
  random sampling, 63–64
  specification, 102–3
Error terms, 103
Error variance, 47
Evaluation design; *see* Design
Experimental control
  contamination, 64–65
  incomplete or improper controls, 64–
    65
Experimental design, 45, 50, 71
  centralized selection, 45
  external validity, 70
  function of significance testing, 91–
    92, 94
  internal validity, 66, 70
  random assignment, 45, 97
  substitute, 61
  threats to internal validity, 62, 64–65
    contamination, 62, 64–65
    external events, 54
    maturation, 55
    selection, 61, 66
    testing, 55
Experimental design function of significance testing, 91–92, 94
Experimental group, 45
  increase of sensitivity, 47
Experimental group mean, 2
Ex-post-facto design, 45, 163–83
  coincidence as source of selection
    bias, 178–82
  compared to quasi-experimental de-
    sign, 163
  concept, 164–68
  contamination, 182
  manipulation, 164
  reconstructed type of study, 168, 175
  retrospectively documented, 164
  significance testing, 95–96
  spuriousness, 165–70, 178
  time-order problems, 182–83
  volunteering, 168–78
External events, threat of, 52–54, 63
  comparison group, 53
External validity, 44–45
  compared in importance to internal
    validity, 70
  generalization, 66–67
  random-comparison group design,
    144
  significance testing, 94
  subobjectives as design, 192
  threat to, 45, 49
  volunteerism, 170

F

Factorial experiment, 42–43
Farquhar, John W., 63
Finding, 193
  benefit-cost analysis, 195

Finding—*Cont.*
  impact analysis, 200–204
  MAUT, 197–98
Fiske, Donald W., 69
Formative evaluation, 25–26
  activities, 31
  implementation of program, 31–32
  subobjectives, 27–31, 35–39
Freeman, Howard E., 63
Fuzzy cut points, 105–7

G
Gabriel, Roy, 156
Gain score analysis, 88–90
Gap, 6–7, 87
Generalizability, 66–67, 69
Generalized-least square estimation, 154
Gentlemen's Agreement, study of evaluative impact, 88, 165
Gewecke, John, 166
Gilbert, John P., 44, 61, 65, 69
Glass, Gene V., 156–57, 160
Glock, Charles Y., 88, 165
Goldberger, Arthur S., 105
Goldman, Jerry, 69, 70
Gramlich, Edward M., 65, 129, 143, 195–96
Guttentag, Marcia, 197

H
Haefner, Don P., 69
Hahn, John C., 166
Hammond, K. R., 65
Hardy, Thomas, 3
Hawthorne, Elizabeth M., 26, 194, 196, 201
Hawthorne effect, 64
Heckman, James, 173
History threats to internal validity, 49–59, 66, 116–17
  attrition, 52, 56–57
  comparison group, 54
  external events, 52–54
  maturation, 52, 54–55
  regression, 52, 56, 59, 71–79
  single-group, over-time design, 65
  testing, 52, 54–55
Hoole, Francis W., 71
Housing subsidy program, research projects, 141–42, 176
Hughes, Edward F., 208
Hyman, Herbert M., 31, 41–42

I
Impact analysis
  comparison with other evaluation techniques, 194–200

Impact analysis—*Cont.*
  definition, 1, 3
  finding function, 200–204
  limiting function, 200, 204–6
  multiple administration outcomes, 194–208
  multiple regression; *see* Multiple regression analysis
  program objectives and constraints, 200–201
  program side effects, 201
  stakeholder, 200
Impact analysis design; *see* Design
Impact assessment, 3, 194
  benefit-cost analysis, 195–96
  data acquisition, 196
  economic theory as basis for extrapolation, 196
  impact analysis, 207
  MAUT, 198
  subjective judgement, 198
Implementation
  activities, 31–32
  assignment of subjects, 62
  contamination, 62
  controls, 62
  delivery of treatment, 62
  formative evaluation, 31–32
Impurity of treatment condition, 182
Incomplete or improper experimental controls, 64–65
Inference of treatment effect, 47
  quasi-experimental design, 180–81
Inherently valued outcome, 11–12
  definition, 15
Inherent problem, 11
Interaction, 143
Interactive effects of volunteering, 170–73
  voluntary attrition, 177–78
Intercept bias
  matched groups, 118–22
  unmatched groups, 122–26
Internal validity, 44–45
  compared in importance to external validity, 70
  random-comparison group design, 142–43
  subobjectives as design, 183, 192
  threats to, 48–49, 52–66, 115–16, 146, 166–67
    contamination, 49
    history; *see* History threats to internal validity
    selection, 44, 58–62, 66
  true experimental design compared to before-after design, 55
Interrupted-time-series design, 132, 147–50, 158
  centralized selection, 181
Interval estimate of treatment effect, 140
Intrasession history, 53

J

Jackson, Bryan O., 139, 141–42, 176, 201
Jason, Leonard A., 58
Jenkins, Gwilyn M., 157
Johnston, J., 102, 139
Judd, Charles M., 27, 44 n, 46, 98, 115, 164–65

K

Kansas City Preventive Control Experiment, 1
Kastenbaum, Robert, 18
Kelling, George L., 1
Kelman, H. R., 18, 67
Kenny, David A., 27, 44 n, 46, 98, 115, 164–65
Kerlinger, Fred H., 69
Kern, F., 65
Kershaw, David H., 7
Kirtland's warbler evaluation, example of use of subobjectives, 35–39
Klein, Malcolm W., 205
Kmenta, Jan, 160
Knowledge subobjective, 33
Koshel, Patricia P., 65, 129

L

Lamborn, K. R., 167
Larkey, Patrick D., 3
Lee, Yon Shik, 26, 160
Leonard, R. C., 48
Leviton, Laura C., 208
Lewis-Beck, Michael S., 149, 152, 164
Light, Richard J., 44, 61, 65, 69
Limiting, 193
  benefit-cost analysis, 195
  impact analysis, 200, 204–6
  MAUT, 198
Local history, 53
Locus of decision, 45
Locus of selection, 45
Lyons, Morgan, 201
Lyons, Thomas, 165

M

McCleary, Richard, 56, 71, 76, 78
McGuire, T. O., 156
Manipulation, 164–65, 168
  selection process, 165
Matched groups, intercept bias, 118–22, 123–24
Matching, 120–21, 124
Maturation threat, 52, 55–56, 59
Mauss, Armand L., 173

MAUT; *see* Multiattribute-utility technology
Mazur-Hart, Stanley F., 154
Means, difference of, 3
Median, 90
Method of subobjectives, 185–91
Mixed designs, 50
Modus Operandi method of demonstrating causality, 186
Mohr, Lawrence B., 125, 139, 141–42, 167, 186, 201–2
Moran, Garrett E., 76
Mosteller, Frederick, 44, 61, 65, 69
Motivation subobjective, 33
Muller, Andreas, 192
Multiple outcome administrative program, 193
Multiattribute-utility technology (MAUT)
  finding, 197
  impact assessment function, 198–99
  limiting, 206
  stakeholders, 197–98
  subjectivity, 207
Multichannel treatment of program organization, 42–43
Multiple outcomes, 39–41, 193–208
  assessing impact, 194
  benefit-cost analysis, 195–97
  common-scaling, 194, 202
  finding, 193, 197–98, 200–204
  impact analysis, 200–208
  limiting, 193, 198, 200, 204–6
  multiattribute-utility technology, 197–99
  weighting, 194, 196–98, 200, 202
Multiple regression analysis, 80
  basic bivariate equation, 81–83
  control variable, 83–87
  as impact statement, 82
  relation to gain score approach, 88–90
  significance testing of impact parameter, 90–96
Murray, Charles A., 56

N

Natural experiment, 164–65
  quasi-experimental, 166
Negative income tax experiments, 7, 11
Newman, J. Robert, 197–98
Noise, 150, 152, 156
Noncontinuous null case outcome, 112
Nonexperimental design, 44–45
Nonrandom measurement error, 108–10
  intentional misclassification, 108–10
Nord, Walter R., 202
Null case curvilinear relations, 111

Null case estimate, 138
Null case interaction, 111
Null case outcome, 47, 87, 100, 112, 137

O

Objective; *see also* Outcome of interest
  compared to outcome, 21
One-group design; *see* Single-group design
One-Shot Case Study, 49
Operationalization, 68
  outcome dimension, 69
Outcome line, 12–17, 204
  acknowledging counterfactual, 21
  construction, 14
  cowbird control program, 38
  distinction between outcomes and activities, 13
  distraction from problem, 19
  home energy audit, 16–17
  levels of coverage, 20–21
  multichannel treatment, 43
  problem definition, 21–23
  program theory, 14
  recognition of multiple concerns, 19
  recognizing targeted problem, 19–20
  relation of problem to, 18–21
Outcome of interest, 2–3, 10–11, 204
  inherently valued, 15
  limiting outcomes, 204–5
  outcome line, 12, 14–18
  subobjectives, 28
Outcomes, 11
  compared to objectives, 21
  distinguished from activities on outcome line, 13
  inherently valued, 11–12
  limiting, 193, 198, 200, 204–6
  multiple; *see* Multiple outcomes
  null case, 47, 87, 100, 112, 137
  and problem, 10–23
  random measurement error, 107
Outlier point, 137
Outward Bound program evaluation, 40
Over-time design, 59

P

Padia, William L., 156
Partisan program evaluation, 203–4
Parts, 39–41
  definition, 40
  examples, 40
Passive observation, 161
Patton, Michael Q., 12
Payne, Beverly C., 165
Pearson correlation, 27
Planned impact of program, 4
Political campaign evaluation, 43
Pooling of data, 159–60

Population, 45
Population at risk, 7–8
Population norm, 133
Population of concern, 134–35
Population treated, 7
Posttest, 46, 54, 82, 117, 118
  R-comparative design, 46–48, 53, 59
Predictor, 47
Predictor variables, 48
  random measurement error, 107
Presumptive reasoning, 57, 129, 132–33, 137, 181, 185
Pretest, 46–48, 53
  comparative-change design, 115, 117–18
  contamination, 48
  control variable, 84
  function in evaluation research, 118
  interaction with treatment, 54, 69
  random-comparison group design, 135–36, 141
  random measurement error, 107, 130–31
  spuriousness, 169
  threat of history, 54–55
  used as denominator, 89
Pretest data, 111
Probability distribution, 90–91
Problem, 2, 10–12
  beneficial impact, 11
  counterfactual, 11
  defined, 22
    relative to a given program, 10
  relation to outcome line, 18–23
  relevant condition, 10
Professional program evaluation, 202–3
Professional Standards Review Organizations (PSROs) program evaluation, 40
Program, 1
  basic concepts, 39
  beneficial or detrimental impacts, 11–12
  comparative methods, 41
  constraints, 200–202
  defined, 193
  diverse elements within, 39–43
  multichannel treatment, 42–43
  multiple outcomes, 39–40, 193–209
  objectives, 200–202
  organization for research, 39–41
  outcome line, 43
  parts, 39–41
  quantifiers of effectiveness, 2–9
Program evaluation
  function of, 209
  framework for study, 2
  partisan, 203–4
  professional, 202–3
  quantifying effectiveness, 2–8
  utilization, 208–9

Program impact, 3
  beneficial or detrimental, 11–12
  planned, 4
  setting, 67
Program personnel, 13–14
Program theory, 1
  outcome line, 14
  multiple outcomes, 193–201
  testing, 1–2
Proportional-gain expectation, 89–90
Proportions, difference of, 3
Prospective evaluation technique, 194,
  197
Pseudotreatment effect, 107
Psychological effect of treatment, 64
Pindyck, Robert S., 160

Q

Quantifiers of program effectiveness,
  2–7
  coverage level of, 7–8
Quasi-experimental design, 45
  assignment, 97
  centralized selection, 49–50, 181
  characteristics of, 49–50
  comparative-change design, 115–31
  ex-post-facto design, 163
  nonrandom assignment, 49
  random comparative-group design,
    132–45
  significance testing, 94–96
  subobjectives, 188
  threats to validity, 52, 59, 63, 66, 115
  time-series design, 146–62

R

R^2, 124–25
Random assignment, 42
Random-comparison group design,
  132–45
  concept of design, 133–34
  estimating treatment effect, 135–42
  ex-post-facto design, 176
  population of concern, 134–35
  population norm, 133–34
  regression models, 81
  subobjectives, 188
  threats to validity, 142–45
    external validity, 144
    interaction, 143
    internal validity, 142–43
Randomization, 45–46, 55, 57–61, 63,
  66, 98
  function of variables in evaluation
    design, 84
  significance testing, 91–92
  threats to validity, 115
  unhappy; *see* Unhappy
    randomization
Randomized-comparative-change design; *see* R-comparative-change
  design

Randomized experiment, 44
Random measurement error, 107–8,
  130–31, 143
Random-sample survey, 91
Random sampling, 91
Random sampling error, 62, 64
Range, 90
Rauma, David, 99, 108, 110
R-C, 3, 11
R-comparative-change design, 46–48,
  61, 105
R-comparative-posttest design, 46–48,
  53, 59
Reconstruction studies, 168
Recursive structural equation, 187
Regression algorithm, 101, 103
Regression analysis, 28–29; *see also*
    Multiple regression analysis
  interrupted-time series data, 151
Regression artifact, 71–79
  basis underlying the standard ac-
    count, 73–74
  logic of, 76–77
  relevance for impact assessment, 74–
    75, 78–79
  weakness of the standard account, 74
Regression coefficient, 3, 83
Regression discontinuity design, 81,
  97–114
  comparative-change design com-
    pared, 81
  logic of, 99–104
  major weaknesses, 97–98
  operation, 97
  threats to validity, 104–14
    contamination due to treatment or
      control, 105
    curvilinearity, 110–14
    fuzzy cutpoints, 105–7
    nonrandom measurement error,
      108–10
    random measurement error, 107–8
    treatment effect, 99, 104, 109
Regression effect, 78–79
Regression parameter, 82
Regression slope coefficient, 84
Regression threat to validity, 52, 56, 59,
  71–79
Reichardt, Charles S., 107–8, 128, 130
Relevance condition, 10
Remedial social programs, 112
Resources as subobjectives, 33
Resulting state of the world, 3
Retrospective evaluation techniques,
  194
Rigid assignment, 101, 103, 105
Rist, Roy C., 64
Rosenbloom, David H., 31, 200, 202
Rosenstock, I. M., 8, 56, 69

Ross, H. Laurence, 164
Rossi, Peter H., 203
Rubinfeld, Daniel L., 160

S

Sample, 90
  independent, 180–81
  random, 90–91
  size of, 180
Sample mean, 90
Sampling distribution, 90–92
  definition, 90
Scatterplot, 136
Scriven, Michael, 25, 186
Selection, 45
  centralized or decentralized selection, 45, 49, 97, 165
  experimental design, 45
  manipulation, 165
  self, 166
  threat to internal validity, 58–62, 66
Selection effects, 60
Selection bias, 60–61
  regression-discontinuity design, 104
  spuriousness, 168–70
Selection-P bias, 60, 166
Selection-Q bias, 60, 62, 76, 133, 143, 166
  comparative-change design, 117–30
  intercept bias, 118–26
  slopes, 126–30
Self-selection, 166
Selltiz, Claire, 167
Sensitivity, 44 n, 46–47, 54
Sensitivity analysis, 177, 199
Set of subjects, 44, 45
Setting of program, 67
Sherrill, Sam, 194, 201, 203
Significance testing, 46
  causal inference function, 91–92
  econometric function, 92–93
  experimental design function, 91–99
  ex-post-facto design, 95–96
  function of, 90
  impact parameter, 90–96
  information communication, 92
  quasi-experimental design, 94–96
  randomization, 91–92
  regression-discontinuity design, 98, 103, 105
  strength of relationship function, 93–95
  survey-design function, 91, 94
  uses in impact analysis, 94
Single-group design, 53–54, 64–65
  over-time design, 64–65
Skipper, 48
Slopes, bias in, 126–30
Smith, Mary L., 40, 156
Smith, William G., 63

Somers, Gerald G., 166, 173
Specification error, 102–3
Spuriousness, 165–70, 178–79, 188
Stakeholder, 197, 200
Standard deviation, 90
Standard scores, 74
Stanley, John C., 44, 49, 52, 54, 62, 72, 97, 99, 112, 117, 164, 168, 171, 181
State of the world (treated subjects), 3
Statistical conclusion validity, 444
Statistical significance, 2, 188
Statistics, 2, 90
Steinburn, Thomas W., 65, 69, 177
Strength of relationship function, 93–95
Stromsdorfer, Ernest W., 166, 173
Structural-equation model, 187
Subobjective, 2, 10, 12–13, 70
  behavior prerequisites, 33–34
  control variables, 84
  as design; *see* Subobjectives as design
  discovery; *see* Discovery subobjective
  formative analysis, 25, 27–31
    use of, example, 25, 27–31
  omission of, 34–35
  operation of, 32–39
  summative evaluations, 25–26, 30, 37
Subobjectives as design, 185–91
  application of method, 191–92
  causality, 185–86, 189–91
  internal validity, 185
  logic of method, 187–91
    program, 187
    validation, 107
  outcome of interest, 28
  spuriousness, 188–90
Summative evaluation, 25–26, 30
  cowbird control program, 37
Surette, Ray, 205
Survey design function, 91, 94

T

Target audience, 42
  random assignment, 42–43
Tashman, L. J., 167
Testing; *see also* Posttest *and* Pretest
  basic threat of history, 52, 54–55
  program theory, 1–2
  significance; *see* Significance testing
Test-retest correlation, 72
Threats to validity; *see* Validity, threats to
Tiao, George C., 156–57, 160
Time ordering, 182–83
Time-series analysis, 146
Time-series design, 146–62
  after-the-fact, 165

Time-series design—*Cont.*
  ARIMA modeling, 154, 157–58
  comparative, 158–62
  effect of history, 159–61
  interrupted; *see* Interrupted time-series design
  law introduced in experimental state, 161–62
  regression analysis, 151–54
Transfer function, 150–52
Treatment delivery contamination, 64, 66
Treatment effect, 82–83, 100, 109
  comparative-time-series design, 159
  interval estimate, 140
Trochim, William M., 98–99, 110, 113
True experiment, 45; *see also* Experimental design
  contamination, 64–66, 71

U

Understated variance, 153
Undesirable conditions, 6–7
Unhappy randomization, 46–48, 57, 61, 94
Unmatched groups, intercept bias in, 122–23

V

Validity, threats to, 104–14, 166–67
  comparative change design, 115–31
  curvilinearity, 110–14
  external validity; *see* External validity
  fuzzy cutpoints, 105–7

Validity, threats to—*Cont.*
  internal validity; *see* Internal validity
  nonrandom measurement error, 108–10
  random-comparison group design, 142–45
  randomization, 115
  random measurement error, 107–8
  regression, 52, 56, 59, 71
  regression-discontinuity design, 104–14
Visual analysis, 150, 154–57
Volpe, Anne, 18
Volunteerism, 135, 142, 165, 168–69
  additive effects, 170, 173–77
  attrition, 177–78
  interactive effects, 170–73, 177–78

W–Z

Waldo, Gordon P., 69
Warner, Kenneth E., 32
Webber, Melvin M., 53
Weighting, 194, 207–8
  benefit-cost analysis, 196–97
  impact analysis, 200, 202
  MAUT, 199
  multiple outcome evaluation, 202
Weiler, Daniel, 65, 203
Weisbrod, Burton A., 166
White noise, 150, 157
Wright, Charles R., 31, 41, 42
Zimring, F. C., 149
Z-variables, 173

About the Author

Lawrence B. Mohr is Professor of Political Science and Public Policy at the University of Michigan, where he teaches statistics, organization theory, and the philosophy of social research in the Department of Political Science, and organizational design and program evaluation in the Institute of Public Policy Studies. He received his Ph.D. in political science from the University of Michigan in 1966. His publications include *Explaining Organizational Behavior: The Limits and Possibilities of Theory and Research* and numerous articles in organizational behavior and program evaluation. He is a former employee of the U.S. Public Health Service and has consulted widely with local and federal agencies, including the National Science Foundation, National Institute of Education, National Institute of Justice, Office of Personnel Management, and General Accounting Office.